THE EARLY CIVILIZATION OF CHINA

FRONTISPIECE A bronze Shang wine mixer, *kuang*, excavated at Shih-lou, Shansi. Dating from between the fourteenth and eleventh century BC, this *kuang* monster has the blunted horns of a sacrificial victim and is decorated with snake-like dragons.

THE EARLY CIVILIZATION OF CHINA

YONG YAP & ARTHUR COTTERELL

WEIDENFELD AND NICOLSON LONDON

For Alan

Designed by Margaret Fraser
for George Weidenfeld and Nicolson Ltd
11 St John's Hill, London SW11

ISBN 0 297 76991 X

Poetry in this book has been quoted by kind
permission of the following publishers:

Constable Publishers, London 164–5. George Allen &
Unwin Ltd, London (*The Book of Songs*, A. Waley) 31.
George Allen & Unwin Ltd, London (*The Poetry and
Career of Li Po*, A. Waley) 162. Grove Press, New York
(*Anthology of Chinese Literature*, C. Birch) 31, 42, 163,
164, 166. Alfred A. Knopf, Inc., New York
(*Translations from the Chinese*, A. Waley; copyright
1919 and renewed 1947 by A. Waley; copyright 1941
and renewed 1969 by Alfred A. Knopf, Inc.; reprinted
by permission of the publisher) 162, 164–5. Penguin
Books Ltd, London (*The Poems of Wang Wei*,
translated by G. W. Robinson, Penguin Classics 1973,
© G. W. Robinson, 1973) 158.

Printed in Great Britain by
Tinling (1973) Limited, Prescot, Merseyside

Acknowledgments

The author and publishers would like to thank the following museums, institutions and photographers for permission to reproduce illustrations and for supplying photographs:

Bibliothèque Nationale, Paris *153*; British Museum 75, 84, *114–15*, 160–1, *218–19*; Bulloz, Paris *153*, 226; Camera Press 34, 72–3, 84–5, 91, 111; Cleveland Museum of Art, Ohio 157; Collection of J. M. Crawford Jr, New York 212–13; Dominique Darbois 169; Field Museum of Natural History, Chicago 145; The Government of the People's Republic of China 19, 20, 27, 36, 43, 46–7, 70, 70–1, 78, 88–9, 170, 185 (below); Richard and Sally Greenhill 194–5; Robert Harding Associates 2, 19, 20, 21, 25, 27, 36, 43, 46–7, *50*, 66–7, 69, 70, 70–1, 78, 88–9, *113*, 170, *179*, *180*, 185 (both), 232; Michael Holford Library *49*, *75*, *97*, *220*; Imperial Palace Museum, Peking 26; Keystone Press Agency 102–3, 129; Paolo Koch 172, 190, 204–5, 230; Mansell Collection 57, 139, 149; Musée Cernuschi, Paris *49*; Musée Guimet, Paris *154*, *220*; Museum of Fine Arts, Boston *back jacket*, 76; National Palace Museum, Taiwan 210–11, 222; Joseph Needham (*The Development of Iron and Steel Technology in China*, W. Heffer & Sons Ltd) 104; Joseph Needham (*The Grand Titration*, Allen & Unwin) 23, 32, 45, 87, 202; Joseph Needham (*Science and Civilisation in China*, Vols 1–6, Cambridge University Press) 26, 29, 39, 47, 54, 71, 93, 98, 107, 151, 198, 203; Outlook Films Ltd *front jacket*, 53 (both), 82, 106, *217*; Popperfoto 52–3, 101, 105, 108, 118, 123, 131, 135, 150, 206 (both), 224; Radio Times Hulton Picture Library 63, 142–3, 146, 174; The Ronald Press Company, New York (*Gardens of China* – Osvald Sirén) 173 (below); Osvald Sirén 159, 162, 173 (above); Snark International, Paris *back jacket*, 76, 80, *116*, 148, *154*; John Massey Stewart 193; Staatliche Museum für Völkskunde, West Berlin *116*; Victoria and Albert Museum 136, 197, 214; Werner Forman Archive *endpaper*, 14, 125, 133, 165, 182–3, 187–9, 227

Picture research by Susan Pinkus
Maps by Edward MacAndrew Purcell
Numerals in italics indicate colour illustrations

Maps

Contents

METRIC MEASUREMENTS

Some readers may be less familiar with the metric measurements
used throughout this text. The following is a guide to
their English equivalents:

1 millimetre	0.04 inch
1 centimetre	0.39 inch
1 metre	3.3 feet (1.1 yards)
1 kilometre	0.6 mile
1 square centimetre	0.155 square inch
1 square metre	11 square feet (1.2 square yards)
1 square kilometre	0.386 square mile
1 hectare	2.5 acres
1 kilogram	2.2 pounds
1 tonne	0.98 ton

Introduction

Cathay is one of the most evocative words that we have in the English language. It retains something of the awe and wonder felt by Marco Polo when he encountered at first hand the magnificence of the Great Khan, the far-reaching and cosmopolitan nature of the Mongol Empire, and the wealth and civilization of China. Kubilai Khan has become a European legend and the Venetian traveller's description of Hangchow has not ceased to amaze readers of *The Travels* today. 'At the end of three days,' wrote Marco Polo, 'you reach the noble and magnificent city of Kin-sai, a name that signified "the celestial city", and which it merits from its pre-eminence to all others in the world, in point of grandeur and beauty, as well as for its abundant delights, which might lead an inhabitant to imagine himself in paradise.' Innumerable streets, squares and parks fitted on to a lattice of canals that gave access to a freshwater lake on one side of the city and the Che River on the other. Spanning these waterways were twelve thousand bridges; those thrown over the principal canals and connected to the main streets, noted the visitor from a city whose own Grand Canal could not boast the famous Rialto until the sixteenth century, 'have arches so high, and are built with so much skill, that vessels with their masts can pass underneath them, whilst at the same time, carts and horses are passing over their heads – so well is the slope from the street adapted to the height of the bridge'. Commerce and industry flourished alongside every form of pleasure and entertainment. The market-places, on three days each week, attracted more than forty thousand persons, seeking all kinds of manufactured goods and commodities. 'In certain shops nothing is vended but the wine of the country, which they are continually brewing, and serve out at a moderate price.' With some hesitation Marco Polo admits that 'in every part of the city courtesans are to be found, adorned with much finery, highly perfumed, occupying well-furnished houses, and attended by female domestics. These women are accomplished, and are perfect in the arts of blandishment and dalliance, which they accompany with expressions adapted to every description of person, insomuch that strangers who have once tasted their charms, remain in a state of fascination, and become so enchanted by their meretricious arts, that they can never divest themselves of the impression.'

Observing the daily life of Hangchow *The Travels* explain:

> The inhabitants of the city are idolaters, and they use paper money as currency. The men as well as women are handsome. The greater part of them are always clothed in silk. . . . Among the handicraft trades exercised in the place, there are twelve considered to be superior to the rest, as being more

generally useful; for each of them there are a thousand workshops and each shop furnishes employment for ten, fifteen, or twenty workmen, and in a few instances as many as forty, under their respective masters. The opulent principals in these manufactures do not labour with their own hands, but, on the contrary, assume airs of gentility and affect parade. Their wives equally abstain from work. They have much beauty, as has been remarked, and are brought up with delicate and languid habits. The costliness of their dresses, in silks and jewellery, can scarcely be imagined. . . . Their houses are well built and richly adorned with carved work. So much do they delight in ornaments of this kind, in paintings, and fancy buildings, that the sums they lavish on such objects are enormous. The natural disposition of the native inhabitants of Kin-sai is pacific, and by the example of their former kings, who were themselves unwarlike, they have been accustomed to the habits of tranquility. The management of arms is unknown to them, nor do they keep any in their houses. Contentious broils are never had among them. They conduct their mercantile and manufacturing concerns with perfect candour and probity. They are friendly towards each other, and persons who inhabit the same street, both men and women, from the mere circumstance of neighbourhood, appear like one family. In their domestic manners they are free from jealousy or suspicion of their wives, to whom great respect is shown. . . . To strangers also, who visit their city in the way of commerce, they give proofs of cordiality, inviting them freely to their houses, showing them hospitable attention, and furnishing them with the best advice and assistance in their mercantile transactions. On the other hand, they dislike the sight of soldiery, not excepting the guards of the grand Khan, as they preserve the recollection that by them they were deprived of the government of their native kings and rulers.

And much more besides. The richness of this description, so greatly did Hangchow excite the admiration of Marco Polo, carried over into the minds of his contemporaries in the West a marvellous image of China during the reign of Kubilai Khan. Yet this impression could not have been more partial and one-sided, if a deliberate attempt had been made to undervalue the Chinese achievement. Although Marco Polo served in the Yuan, or Mongol, civil service from 1271 to 1297, the year Kubilai Khan died, he remained largely unaware of the recent triumphs of the Sung Empire, whose capital he called Kin-sai. Employment in government service gave him a unique opportunity for observing and collecting information about the Yuan Empire. *The Travels*, the account of his experiences, does provide us with interesting details about Mongol rule, but it lacks real insight concerning the situation of the Chinese. He did not learn the Chinese language and seems to have moved largely in Mongol social circles. Kubilai Khan is portrayed as a great ruler, presiding over a splendid Court, to which all men of worth are welcomed, regardless of origin, race or creed. Marco Polo's amazement and praise at this liberal atmosphere is understandable in the light of the narrow, closed world of Europe at this period; yet, the Yuan Empire was a pale imitation of what had been a general Chinese practice since Han times (206 BC–AD 221). And lost on Marco Polo was the political motive behind the employment of foreign adventurers, namely the Mongol desire to exclude Chinese scholars. Ignorant of Chinese history and culture, he misunderstood the aversion to soldiers, whose social status had been lowered during the period of the Warring States (481–221 BC). Technology, too, seems not to have exercised his curiosity. A distinguished ancestor of the twelve thousand bridges in Hangchow was the An-chi bridge at Chao-hsien. Built by the Sui Emperor Wen-ti in AD 610, this span over the Grand Canal, which was dug to join the Yang-tze and the Yellow river systems, is the earliest segmental arch bridge known in any civilization. Against Genghiz Khan, the 'pacifist' dynasty of the Sung had used the most advanced arsenal of weapons ever developed. Gunpowder, explosive grenades and bombs launched from catapults, rocket-aided arrows and flame-throwers, poisonous smoke and a primitive armoured car had held up the Mongol advance for nearly half a century, the stoutest resistance shown to the fierce, mounted horde from the steppe, before the last Sung ruler perished in a sea battle off what is now Hong Kong (1279).

Apart from the Yuan dynasty (1279–1368) being an alien domination, the period also represents the termination of the early civilization of China. Kubilai Khan ruled an empire already in decline. The violence of the initial Mongol attacks on China had impoverished whole provinces, while a corrupt government was little concerned with the welfare of the Chinese people. Below the surface the forces of rebellion that were to overthrow and expel the Mongols steadily gathered in force. All this, and the great tradition of early Chinese civilization, went undocumented by Marco Polo. But the idea of Cathay made a profound impression so that to some extent we have all absorbed an odd view of the early civilization of China. During this period the 'Celestial Empire' was better known to Europe than at any time till the twentieth century, because Mongol control of so much of the world ensured that roads were safe and travel easy, and the prejudice against Chinese offered employment possibilities to foreign adventurers.

This book is an attempt to supplement the picture of China as presented in *The Travels*. It traces the origins and development of Chinese civilization until the Mongol Conquest, which effectively ended the first and early phase of that great tradition, the oldest continuous one surviving today. The Ming Empire (1368–1644), which followed the overthrow of the Mongols, was an age of restoration, a conscious recovery of the blighted national heritage. We wish to introduce the reader to a most fascinating period in the history of the world – more than two millennia of the most outstanding human achievement. That is, the formation of China, not Cathay.

1

Prehistoric and Feudal China
From earliest times to 771 BC

Original environment plays a decisive part in the shaping of a culture. In the case of China the geographical setting has acted as more than a background for historical development; it has influenced profoundly the whole fabric of this self-contained civilization. Indeed, there are those who would maintain that geography enters vitally into the pattern of differences that exists between the cultures of China and Europe, those twin poles of mankind.

The first impression of the People's Republic is its immense size; it is the third largest country in the world. Although the present political boundaries enclose a much larger land area than did the first Chinese Empire (221 BC), China is an exception in the pre-modern world to what would appear to be a rule that units of such magnitude are not stable entities over long periods of time. For the Chinese rightly see themselves as the direct descendants of an ancient civilization, largely isolated from the rest of the world. There has been a steady and continuous expansion of frontiers, particularly in a southward direction, that is still in progress today. The power of absorption in Chinese culture has often been remarked upon by visitors: no territory once incorporated has ever left the cultural area, despite long periods of barbarian invasion and partition.

Three great rivers and their innumerable tributaries, the veins that carry the life blood of the country, give form to three main geographical divisions, excluding Manchuria and the new lands north of the Great Wall. From the Pamirs, 'the roof of the world', and the Tibetan Plateau all water courses flow eastwards to the Pacific. In the south the West River, which reaches the coast at Canton, long a focus of both culture and commerce, defines a clear region in its drainage system, whilst central China is served by the Yang-tze River, whose course includes the Red Basin of Szechuan and the lake-studded middle section where modern Wuhan has become a leading industrial centre, before entering the Yellow Sea near Shanghai. The north is dependent on the Yellow River, sometimes called 'China's Sorrow', because of its tendency to change course on the great coastal plains. In 1851 the Yellow River moved its outlet from south of Shantung to a point nearly five hundred kilometres north; besides devastating large tracts of countryside the human toll ran into millions of lives. Yet the middle course of this great turbulent river was the original centre of China, 'the land within the passes'. Here it was that the earliest Chinese civilization developed over five thousand years ago. By 1000 BC the Chinese had spread eastwards along the Yellow River valley and begun to

'The land within the passes'; the loess countryside around Sian, the modern city which has grown from Ch'ang-an, the ancient imperial capital.

move southwards to the valley of the Yang-tze. Into the cultural area many different peoples were absorbed; others have been dispersed to less accessible highlands and wastelands.

The West River estuary is one thousand six hundred kilometres south of the present outlet of the Yellow River. This immense distance alone ensures that climatic conditions differ profoundly in the three river basins. A tropical climate, with hot and humid summers and warm and sunny winters, permits a twelve month growing period in the valley of the West River. Though a similar hot and moist summer is usual in the Yang-tze basin, the winter months are much colder. Bitter north winds bring heavy frost in January and February, when snow often falls too. A growing season of nine months is the average; rice is the predominant crop, though it faces competition by wheat and barley in the north. Of the three river basins it is the northern one, the plain of the Yellow River and the mountainous lands of its upper course, that has the least favourable climate. Winters are long, cold and dry; bitter north-west winds from Mongolia sweep over the hills and descend to the plain, causing heavy dust storms. Summer rainfall is sparse and unreliable, whilst sudden cloud-bursts or hail storms can be very destructive to the loess soil. In years of drought the dust storms in summer are worse even than those in winter. The sheltered valley of Wei, the heartland of China, suffers less from these hazards than any other part of the region.

'The land within the passes', wedged between the Lu Liang and Chin Ling Highlands to the south of the Ordos Desert, is loess country. Thick deposits of windblown yellow earth, varying from thirty to over one hundred metres, cover the landscape. This fine soil originated from the Mongolian desert, and it is very fertile when well watered. Although the period when the great winds carried the loess down from the desert lands ended after the Ice Age and erosion of these deposits began, associated with the gradual uplift of the continental platform, the present-day dust storms are a gentler continuation of this age-old geological process. Similarly, the flood plain of the Yellow River, below 'the land within the passes', provides evidence of the massiveness of natural change, those immense environmental influences that necessarily modify the life and ways of man. An artesian well, bored in 1936, discovered that the Yellow River had responded to the sinking of the coastal region by piling up silt to a depth of 875 metres.

The physical environment not only preserved the uniqueness of the Yellow River culture by formidable barriers which separated this society from other great centres in the Ancient World but also it had a great formative effect on Chinese civilization. Early man was at the mercy of natural forces: the seasons, rainfall, the flow of the great rivers and the prevalence of earthquakes. As a result his whole way of life, his beliefs, superstitions, fables, work and leisure, were all dominated by them and their potency. To survive, the earliest beginnings of Chinese civilization had to develop in accord with this demanding environment. The first inhabitants of the Yellow River came to see themselves as members of a vast order of living things, with whose processes they had to seek a harmonious relationship. This profound sense of reciprocity found expression in the ancient theory of Yin-Yang, which has remained a basic concept of the Chinese mind. Upon the delicate balance of these two interacting forces the peace and prosperity of mankind entirely depended.

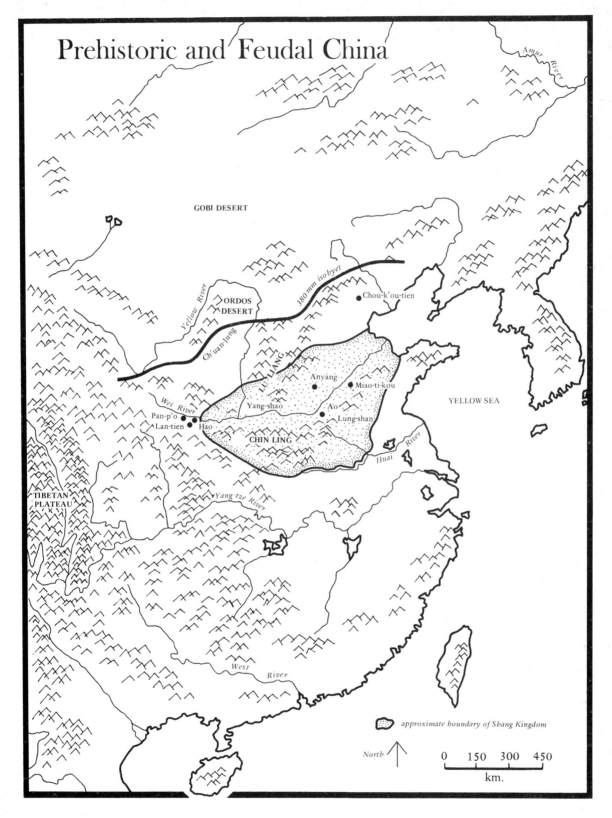

Prehistoric and Feudal China

GOBI DESERT

Amur River

Yellow River

ORDOS DESERT

380 mm isohyet

Chou-k'ou-tien

Ch'uan-jung

LU LIANG

Anyang

Miao-ti-kou

YELLOW SEA

Wei River

Yang-shao

Ao

Pan-p'o

Lung-shan

Lan-tien

Hao

CHIN LING

Huai River

TIBETAN PLATEAU

Yang-tze River

West River

approximate boundary of Shang Kingdom

North

| 0 | 150 | 300 | 450 |

km.

The very nature of the loess soil inaugurated what was to be the foundation of Chinese civilization; it encouraged the development of water control. The ancient kings preserved the people by maintaining a proper relationship with the heavenly powers and undertook large-scale conservancy schemes to make the countryside safe from floods and well irrigated for agriculture. Because loess soil is so fine a texture it holds moisture easily, a capillary effect bringing to the surface this 'underground' water. One reason for the ability of China to maintain a large population in high densities from such an early time,

> lies in the self-fertilizing capacity of loess when there is sufficient water, and the capacity for self-renewal of the rich silt deposits in the alluvial plains, which are constantly rejuvenated by erosion, either through controlled irrigation or natural flooding. In the latter case the benefit is counter-balanced by damage, but, in the long run, it keeps the soil young and productive and free from the danger of depletion. This is the reason why China could stand many centuries of intense agriculture without recourse to scientific repletion of the soil by mineral fertilizers.

Before considering Chinese traditions about the remote past – antiquarian study is known to have existed in China as early as 200 BC – the recent discoveries of scientific archaeology merit attention. In the 1920s a series of finds in a cave at Chou-k'ou-tien, to the south of Peking, established the great antiquity of the human race in the valleys of China and furnished proof that civilization here was as old as Chinese myth would suggest. The remains of *Sinanthropus pekinensis*, or Peking Man, as the creature is called, date from 400,000 BC. Physical features still retained in modern Chinese people are found on the skull of Peking Man. In the evolution of the human race, he represents a rather advanced stage when the four limbs and trunk had already acquired human proportions. A hunter, with the knowledge of fire, he used flaked and chipped stone tools in a terrain that 'abounded with other mammals such as rhinoceroses, ancient horses, pigs, deer, buffaloes, sabre-toothed tigers and cats as large as lions'.

At this time the Ordos was a considerable oasis on the edge of the desert lands. Along with this upper stretch of the Yellow River, the 'land within the passes' must have been a well-watered pasture, ideal as a roaming ground for big game and for the ancestors of mankind. Confirmation of these conditions came in 1963 and 1964, when a 'distant cousin' of Peking Man was discovered in a cave near the shores of a lake on the Wei River. The site at Lan-t'ien, sixty kilometres south-east of Sian, has given the creature its name, *Sinanthropus lantianensis*, and like Peking Man its remains and stone implements are associated with mammal fossils such as tigers, dogs, elephants, boar and deer. From the comparative thickness of the skull and its small cranial capacity it has been deduced that Lan-t'ien Man is more primitive than both Peking Man and Java Man, probably around 500,000 to 600,000 years old.

The gap between Peking Man and the Yang-shao culture of the New Stone Age (from 5000 BC), which is characterized by painted pottery and was found in 1922, remains largely uncharted, though recent finds have started to show a continuity of development throughout the Stone Age. The most thoroughly investigated Yang-shao site, that of Pan-p'o, also in the Wei valley, has distinct

STONE AGE
ARCHAEOLOGICAL
DISCOVERIES

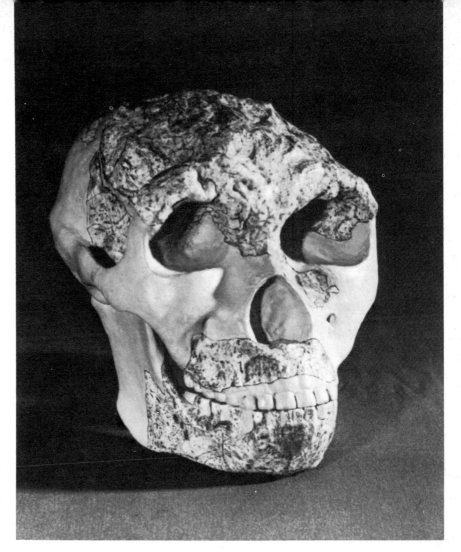

Sinanthropus lantianensis; casts of the skull and lower jaw of Lan-t'ien Man found near Sian in the Wei valley in 1963 and 1964. It dates from about 500,000 BC.

areas for habitation, pottery kilns, and burial. In the centre of this settlement, which covers almost 70,000 square metres, there is a large communal hall with a floor space of 160 square metres. Other houses and storage pits around this construction show that the dwelling site, enclosed by a defensive ditch, was inhabited for a long time. Slightly away from the ditch are the cemetery and several kiln sites. Agriculture was the main activity of the village, whose population at its height was between 500 and 600 people. Millet was the staple crop, whilst newly domesticated animals like pigs supplemented the produce of hunting and fishing expeditions. More than half a million pieces of pottery have been unearthed at Pan-p'o. Of these nearly a thousand are sufficiently well preserved to display the remarkable achievement of Yang-shao ceramics. The usual colour is red. Geometrical patterns and later a fish design are painted on in white and black pigments. Many pieces had a funerary purpose, for seventy-six children have been found in pottery urns, buried within the settlement; adult graves were located beyond the defensive ditch but, in spite of several examples of secondary burial, the later Chinese custom of placing the bones of the deceased in an urn once the body has properly decayed is absent. Most significant, however, are the two pottery vessels that were intended for cooking. First, the *li*, three pots joined as a tripod, marks an enormous advance in terms of using heat, since the hollow legs both provide support and present a greater surface to the fire, whilst the internal division allows the preparation of several things at once. Secondly, there is the *hsien*, in which a lower vessel similar to a *li* is surmounted by another one with a perforated bottom and a cover, so that cooking can be achieved by steam. Originating in Yang-shao culture, these forms reappear in later stages of Chinese development and suggest that Chinese skill in cooking is very old.

The loess soil assisted the initial building of Pan-p'o, since the early houses are all semi-subterranean. It makes clean mud-pies as well as tunnels and niches; the villagers designed in it cupboards, cellars, walls, fireplaces, seats and beds. Downstream on the flood plain of the Yellow River people of another Neolithic culture, the Lung-shan, made a careful selection of places for settlement. Their villages are found on the upper stretch of a gentle stream or within sight of a hill, and a thick wall for protection against minor flood is common. A more advanced pottery industry produced thin, highly polished ware, either grey or black in colour. It shows signs of having been made on a wheel, unlike the 'coiling' process employed by the earlier Yang-shao potters. The relation between these two New Stone Age cultures is still the subject of debate, although excavations at Miao-ti-kou on the lower course of the Yellow River suggest that Lung-shan may have developed directly from Yang-shao. The Lung-shan culture flourished down to about 1500 BC, the end of the Stone Age in China. Archaeology has recovered nothing that would question the view that sees Chinese civilization as always predominantly agricultural. A settled way of life, based on cultivation and the domestication of animals, especially the pig, appears from the very earliest traces of society. The loess country permitted accelerated development towards civilization. It seems that the Chinese people never passed through a pastoral period. Milk and milk

Shallow red pottery bowl with a mask painted in black from the Yang-shao culture of the Neolithic period, fifth to fourth millennium BC. It was excavated at Pan-p'o, Shensi.

products are absent from diet, whilst agricultural metaphors are common in the language from time immemorial.

A singular contribution of the Lung-shan people to Chinese civilization was a primitive form of scapulimancy, which is not found outside the Chinese cultural area. Divination took the form of observing the cracks that resulted from heating ox and deer *scapulae*, or shoulder bones. These were obtained either by scorching the surface of the bone directly, or by applying a burning stick to a prepared, round depression in the bone. During the Shang dynasty oracle-bones, usually tortoise shells, had the omen inscribed on them.

CHINESE
HISTORICAL
TRADITIONS
AND MYTH

The archaeological record does not extend beyond the Shang dynasty (1500–1027 BC), and even this confirmation of Chinese historical tradition occurred only in 1935 when the later Shang capital at Anyang was uncovered. Until these finds there was general scepticism concerning everything before the Chou dynasty (1027–256 BC). At the moment the threshold of historical knowledge remains at the beginning of Shang, but we should not be deterred from examining the traditions and myths surrounding the origins of Chinese civilization. Because ancient China was isolated from the other early centres of

A Shang pottery steamer, *hsien*, with a corded surface, dating from the sixteenth or fifteenth century BC. It was found at Cheng-chou, Honan, in 1953.

civilization – Egypt, Mesopotamia and the Indus valley – the first thoughts of the Chinese, their legends, belong to them alone. From these tales we may be able to identify what were the original and distinct elements in the Chinese consciousness.

A legend of the creation of the universe concerns P'an-ku, primeval man. At the outset the universe was an egg. One day the egg split open. The top half became the sky and the bottom half the earth. P'an-ku, who emerged from the broken egg, grew three metres taller every day, just as the sky became three metres higher and the earth three metres thicker. After eighteen thousand years P'an-ku died. Then, like the original egg, he split into a number of parts. His head formed the sun and moon, his blood the rivers and seas, his hair the forests, his sweat the rain, his breath the wind, his voice thunder and, last of all, his fleas became the ancestors of mankind.

What stands out most in this story for a Westerner is the lowly position the Chinese have ascribed to man: not the centre of creation, not a colossus in the landscape, but rather a small figure in the great sweep of natural things. The insignificance of men, as formulated in the P'an-ku myth, was to find perfect expression in Chinese landscape painting, where tiny figures are set down amid the magnificence of the natural world, mountains and valleys, rivers and lakes, clouds and waterfalls, trees and flowers. Today, the popular Chinese proverb, 'Mountains make great trees', still expresses the idea that noteworthy landscape moulds men of great character. Such a viewpoint could not have been more appropriate for the first inhabitants of the Yellow River communities, members of a vast order of living things, with whose processes they had to seek a harmonious relationship if their society was to continue from generation to generation.

After P'an-ku came a series of emperors, about whom little is known except their divinity; Ssu-ma Ch'ien (145–90 or 79 BC), who wrote the first general history of China, only recognized Huang Ti, the Yellow Emperor, and his four successors, Chuan Hsiu, K'u, Yao and Shun, as the earliest mortal rulers. The earlier divinities made important contributions, such as architecture, farming and herbal medicine, to the development of Chinese civilization, but the Yellow Emperor is attributed with the impulse that led to the firm foundation of China. He is the cultural founder-hero. Apart from defeating the Miao tribes and establishing Chinese supremacy in 'the land within the passes', the Yellow Emperor introduced governmental institutions. Some traditions credit him with the invention of the compass and coined money, which replaced cowrie shells as the medium of exchange, whilst his wife excelled in sericulture and household skills. Under his firm and benevolent rule the people prospered and civilization advanced: his chief minister first devised written signs, whereupon 'all spirits cried in agony, as the innermost secrets of nature were thus revealed'.

The throne was not passed on to the next emperor according to birth, each successor being chosen by merit. Possibly this tradition recalls dimly some arrangement whereby a confederation of tribes elected a paramount chieftain to lead them in times of attack from barbarian peoples entering their land. However, the moral predilection of Chinese historians has led them to conclude that selection was determined by each candidate's 'outstanding virtue and abilities'. Yao, 'able and virtuous', united all the states 'so the black-haired

Yu the Great Engineer. This late Ch'ing illustration shows the legendary hydraulic engineer, who spent thirteen years 'mastering the waters', leaving home.

禹娶塗山圖

大禹　啟　禹妻

people were transformed. The result was universal concord.' Moreover, he instituted astronomical observation and established the calendar, 'so to deliver respectfully the seasons to be observed by the people'. Flood control is mentioned during the reign of Shun, who 'deepened the rivers', but Yu, the Great Engineer, is the person forever connected with hydraulic conservancy works because of his success in containing the Great Deluge.

'The inundating waters seemed to assail the heavens', Yu said, 'and in their extent embraced the hills and overtopped the great mounds, so that the people were bewildered and overwhelmed. . . . I opened passages for the streams throughout the nine provinces and conducted them to the seas. I deepened the channels and conducted them to the streams.' Thirteen years Yu spent 'mastering the waters' without once returning home to see his wife and children. By his extensive water-control works he brought 'water benefits' to all the people – floods ceased and fields were irrigated; to his own family came the privilege of founding the first dynasty, the Hsia. This elevation of Yu's kinsmen indicates how important hydraulic conservancy must have been in ancient China. 'The fact that irrigation channels, surface tanks, drainage and flood-control works and artificial waterways were mostly built as public works links them closely with politics.' From 2205 BC the descendants of Yu are supposed to have reigned down to 1500 BC, when the last Hsia king, Chieh, was overthrown by the Shang.

Of the Hsia dynasty there is no archaeological trace. This is not the case with Shang China, though dismissed as unhistoric prior to the excavations at Anyang in the 1930s. It was maintained that Ssu-ma Ch'ien could not have had reliable source materials for his account of what happened a thousand years before his own time. When the oracular inscriptions on bone excavated at Anyang were studied, there was general astonishment that they confirmed almost in its entirety the king-list for the Shang dynasty as preserved in the histories.

SHANG (1500–1027 BC)

According to the *Shu Ching* (*Book of History*), the last sovereign of the Hsia, Chieh, was a cruel tyrant, whose wickedness brought retribution on his house. Infatuated with an outstanding beauty, Mei Hsi, the king neglected government and indulged in all kinds of perverted pleasures. Around her ornate chamber, decked out with all the precious stones of the royal treasury, he heaped up mounds of meat, hanging dried joints on all the trees, filled a pond with wine until they could row a boat on it, while three thousand people would appear at the beat of a drum and drink up the liquor like so many oxen. The vices of Chieh are almost parallel to those of Chou Hsin, the final Shang monarch, against whom another successful rebellion was to arise in 1027 BC. It has been suggested that the *Shu Ching* relates garbled and unfriendly accounts of a religious festival to the fertility gods. But whatever the truth behind these tales the traditional view is unequivocal in its praise for the just overthrow of such rulers.

When T'ang, the leader of the Shang against Chieh, doubted the wisdom of ascending the throne and said that he was 'afraid that in future ages men will fill their mouths with me as an apology for their rebellious proceedings', his chief minister replied thus:

A Shang bronze ritual
cauldron, *ting*, dating
from between the
fourteenth and eleventh
century BC. It was used in
ceremonies connected
with ancestor worship and
the faces serve as
reminders of the Shang
custom of human
sacrifice.

Oh! Heaven gives birth to the people with such desires that, without a
ruler, they must fall into disorders; Heaven again gives birth to the man of
intelligence to regulate them. The sovereign of Hsia had his virtue entirely
obscured; the people were as if they had fallen amid mire and burning charcoal. Heaven hereupon endowed our king with valour and prudence to
serve as a sign and direction to the myriad regions and to continue the old
ways of Yu. You are now following the proper course, honouring and
obeying the appointment of Heaven. The king of Hsia was an offender,
falsely and calumniously alleging the sanction of supreme Heaven to spread
abroad his commands among the people. On this account God viewed him
with disapprobation, caused our Shang to receive the appointment, and
employed you to enliven the multitudes of people.

Legitimacy of virtue, not birth, is being postulated here. Only the most virtuous men were entitled to rule, like Yao and Shun. Much later the philosopher
Mencius (*c.* 390–305 BC) was to construct a theory of the Right of Rebellion
from the fall of Chou Hsin, the Shang tyrant.

But T'ang was noted for both his military exploits and the attention he paid
to domestic affairs. An efficient and just government coupled with the promotion of increased agricultural production, upon which during campaigns he
could support his army, now equipped with the chariot and bow, gave

supremacy to the Shang dynasty. The period which he inaugurated marks a new phase in Chinese civilization. The Shang people distinguished themselves by the achievement of important advances in arts and technology; the Stone Age was replaced by the Bronze; an effective and centralized kingdom evolved, embracing the different tribal groups; and, not least, written language was invented. China had moved from prehistory into history.

Bronze appears with apparent suddenness after 1500 BC, and it is soon followed by a mature Bronze Age culture. The quality of Shang bronzes – primarily ritual vessels used in ancestor worship – is striking, their designs having the finality associated only with highly developed art. Indeed, the rapid success of bronze-casting in China was probably the outcome of experience gained with pottery kilns of advanced design, as existed already in the New Stone Age. Recent archaeological discoveries reveal too the ceramic origin of several vessels previously thought to be peculiar to bronze.

The Shang king in person attended to the affairs of his kingdom. Inscriptions tell us that all government decisions were the monarch's decisions. Likewise he officiated as chief priest in the rituals that ensured the prosperity of both nobles and people. Since agriculture was the main occupation he would preside ceremoniously at the times of sowing and harvest. Crops included millet, wheat and rice; the former seems to have been the main staple as well as an ingredient for making wine. There were oxen, goats, chickens and pigs, whilst dogs are the usual animals found in tombs and graves. Anyang, the chief Shang site, was a carefully planned city which fitted well into the bend of a river. The remains of an extravagant royal palace are surrounded by carefully segregated semi-subterranean dwellings for the lower orders, and foundations were frequently consecrated with animal and human victims. At Anyang too

A Shang chime-stone excavated from one of the royal tombs at Anyang, dating from between the fourteenth and eleventh century BC. The face is engraved with a stylized tiger.

very large numbers of bones and tortoise shells with oracular inscriptions have been uncovered. The continuity of Lung-shan culture and Shang civilization is evident; the important difference for us is that the scribes responsible for divination in Shang China evolved a written script and often used it to inscribe the questions and sometimes the answers, on the oracle bone or shell. From these writings a great deal of historical detail has been gleaned.

Most spectacular of all are the Shang tombs, ten of which at Anyang belonged to kings. Some of them are enormous. The Wu-kuan-ts'un tomb has a burial pit with two passages leading out of it, each forty-five metres in length. The southern passage contains two horse pits and one kneeling burial; the northern passage contains three horse pits and a human burial with two kneeling figures. Human burials are also found on the platforms on both sides of the chamber. Another victim has been placed under the coffin in a prone position with a *ko* dagger. In all the number of victims is one hundred and thirty-one – fifty-two animals and birds, and seventy-nine human remains.

ANCIENT RELIGION

Behind the funeral megalomania of the Shang kings, akin to the extravagances of their peers in Bronze Age Egypt and Mesopotamia, stood a body of religious ideas and cultic practices which were later transformed by Confucius (551–479 BC) and his followers into the state religion of China. Human sacrifice declined before Confucian teaching – there is no mention of such in the *Analects* – and, in the first century BC, a Han prince was severely punished for forcing slave musicians to follow him into death: his lands were confiscated and his son disinherited by the emperor. The continuity of Shang and the rest of early Chinese civilization lies in the rites of ancestor worship performed by the priest-king. The Shang nobles were a closely-knit kinship group, whose chief member, the king, traced his line of descent from their supreme god, Shang Ti, the founder-ancestor of their people and the present ruler of the natural world. Shang Ti was thought of as ruling on high, and his realm extended beyond the world of their deceased ancestors to include control of the great natural phenomena – sun, moon, stars, rain, wind and thunder. When a king died, he went up to heaven to join his great ancestor, bequeathing to his eldest son the role of chief worshipper in the ancestor cult. Upon the

Shang bronze *ko* blade of the sixteenth or fifteenth century BC. The bronze-bladed halberd was the chief Shang weapon and a more ornate version, the *ko* dagger, was placed in tombs. Singular to early Chinese civilization, the ritual significance of the *ko* in burial rites is obscure.

goodwill of Shang Ti and the deceased forebears everything hung; they received the appropriate sacrifices for the seasons and major events, such as birth, marriage and death, besides providing guidance and help when governmental decisions arose. Hence, political power was linked with spiritual power, and the ruler as Son of Heaven, by his harmonious relation with the spiritual realm, ensured the welfare of the state – a concept that became in Confucian theory the basis of authority. The unworthiness of a monarch would be reflected in the attitude of the heavens, just as 'the earth shook' and 'rivers were dried up' during the last years of Chieh. In this context later imperial interest in seismology is readily explained; the scientist, Chang Heng, set up the first known practical seismograph about AD 130.

In order to consult the ancestral spirits about the future two methods of divination were employed. A yes-or-no answer was given by scapulimancy and the drawing of lots, though this latter procedure did not acquire an equal status until the Chou period. Oracular inscriptions graphically outline the ancestral relationship, like these very ancient examples:

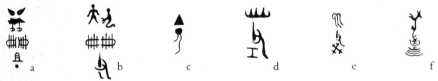

The first set of characters (a) are divided by the balustrade of the temple. Above, in the sanctuary, the eyes of the ancestor stare at the hide of a slaughtered victim, stretched on two-stakes; below, outside the temple entrance, there are offerings of raw meat and wine. In (b) the rites of ancestor worship are given even clearer exposition for, in a fit of rapture, the offering son is spiritually transported beyond the balustrade into the sanctuary, where he kneels before the very presence of the ancestor. The bottom character represents the smell of offered meat. Since the spiritual realm had to be informed of important events, it was the custom to present a new-born child to the sight of the ancestor (c). Intercession was the royal prerogative when the chief elements were involved, such as mountains (d), clouds (e) and rain-making dragons (f).

Beneath the noble class existed the vast peasantry, barely advanced beyond the Stone Age economy. Of their religion little is known. Since their chief concern was with agriculture, their deities had charge of the soil and those mysterious processes that sprout and ripen grain. Hou T'u, or She, 'prince of the earth', had a shrine in every village, and of no less importance was Hou Chi, or Ku, 'he who rules the millet'. It has been pointed out that the Shang dynasty made an unsuccessful attempt to introduce new religious customs amongst the peasants; T'ang vainly tried to change the god of soil. The chthonic religion of the people proved too firmly rooted to be downgraded by royal decree. Its customs were woven into the daily life of the countryside.

Whereas the noble married, with great and elaborate rites and ceremonies, the daughter of some other noble clan, who after her marriage would be associated with the rites of her husband's ancestral temple, the peasants celebrated every spring a festival in which the youths and girls of neighbouring villages met in free association, only translated into formal marriage in the autumn if the girls were with child.

The legendary Emperor Shun and his ministers consulting the oracles of the tortoise-shell and the milfoil. A late Ch'ing illustration.

The peasants lacked the services of the learned diviners and other priests, drawn from the ranks of the nobility, who assisted the king in the worship of Shang Ti, but there were other adepts ready to help them. The *wu*, female and male, acted as sorcerers and magicians, whose sympathetic magic eased the lot of the hard-worked peasants by placating malignant spirits and invoking aid from those more kindly disposed. Details of a ceremony of exposure survive; it suggests that the drops of sweat shed by the *wu*, dancing within a circle under the blazing sun, were expected to induce drops of rain. Most probably there were *wu* with psychic powers too. These mediums could make contact with the dead and the spirit world, though their abilities in this direction were unappreciated by the nobility. The *wu* magicians, with the whole tradition of peasant religion, remained beyond the pale, utterly divorced from respectable worship. Not for nothing did the later Taoism, in opposition to Confucian orthodoxy, draw upon the primitive strength of the *wu*. At this early stage in Chinese civilization there had already developed, in embryo, an alternative approach to the universe. As Lao-tzu (born 640 BC), the moving spirit of Taoism, was to assert, there were better ways of apprehending the nature of things than serving within the confines of the feudal Court.

Finally, a word needs to be said about the Yin-Yang theory. The visual representation of these two interacting forces illustrates their characteristics exactly. They were not thought of as being in conflict, but existing together in precarious balance, which if disturbed would bring disasters to mankind. The harmony of the universe depended upon this balance – Yin, negative, female, dark, the Earth; Yang, positive, male, light, Heaven. As the source of weather, Heaven was looked upon as the greater, the realm of Shang Ti, whose benevolence had to be entreated with sacrifices made by the One Man, the Son of Heaven. This perception of the natural forces, we have already noted, stemmed from the everyday experience of early agriculturalists in the loess country, where a sudden downpour could alter the landscape drastically. What is significant in this viewpoint, for both Chinese philosophy and science, turns on the cyclical nature of the world implied. Nature was a single intricately balanced organism, undergoing continuous alterations, with which man must learn to respond correctly. Attunement was vital. Just as Yu dug the beds of rivers deeper and kept the dykes low, conducting the waters to the sea, interdependence, not the idea of succession, was stressed. Thus events were not seen as the result of mechanical processes, like a 'billiard-ball' system of causality, in which the prior impact of one thing is the sole cause of the motion of another; but as part of one timeless pattern. Throughout the three and a half millennia of recorded history for Chinese civilization the Yin-Yang idea has had a tremendous influence on the way the black-haired people have thought and lived.

LANGUAGE   Shang script was built on pictograms. These 'pictures' gave rise to the non-alphabetical and non-phonetic character of the Chinese language. Characters developed value as ideas rather than sounds. Sound signs were added during the Chou period but a general decay set in and etymology became confused. Confucius himself complained of the scribes who were obliged to leave blank the characters they could not write. With typical ruthlessness the First

Emperor, Ch'in Shih Huang-ti, had his chief minister, Li Ssu, revise the language and issue an official index (213 BC). His collection contained 3300 characters, each written in its 'correct' manner, though Li Ssu misinterpreted some old forms. During the Han Empire (206 BC–AD 221) the number of characters multiplied three-fold in spite of attempts to establish a standard dictionary. Literacy was spreading – there were more than thirty thousand students at the Imperial Academy alone in the reign of Emperor Han Huan-ti (147–168), whilst the size of the country had grown too – and new forms were readily devised. 'Good' characters jostled with 'bad'. Although this tendency has continued down the centuries, the writing system was rationalized and characters grouped according to their radicals, or roots. Today, there are two hundred and fourteen such categories for the thousands of existing characters, of which a literate Chinese will have mastered at least two thousand.

In Chinese the sound of a word does not necessarily bear any relation to the way in which it is written. The meaning of the written character is fixed so that it is accessible to speakers of different dialects, even to a Japanese or a Korean in the case of some borrowed words. For example, the character for king, 王, is pronounced *wang* in Mandarin, the educated speech form, *ong* in the Hokien dialect, and *w'ong* in the Cantonese dialect. This common script, unrelated to dialect sound, has been a contributory factor in the age-long unity of China. The oldest surviving language, it is used by the largest number of people in the world at the present day.

The Shang scribes who first invented the written language and their descendents, the *shih* of later times, never lost their privileged place in society. Learning and scholarship brought prestige as well as access to public office, once the philosophy of Confucius had become dominant.

The histories paint Chou Hsin, the last Shang king, in even more lurid colours than the tyrant Chieh. Not only did Chou Hsin indulge in licentious games and bouts of excessive drinking, but Ta Chi, his beautiful lover, exhibited a sadism that alienated all the nobility. She devised two new instruments of torture with which to punish those who accorded the throne insufficient respect. One of them was called 'the heater' and consisted of a piece of metal, made red-hot in a fire, which accused persons were obliged to grasp with their hands. The other was a metal pole, greased all over, and placed above a pit of burning charcoal. The victim had to walk across the pillar and when his feet slipped and he fell down into the flames, Ta Chi would burst out laughing. This was known as 'roasting'.

Despite efforts by leading members of the nobility to get Chou Hsin to see the error of his ways, the kingdom tottered towards ruin as revolts grew more frequent. A rising power was Chou, an outlying territory in the west, whose chief, Ch'ang, was imprisoned by the king on suspicion of treason. During his incarceration Ch'ang studied the *I Ching* (*Book of Changes*), and composed a considerable portion of the commentary on its mysterious diagrams. This ancient text of divination became one of the Classics, the majority of which date from the Early Chou period. But Ch'ang was not a rebel, and after his release obtained the abolition of the punishment of 'roasting' and did much to restore the kingdom until his death.

EARLY CHOU
(1027–771 BC)

The Chou people claimed descent from Ch'i, the minister of agriculture to Shun, but we do not know a great deal about their origins. Half nomadic and half agricultural, the tribe had roamed from place to place until it settled in the fertile Wei valley. Wu-wang, the successor of Ch'ang, founded a new capital at Hao, near modern Sian. Perhaps the firmer economic base of the Wei valley and a residue of semi-barbarian vigour in arms combined to replace the Shang kingdom by the Chou. Discrepancies in the historical record suggest that the Chou, as they came to power, replaced the Shang version of history with their own. But the traditional Chinese view is that Wu-wang overturned the unjust and repressive rule of Chou Hsin. Since the first certain date of Chinese chronology is 841 BC, when rebellion against a Chou king, Li, led to a regency that can be accurately dated, there are several possibilities for the end of the Shang period. The capture of Anyang occurred in 1122, or 1050, or 1027 BC.

It has been argued that the fall of Shang was not the result of a popular uprising but, on the contrary, a deliberate conquest of one powerful state by another. The issue of the struggle was certainly long in doubt. The fourth son of Ch'ang, Tan, the Duke of Chou, finally established the new dynasty, when after the death of Wu, he acted as regent for the young king, Ch'eng. This elder statesman was credited with great wisdom by later generations. Looking back on these early years from the confusion at the end of the Chou dynasty, many people, the philosopher Confucius among them, regarded this period as a lost ideal. The Duke of Chou had shown proper respect for the fallen royal house – one of the remaining Shang princes was invested with the fief of Sung in order that the ancestral sacrifices might be continued – and his treatment of the scholar officials was a sign of the value he attached to peace. They were, in fact, added to the Chou civil service. The Duke of Chou addressed them, thus:

> The king says, 'I declare to you, ye numerous officers of Yin (Shang), I have not put you to death and therefore I reiterate the declaration of my charge. I have now built this great city here in Lo, considering that there is no central place in which to receive my guests from the four quarters and also that you, ye numerous officers, might here with zealous activity perform the part of ministers to us, with the obedience ye would learn. Ye have still here, I may say, your grounds and may still rest in your duties and dwellings.'

Order, harmony, respect for elders and learning – these were the virtues that Confucius thought he saw. How correct such wistful glances in the past were it is impossible to know. Certainly the *Shih Ching* (*Book of Odes*), contains this famous verse:

> Broken were our axes
> And chipped our hatchets.
> But since the Duke of Chou came to the East
> Throughout the kingdom all is well.
> He has shown compassion to us people.
> He has greatly helped us.

The relative backwardness of the Chou people may have inclined them to adopt the structure of the Shang state. Their early bronze vessels were perhaps less fine than late Shang, but not for long, and their contributions in both religion and politics brought the feudal system to full maturity. The country

was partitioned into fiefs, held by the great nobles, who were liable to render war services at the king's behest. The nobility was divided into grades, duke, marquis, count and baron, whilst the gentry, 'sons of lords', served both the king and the feudal lords. Supporting the whole system was the work of the peasant-farmers; they sustained society by producing an agricultural surplus and by providing unpaid labour in the form of the corvée. There was not a slave class of any significant size, unlike Greece and Rome. The general absence of this degrading institution is one of the notable features of Chinese civilization.

Shang Ti, because of the sufferings of the people, had called Chou to punish the wicked Chou Hsin. 'Unpitying Heaven', the Duke of Chou told his brother, Prince Shih, 'sent down ruin on Yin (Shang). Yin has lost its mandate to rule, which our house of Chou has received.' This justification for rebellion and seizure of power reinforced the old claim of legitimacy of virtue, originally made by the first Shang king, when the Hsia dynasty was deposed. It was accepted by the Middle Kingdom, as China was now called, and four hundred years of peace ensued. Not until 771 BC did the feudal system break down as a result of an alliance of barbarian tribesmen, the Chu'an Jung, with the relatives of the queen, who had been set aside because of King Yu's infatuation with a favourite concubine. Hao was sacked and the king slain. The house of Chou never recovered from this catastrophe, though a new capital was established downstream at Loyang (770 BC). Royal authority was broken and power transferred to the nobles holding great fiefs, soon independent states in all but name. Yet nominally the Chou was destined to be the longest dynasty in Chinese history, not disappearing till 256 BC.

In the century before this barbarian invasion, Chou society had begun to show signs of instability. Population growth and economic development put severe strains on the feudal structure. As population pressure built up in the middle course of the Yellow River there was a movement eastwards to the flood plains and southwards into the river systems of the Huai and the Yangtze where reliable rainfall encouraged a more diverse agriculture, and the population continued to expand. As the Chinese moved south they encountered a milder climate and different cultures. From the sub-tropical rain forests of the Yang-tze valley the cultivation of rice gradually spread northwards to rival millet as the staple food. Erosion and flooding were not as destructive in the south: agriculture became wet, since growing rice involved water control through the use of ditches, canals and basins. The shifting of economic activities and the territorial increase encouraged fragmentation. Local interests gathered themselves into definite units of organization, even if like the southern region of Ch'u power rested primarily on non-Chinese peoples. The eastern fiefs of the north steadily acquired the direction of their own affairs. In the north-west climatic conditions proved too hostile for agricultural development and a rift between the peoples of the area was apparent. Beyond the 380 mm isohyet, the limit of rainfall for settled cultivation, a nomadic way of life prevailed. From these lands the Chu'an Jung had descended with such fury on Hao and thereafter the threat of mounted raiders from the north assumed a permanent place in the anxieties of the Chinese mind.

2

The Classical Age
770–221 BC

The name of Ch'un Ch'iu has been given to the period following the destruction of Hao. It comes from the title of an historical work, *Spring and Autumn Annals*, which provides the first accurate chronology of Chinese history. Perhaps its subject, the state of Lu, accounts for the tradition that assigns authorship to Confucius, but this history of his native state does not manifest any positive evidence to support such a claim. There are constant references to it in the *Analects*, but for Confucius history was a rich chronicle of human events, the field for all moral observation. He was the first person in the world to insist that the proper study of mankind *is* man.

The Spring and Autumn period (722–481 BC) exploded the myth that China was a closely-knit feudal state. The Chou kings gradually lost their power and authority, retaining undisputed only a religious function in the small and impoverished royal domain surrounding Loyang. How empty the titles and dignities of the One Man became is recorded in the amusing story of the man from Wen.

A man from Wen migrated to Chou but Chou did not admit aliens.

'Are you an alien?' they asked him.

'No, a native,' he replied. They asked him what lane he lived in and he could not tell them, so the bailiff took him to gaol. The ruler sent a man to question him.

'Why did you call yourself a citizen when you are an alien?' he asked.

'When I was a child and learned the *Book of Odes*, I chanted the verses that went:

Any land with the heavens above it
Is the king's land.
Anyone within the circling sea
Is the king's servant.

Since Chou rules all under the heaven I am the servant of the Son of Heaven – how should I be an alien? This is why I said I was a citizen.'

The ruler of Chou made the officer release the man.

With the decay of feudal obligations and the weakening of central authority, the emergent states fought each other for territories and competed to attract technicians and even peasant-farmers. Primitive Ch'in encouraged immigration of the latter from rival states by offering houses and exemption from military service. Incessant warfare, either between the Chinese themselves or

The Great Wall of China. In 214 BC Ch'in Shih Huang-ti ordered general Meng T'ien to set up a line of fortresses along the northern frontier. The wall was largely reconstructed in the Ming dynasty (1368–1644).

35

The remains of a tiered building at Lin-tzu, Shantung, the capital of the state of Ch'i in the Warring States period.

with invading barbarians, brought about a substantial reduction in the number of states in the Middle Kingdom. There was an overall tendency for the smaller and weaker states to be absorbed by stronger ones. In the eighth century BC two hundred feudal territories existed; by 500 BC less than twenty states could boast their independence.

Some alternative form of order evolved from the *pa*, or hegemon system, whereby the most powerful prince assumed leadership of a confederation of states. The first hegemony, that of Prince Huan of Ch'i (685–643 BC), attempted to maintain the peace and repel barbarian inroads. Conferences were called in order to discuss points of mutual interest, like the sharing of rivers, and the idea of joint action was mooted. Prince Huan led his allies against Ch'u, a semi-barbarian state in the south, and forced its ruler to desist from aggression (656 BC), but such actions on behalf of the Chou monarch were rarely more than a cloak for the hegemon's own policies. The superiority of Ch'i derived from early monopolies in salt and iron, the first appearance of this metal. In one of Prince Huan's conversations it was said, 'The lovely metal (bronze) is used for casting swords and pikes; it is used in company of dogs and horses. The ugly metal (iron) is used for casting hoes which flatten weeds and axes which fell trees; it is used upon the fruitful earth.'

The Iron Age had arrived in China. At first the new metal had little impact on weapons of war, as iron cores to arrow heads and swords started to appear only at the end of the Ch'un Ch'iu period; its immediate and lasting effect was on agriculture, where the efficiency of iron ploughshares made cultivation easier. This increased productivity may partly account for the non-appearance of a large slave population in the early civilization of China: a massive single labour force was not required to work the land.

Prince Huan was regarded as an enlightened leader. Scholars were welcomed in Lin-tzu, the capital of Ch'i, and commerce flourished. Yet during his reign of forty-three years he went to war no less than twenty-eight times. After his death the belligerent tendencies of the states continued to predominate, and within each state itself intrigue and violence deposed many a prince. The hegemony then passed to Sung (650 BC), T'sin (636 BC), Ch'in (629 BC) and Ch'u (613 BC). If these shifts in the balance of power indicated anything, it was that no state had strength enough to unify the Middle Kingdom. In the year 546 BC the chief minister of Sung, one of the smaller central states that had suffered terribly in the prolonged struggle between T'sin and Ch'u, took the initiative in calling a peace conference at Shangch'ui. Surprisingly, the agreement lasted for forty years, when it was breached by Wu, a newly sinicized power, which had not attended the conference. The result of this resumption of hostilities was the last part of the Classical Age, known as the Warring States (481–221 BC). These years witnessed the death throes of feudal society and ended in the unification of all China, the foundation of the first Chinese Empire by triumphant Ch'in.

THE RISE OF CH'IN   In 403 BC the internal troubles of T'sin split it into three separate states: Han, Wei and Chao. This disintegration left Ch'in in a strong position, particularly in the Yellow River valley: taking advantage of the opportunity successive princes developed the power base until Ch'in could rival and defeat Ch'u, the other contender for supremacy. Powerless, the Son of Heaven could only watch as these two great powers, still largely semi-barbarian states on the fringes of the Middle Kingdom, gained territory through the quarrels of their Chinese neighbours. The dilemma of the Chinese states is well expressed in this outline of foreign policy choices that a minister explained to Prince Chien of Ch'i (264–221 BC):

> To the west of Chou and Han lies mighty Ch'in and to the east of them are Chao and Wei. If Ch'in attacks them in the west, Chao and Wei will also take territory from Chou and Han; Han will be defeated and Chou harmed. When they are defeated and harmed Chao and Wei cannot but be troubled by Ch'in.
> Now if Ch'i and Ch'in attack Chao and Wei this would in no way differ from Chao and Wei making use of Ch'in's attack in order to assault Han and Chou. Ch'i allies with Ch'in and attacks Chao and Wei. When they have perished, Ch'in will come east and invade Ch'i. Then will you find help anywhere under heaven?

The swift rise of Ch'in through the turmoil of the Warring States period is not simply a tale of military decisiveness sweeping away the anarchy of decayed feudalism. For this political change in the constitution of the Middle Kingdom, startling though it was to the people of that time, corresponded with a fundamental transformation of the social and economic structure as well as a thorough reshaping of the intellectual outlook of China. This was the Classical Age, when Chinese civilization found its pattern. The four social classes formed below the feudal hierarchy. Water schemes began to improve the countryside. Cities and towns multiplied. Science and technology developed. Great thinkers appeared, leaving their mark on the minds of future generations.

The Ch'in conquest of Shu and Pa added valuable resources and outflanked the rival state of Ch'u (316 BC). But it was the foresight of one of the Ch'in governors, Li Ping, that converted this region into a valuable asset. He persuaded the non-Chinese inhabitants and the new colonists to undertake the construction of a remarkable system of irrigation which established its agricultural prosperity forever. The central work in the scheme was a dam that divided the Min River into two main streams, each of which branched out into numerous minor canals with a network of thousands of irrigation ditches. People soon called the Ch'engtu plain 'sea-on-land'. However, the origin of the famous Chengkuo Canal, which connected the Ching and Lo rivers north of the Wei valley, was an intrigue aimed at bringing Ch'in to ruin. Ssu-ma Ch'ien records:

> That the Prince of Han wished to prevent the eastern expansion of Ch'in by exhausting it with projects. He therefore sent the water engineer, Cheng Kuo, to the Prince of Ch'in to convince him that a canal should be built between the Ching and the Lo rivers. The proposed canal would be 300 *li* long and used for irrigation. The project was half finished when the trick was discovered. The Prince was stopped from killing Cheng Kuo by the engineer's own argument. 'Although this scheme was intended to injure you,' he said, 'if the canal is completed, it will bring great benefit to Ch'in.' The work was then ordered to be continued. When finished it irrigated 40,000 *ch'ing* of poor land with water laden with rich silt. The productivity of the fields rose to one *chung* for each *mu*. Thus, the interior became a fertile plain without bad years. Ch'in, then, grew rich and strong and finally conquered all the other feudal states. The canal was called Chengkuo Canal.

So the plot misfired badly; Han had bestowed on Ch'in the key to eventual victory. The additional grain from this vast area supported extra soldiers and the strategic advantage of the canal was greatly improved communications. The Chengkuo Canal, opened in the year 246 BC, transformed what is now central Shensi into the first key economic area, an economic area where agricultural productivity and facilities of transport permitted a supply of grain-tribute so superior to that of other areas, that the people who controlled it could control all China.

The construction of large-scale hydraulic conservancy schemes became a settled policy on the part of Ch'in. Organizing such public works greatly increased the central authority of the prince, at the expense of the nobility, and a more streamlined state emerged, the predecessor of the bureaucratic system that later comprised the Chinese Empire. The Court ceased to be the preserve of the high-born. A successful and respected minister, Lu Pu-wei, was originally a merchant; he led a group with scientific and technological interests. When the prince of Han sent Cheng Kuo to Ch'in, he must have thought that the semi-barbarian state which was known for its own innovations would fall victim of a grandiose scheme, through inexperience. He could not have judged more incorrectly. If there was one characteristic of Ch'in, it was a fanatical determination. Chengkuo Canal was constructed, though such projects were unusual at the time, because the ethic of the state, the philosophy associated with the name of Shang Yang, who served Ch'in from 350 to 338 BC, subordinated everything to the will of the ruler. In true fascist manner the justification of political organization was war. 'Agriculture and War' is the title of a chapter in the *Book of Lord Shang*: only those occupations that contributed to the war effort merited any reward. To direct all the energies of the state to this end cruelty was introduced. It had to be made worse for people to

A late Ch'ing illustration of the river conservancy schemes of Yu the Great Engineer. Here dykes are being strengthened and sandbanks removed.

導黑水副圖

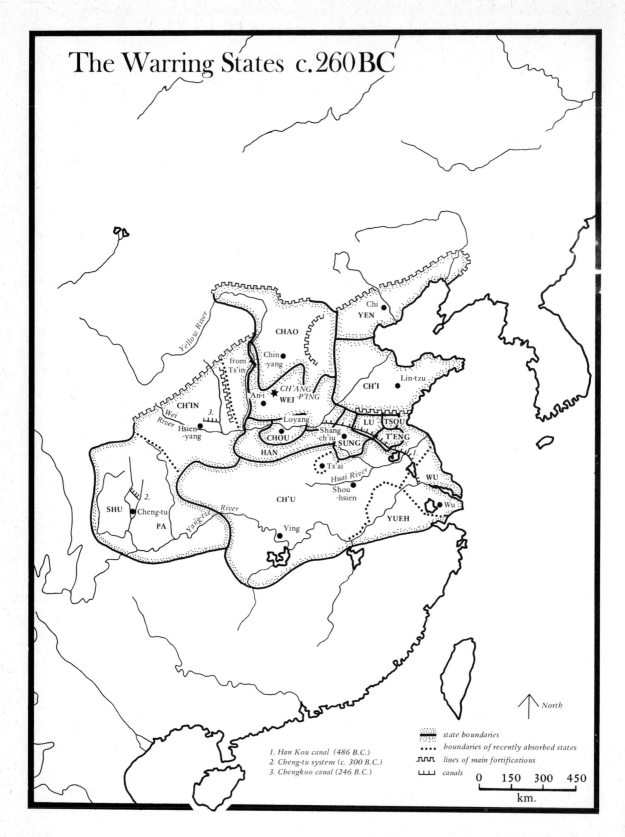

The Warring States c.260BC

CHAO
Chi
YEN
Chin-yang
from Ts'in
An-i
CH'ANG-P'ING
WEI
CH'I
Lin-tzu
CH'IN
3.
Wei River
Hsien-yang
Loyang
CHOU
Shang-ch'iu
LU TSOU
HAN
SUNG
T'ENG
Ts'ai
Huai River
WU
Shou-hsien
SHU
Cheng-tu
PA
Yangtze River
CH'U
Wu
Ying
YUEH

North

1. Han Kou canal (486 B.C.)
2. Cheng-tu system (c. 300 B.C.)
3. Chengkuo canal (246 B.C.)

state boundaries
boundaries of recently absorbed states
lines of main fortifications
canals

0   150   300   450
km.

fall into the hands of the police than to fight the forces of an enemy state. The draconian nature of the punishments recommended by the philosophers of the School of Law underpinned the authoritarianism of the princes of Ch'in.

The second semi-barbarian state of influence was Ch'u, centred in the Yang-tze River valley. Although this area was endowed with a mild climate suited to agriculture, there was no effective exploitation of this resource, unlike in its ruthless competitor Ch'in. Possibly the loess soil of the northern state, with the resulting importance of irrigation, was the lever by which the prince of Ch'in could move his people as a unified force, whereas the prince of Ch'u could achieve much less social cohesion. Another disadvantage of Ch'u was the presence of Yueh, a warlike coastal state, on its eastern flank. Not until 346 BC did Ch'u manage to defeat this troublesome neighbour. Nevertheless, Ch'u was able to expand northwards and the native state of Confucius, Lu, fell to its forces in 249 BC. But not all of the Chinese states were as ineffective as Han in resisting the encroachment of Ch'in and, to a lesser extent, Ch'u. One of the innovators of the Warring States period was Wu Ling, Prince of Chao (325–299 BC). Disregarding tradition and the laughter of his peers, Prince Wu Ling bade his people adopt 'barbarian' dress, for he took over not only the Hu tactic of cavalry but even the trousers worn by these Mongolian tribesmen. It was the death-knell of the chariot, but not sufficient as a military weapon to protect the territories of Chao. At the battle of Ch'ang P'ing the army of Chao was overwhelmed and the Ch'in generals put to death four hundred thousand prisoners (259 BC). A shock went through Chinese society. Then, again, three years later Ch'in struck a blow at the very heart of the Middle Kingdom. Chou was attacked and the Son of Heaven forced from his little throne. The Chou dynasty passed into history, its ancestral spirits into neglect. From this moment onward all eyes apprehensively watched as Ch'in destroyed one state after another, in the words of Ssu-ma Ch'ien, 'like a silkworm devours a mulberry leaf'.

With the elevation of Prince Cheng in 246 BC Ch'in girded itself for the final struggle: preparations lasting for more than a decade were made under the direction of two outstanding ministers, Lu Pu-wei and Li Ssu. There is some archaeological evidence, not yet too positive, that steel weapons were developed. Han went down in 230 BC, soon followed by Chao (228 BC), Ch'i (226 BC) and Wei (225 BC), but the decisive encounter did not occur till the year 223 BC, when the rival state of Ch'u was completely overrun. Another year brought the end of remote Yen and the 'Tiger of Ch'in', as Prince Cheng was called, proclaimed himself Shih Huang-ti, 'the First Emperor'.

SOCIETY IN
TRANSITION

A sense of loss haunted many of the philosophers of the Warring States period. In the centuries of ever-increasing turmoil down to the triumph of Ch'in it was not unnatural to look back with nostalgia at the early Chou kingdom, when, according to the *Shih Ching (Book of Odes)*, feudal society was in a state of perfect repair. But this conviction that the Golden Age had passed and that civilization was in decline reflected not only the change in political realities; much of its strength was drawn from the great social upheaval that accompanied the end of feudalism. Alongside the process of centralization that led to the foundation in 221 BC of a unified empire organized by bureaucratic officials, an equally significant social revolution was happening. In place of the old feudal structure, with its sharp division between a hereditary nobility and the peasantry, a more complex community evolved, so that all sections of society became the First Emperor's subjects, likewise divided, but by less insurmountable barriers than birth. Under the first purely Chinese dynasty, the Former Han (202 BC–AD 9), the last vestiges of feudalism disappeared and the political structure assumed a pattern that was to serve China until 1911, when the Empire was overthrown and the Republic founded. The twin pillars of this society, which supported the world's largest enduring state, were a progressively more privileged bureaucracy closely connected with the landowning class, and the great multitude of farmers, no longer tied to a feudal lord but now liable to taxation, labour on public works, and military service. Here we are concerned with the transition of Chinese society from feudalism to the new order of the imperial era, because in these far-reaching changes can be discerned the lasting fundamentals of social organization.

The *Book of Odes* has recorded the ideal life of the feudal manor in several fine poems based on the rural calendar. This verse describes some of the service rendered by the peasants:

> In the fourth month the milkwort is in spike,
> In the fifth month the cicada cries.
> In the eighth month the harvest is gathered,
> In the tenth month the boughs fall.
> In the days of the First we hunt the racoon,
> And take those foxes and wild-cats
> To make furs for our Lord.
> In the days of the Second is the great Meet;
> Practice for deeds of war.
> The one-year-old boar we keep;
> The three-year-old we offer to our Lord.

The picture given is one of peace and prosperity, of an orderly rural life, and cordial relations between noble and peasant, but there can be little doubt that life was hard for the tillers of the soil. They had to work from dawn to dusk and were at the beck and call of their masters. Yet the fundamental importance of the peasant-farmers to Chinese civilization was fully recognized by the nobility and their welfare was achieved by the construction of mud-walled villages that afforded winter shelter as well as protection from marauders. Permanent fields had replaced the primitive system of burn-and-clear agriculture during the Early Chou period. In 594 BC the state of Lu levied the first land tax of which there is a record.

Throughout the Classical Age there was a gradual loosening of feudal ties. In some states, like Ch'in, the process was deliberately accelerated as a policy aimed at strengthening the central authority of the prince; in others, various economic factors played their part in hastening or retarding the break-up of the simple model described in the *Book of Odes*. Whilst the apex of the feudal hierarchy remained, those ancient families connected with the royal house and bearing the titles of duke, marquis, count, viscount and baron, the power base of this hereditary group, were under mounting pressure. The challenge was two-fold – external and internal. In 598 BC the prince of Ch'u invaded the small state of Ch'en because its ruler had been assassinated by a minister and the culprit deserved punishment; but conquest led to annexation, not a restoration of the native house. Then, again, the prince of Lu was reduced to a puppet during Confucius' lifetime. Just as the prestige and influence of the Chou kings had declined, within the various states, except Ch'in, there was a tendency for the clans of principal ministers to usurp power at the expense of the ruler. These powerful families as well as the nobler families they eclipsed were to be uprooted and dispersed by the First Emperor. After the foundation of the Empire, particularly in the Former Han period, the aristocracy was confined to relatives of the reigning imperial house; its members, carefully watched and kept out of the administration, ceased to have any influence in public affairs.

Iron moulds for casting sickle-blades dating from the fifth or fourth century BC in the Warring States period; excavated at Hsing-lung, Hopei, in 1953.

If uncertainty and confusion were normal within the feudal Court itself, the experience of social change for the rest of the population, though less dramatic, was even more decisive. It was at this time that four famous estates were first recognized. These classes, in order of precedence, were *shih*, the lesser nobility, that is the gentry, knights and scholars; *nung*, the peasant-farmers; *kung*, the artisans; and *shang*, the merchants. Before considering each estate in turn, it is necessary to notice the significance of the social order. The low position of the merchants was the natural outcome of economic development in the Classical Age, because princes assumed most of the responsibility for industry and hydraulic conservancy works. Metal working was more than an adjunct of state policy: iron agricultural tools were called 'a matter of life and death to the peasantry' and iron weapons may have contributed to the victory of Ch'in. In the Han Empire there were further extensions of nationalization, placing under imperial control the salt and iron industries as well as the making of wine and beer. At the same time there was an attempt by law to prevent merchants from owning land, though it is doubtful if it was effective in curbing speculation. Another emphasis unusual to people brought up in the West is the long-standing Chinese distaste for the military. 'Good iron is not made into nails, nor good men into soldiers', runs an ancient proverb. Later, the harshness of Ch'in rule only served to confirm this view, though it is likely that a large part of the original impulse came from the philosophy of Mo-tzu (fifth century BC), who taught the folly of war and insisted upon the brotherhood of all men. Yet the importance attached to learning by Confucius, and the consequent respect for one's teacher, ensured that the pattern of Chinese society was based on a civil ethic. Good behaviour meant the performance of the duties of a citizen. The poor status of merchant and soldier has remained down the centuries.

Out of the struggle for power between states and within states emerged a new social class, just below the feudal hierarchy. It was the *shih*. With the blurring of feudal distinctions and the disappearance of so many states, the rights of birth seemed to count for less than ability and talent. A growing surplus of younger sons from noble families, educated but without rank, took advantage of whatever opportunities offered themselves. These *shih* were forced to rely on their own exertions. Since they usually inherited sufficient property or means to be able to survive without undertaking manual toil, the lot of peasant-farmer seemed unattractive to them, whereas a career of service with a state or noble family did not. 'In the thirteenth year (of Prince Wen, or 753 BC) Ch'in for the first time appointed scribes', Ssu-ma Ch'ien tells us, 'in order to record events.' At this time Ch'in was a young state and the appoint-

The Classical Age

ment of scribes, the beginnings of a secretariat for central administration, was in line with the practice of the older, purely Chinese states. Such posts were open to the *shih*. Promotion might follow, perhaps even a feudal title. During the Warring States period itinerant members of this class were willing to sell their services to the highest bidder. When political intrigue and warfare were incessant, princes lent an ear to any scheme that seemed to promise some new advantage. Finding his own state of Lu uninterested in his ideas for reform, Confucius himself had become one of the first of the 'wandering scholars', moving from one capital to another in a vain search for a ruler who would listen sympathetically to virtuous advice. By the lifetime of his great follower, Mencius, the century in which Ch'in became dominant, only those *shih* with destructive projects were welcomed. War, of course, was another career, as officers were needed for the large armies that battled with each other campaign after campaign. Other *shih* must have been tempted into commerce, as the name *shang*, meaning merchants, was the same as that of the Shang dynasty.

The *nung*, the peasant-farmers, retained their social importance in spite of the dissolution of the old communal structures of feudalism. Their work was considered productive and fundamental, for it supplied food for society. The work of artisans and merchants, however, was non-productive and secondary. Hence, throughout the ages Chinese writers have praised the diligent farmer, satirized the official, and attacked the cruelty of the military officer. This does not mean that there was no rural distress. On the contrary, the poverty of peasants is a perennial theme, though successive governments have sought to protect the honest countrymen. What did not occur in China – and all the reasons for this unique historical course of social development are yet un-known – was the institution of large-scale slavery as understood in the Ancient World: Egypt, Mesopotamia, Greece and Rome. It is impossible to give dates for the series of events that led up to the creation of a free peasantry. Certainly the introduction of private ownership of land in Ch'in, a policy of Shang Yang, cannot be ignored, because it was this state that founded the First Empire. Nevertheless, the buying and selling of land was general in Wei at the same time, and, noted in several states, was the plight of the small farmer, squeezed by taxation and labour duty, whose accumulating debts forced him to sell and become a tenant or share-cropper. The *ching tien*, or 'well-field' system, was the normal arrangement for land tenure, though Mencius advised the Duke of T'eng to adopt a more flexible policy in areas of dense population. He said:

> In the remoter districts, let the nine-lot division be observed, and let one lot be set apart as a 'helping lot' – a lot which the eight families help each other to cultivate as land for the lord. In the city and suburban areas, let the people pay a tax of a tenth part of their produce, and render military service.

We have already referred to the way in which Ch'in competed for population, by offering immigrant *nung* land, houses and exemption from military service. Likewise, valour displayed in battle by subjects of Ch'in was rewarded with grants of land. Shu and Pa were deliberately settled with a free peasantry. The princes of Ch'in shifted the internal balance of power within their state against the nobility by encouraging the growth of a free smallholding class. But it was the spread of iron technology which most probably hastened the disintegra-

Intensive agriculture around the walled-city-in-the-country; an illustration of the famous statement in the *Shu Ching*, 'Heaven sees according to what the people see, Heaven hears according to what the people hear'.

視聽自民圖

tion of feudal bonds. 'The ugly metal' provided more efficient hoes, plough-shares, picks and axes; it permitted the effective working of the land by smaller numbers of peasant-farmers. The rapid strides in iron metallurgy, leading to the production of cast iron in China over seventeen centuries before the West, may have been the chief economic factor that shaped Chinese society, putting an end to the Shang legacy of slavery. As decisive an influence on social structure could have been the crossbow, another early technical achievement. The *nung* called out in feudal levies were armed with such bows. These powerful offensive weapons explain the strategy of military walls, which were constructed along frontiers during the Warring States period. On the northern and north-western frontiers these extensive fortifications were designed to resist nomad attacks. The veteran-farmers settled nearby would man them in an emergency as an infantry force armed with the crossbow. In conflicts between or within states, the deadly shafts could be brought to bear on noble and commoner alike. Armour was rudimentary, composed of bamboo and wood; hence, the Chinese feudal lord was vulnerable in contrast with the later Western knight, protected by his steel armour, lance and sword, and mounted on an armoured horse. The *nung* were at no such tactical disadvantage, and Mencius could argue the right of the people to overthrow tyrants.

Around the feudal courts groups of *kung*, artisans, gathered as demand rose for luxury items. These craftsmen were skilled in carving jade, ivory and bamboo, besides working with precious stones and metals. From Shang times the Chinese had displayed a pre-eminence in the casting of bronze vessels that were used in the ritual associated with ancestor worship. As the agricultural base of the economy improved, with increased production from reduced manpower, a regular supply of food became available for the *kung*, whose usefulness was evident in the arts of peace and war. Chariots, swords and the firing mechanism for crossbows formed the staple ingredients of the arms race, so that princes and the great noble families vied with each other to attract the best technicians of the day. Their arsenals and workshops were the prototypes of imperial manufacturing works established in the Han period.

The complexities of production and distribution gave the merchants, the *shang*, their chance. Iron had to be brought from the mountains of what is now Szechuan; salt, fish, lacquer, silk and musical instruments needed moving out of Shantung; from the North could be obtained wood and precious stones; and within the various states a local speciality of one kind or another usually justified commercial enterprise. Improved communications, road and canal, facilitated trade between the cities, now often with populations in excess of 100,000. Coins had replaced barter and cowrie shells well before the Warring States period, as state mints issued copper and gold denominations. Many merchants acquired great wealth but their position was never secure. Princes were loath to lose control of economic policy and the scholar officials closed their ranks against the sons of wealthy merchants. The *kung* had a more favourable legal position than the *shang*, who were debarred from wearing silk garments and riding on horses or in carriages. Social mobility was to be the price of affluence in imperial times, when sumptuary laws and swingeing taxation were the means of periodical control. Prestige could be gained by associating with those honoured by society, the nobles and the officials, but the source of the merchant's wealth remained a liability.

A tamped or rammed earth wall under construction.

BELOW A brick dating from the Ch'in dynasty decorated with hunting scenes.

Common to all classes was the family, the keystone of Chinese society. Ancestor worship would suggest that it should have been the basic social unit. 'The hundred families' had long been a name for the Chinese nation, and there were many large families.

Yet the family as an institution was threatened, like much else in feudal society, by the philosophy of Ch'in. Shang Yang passed a law that imposed a double tax on persons with two or more adult sons living with them. Communal ownership gave place to individual possessions and nuclear families. Opposed to this view was Confucian philosophy, ultimately the dominant one in Chinese civilization. Possibly Ch'in and, to a lesser extent, Ch'u represented a semi-barbarian kinship system. In conversation with the Duke of She, elder statesman of the southern power and a man of moral principle, Confucius disagreed about this very issue. Whereas the duke saw an individual's first loyalty to the state, the philosopher maintained it was to the family. 'The Duke of She said to Confucius, "Among us there are those who are so upright that if his father steals a sheep, the son will testify against him." Confucius replied, "Among us the upright act quite differently. The son shields the father, and the father shields the son; we regard this as uprightness."' What might be called an off-shoot of large families, or clans, were the numerous secret societies. These associations may have grown up in response to the general decay of society during the Warring States period. They provided protection in uncertain times, such as during the decline of a dynasty, and were often directly connected with popular rebellions.

TECHNOLOGY Significant technical advances in various fields occurred during the Classical Age. These new developments in technology were largely responsible for the transformation of China into a centralized, well-organized state by 221 BC. They provided an economic capability that ensured China could maintain its civilization entirely independent of other parts of the Ancient World, thus preserving the cultural pattern they had helped create. The improvements were in building, communications, hydraulics and metallurgy.

Building technology was concerned primarily with the construction of walls. The ubiquity of walls in Chinese civilization has often been remarked. Every Chinese city had its surrounding wall, whilst there was hardly a village of any size in northern China which had not at least a mud wall around its huts and stables. Within the city itself, walls divided the dwelling areas into lots and compounds, sections and districts. Gates, sometimes set in large watch towers, controlled the means of access from one part to another. Cities were planned and the arrangement of walls reinforced the power of the authorities – the prince and his officials. The chief method of wall construction was tamped or rammed earth. Wooden shuttering was used, dry earth being rammed inside until solid. Then, the shuttering would be removed and the process repeated at a higher level. Bamboo might be placed between each layer to absorb moisture. 'Earth' walls probably determined the two most characteristic features of Chinese architecture, namely that walls were not in general weight-bearing, and that buildings were furnished with generously overhanging eaves. During the Ch'un Ch'iu period sun-dried bricks were added as a facing for 'earth' walls, and by the end of the Warring States period fire-baked bricks, sometimes highly ornamented, had become available. Archaeological discoveries at the Ch'in capital have revealed water-conduits of thick stoneware.

When the ancient Asian nomads surrounded their camps with a rampart of earth, it is not surprising that the agrarian culture of China erected walls around its earliest cities. The rural landscape was dominated by the walled city, which contained the state granaries that held the grain-tribute or tax upon which organized government depended. This food surplus maintained the army and the conscripted labour force involved in water-conservancy schemes. As canals and irrigation projects became more complex and more general, particularly from the Han Empire onwards, the walled-city-in-the-country was the effective seat of government and administration. Nightsoil being the chief fertilizer in China, it was inevitable that intensive agriculture developed in the fields just outside the walls of cities.

Shang cities possessed extensive fortifications. Those of Ao, due south of Anyang, almost twenty metres wide at the base, enclosed an area of 1,756 square metres. Impetus for advance in the art of fortification came from the collapse of Chou power and the deadly rivalry between the Warring States. City walls were enlarged and strengthened against such devices as tunnels and the diversion of rivers to weaken their foundations. Other military walls were those constructed along state frontiers, especially in the north where the Chinese were reaching lands unsuited to settled agriculture. Here was a cleavage between two environments, the lands of the steppe and the lands of the sown. The various walls built by the Warring States were eventually linked by the First Emperor to form the Great Wall, which was intended to thwart potential cavalry attacks by nomads. The Great Wall is well over three thousand kilometres long and it is thought the only work of man which could be picked out by Martian astronomers.

There can be no doubt concerning the superiority of ancient Chinese roads to Roman ones. At the same time that Rome was forming its impressive road network in the West, there already existed in the Yellow River valley an

A Shang bronze vessel in the shape of a man being protected by a tiger dating from between the fourteenth and twelfth century BC. It was either a ritual wine vessel, a *yu* or a pourer used for ritual ablutions, a *ho*.

advanced communications system. Whereas the Roman road might be described as a heavy wall laid on its side, the Chou road was essentially a thin, convex, watertight 'shell', resting on ordinary subsoil. In this use of a light and elastic road surface the Chinese avoided the problems of temperature change and anticipated the technique of John McAdam by two millennia. During the Warring States period there was much road-building activity both for military and commercial purposes. A factor in the success of Ch'in may have been its development of communications, road and canal. In a debate about policy Ts'ai Tse told the Marquis Ying, the chief minister, that he had heard of his plans which 'would control the Lords from where he sits, would direct wealth from the land of Three Rivers so that it bears fruit in Yi-yang, would seal off the way through Sheepgut Canyons, garrison the mouth of the Great Highroad, cut off Fan and Chung-hang's tail and build a long and trestled roadway to Shu-Han so that all the world may fear Ch'in'.

The economic importance of Shu and Pa as the source of iron led to the construction of the several roads from the Ch'in heartland. A southern extension was the famous 'Five-Foot Way', built by the First Emperor. This road ran from Shu to Yeh-yu, near Kunming Lakes, and for many miles there were 'hanging galleries', suspended along the sides of precipitous slopes. The 'hanging galleries' were wooden balconies jutting out from the cliff-face; they carried a road about five metres wide. Along its route there were a variety of bridges, though records exist of more than one bridge over a thousand feet in length, with nearly seventy spans, in the Wei valley. The simple wooden beam bridge had been extended into a trestle structure, resting on piers close to the water-level and likely to disappear from sight at flood seasons. Boat bridges were also in use as well as simple stone arch bridges.

The imperial post-station system was started under the Chou kings. Messengers, coachmen and station-masters were maintained by the states in order to improve communications. Diplomatic missions sent out by the state of Lu increased from 179 kilometres per mission in the late eighth century to 726 kilometres per mission in the late sixth century. Improved vehicles facilitated easier travel. The Shang had chariots with solid wheels, but in the Warring States period these cumbersome wheels gave place to more efficient ones, with a hub, spokes and a rim. An efficient equine harness originated in China at this time too. Unlike the throat-and-girth harness of the Ancient World down to the end of the Roman Empire, the Chinese trace harness and the later, improved collar harness did not choke the horse and so reduce its tractive power by about one-third. Heavy carts, with strengthened wheels and axles, were becoming common at the end of the Classical Age. These vehicles and boats carried goods, grain and military supplies, though water transport was to assume chief importance after the Han Empire.

Navigation was appreciated early in China. The great mechanical advantage which canals offer for the transportation of heavy goods, anticipating the canal building era that accompanied the Industrial Revolution in the West by eighteen centuries, was realized during the Warring States period. In 486 BC the Prince of Wu ordered the construction of the Han Kou Canal, which connected the Huai River with the Yang-tze. His objectives were military; he wanted a means of supplying Wu troops attacking Sung and Lu to the north. This canal – the first practical inland artificial waterway in human history –

A camel train near a western section of the Great Wall.

now forms a section of the Grand Canal, linking Hangchow with Peking, the oldest summit canal in any civilization (thirteenth century). Hydraulic engineering, we have already noticed, has been crucial to Chinese civilization. Of all the countries in the world China's control and use of water has been outstanding. The environment permitted irrigation on a small scale and then encouraged not only irrigation but schemes of drainage and flood prevention on an increasingly larger scale. It should be remembered that Yu the Great Engineer is connected with the origins of feudalism. He founded the Hsia dynasty after organizing the people into a labour force capable of 'controlling the waters'. The corvée provided the manpower required for hydraulic engineering, a vast supply of labour unavailable in primitive collectivist

society. In the long term, of course, irrigation schemes and the construction of artificial waterways undermined the feudal system. The great Chengkuo project only served to increase the central authority of the Ch'in state, but this process of centralization was only completed in 221 BC.

Prince Huan of Ch'i is supposed to have thrown up dykes along the lower reaches of the Yellow River, thereby concentrating the nine streams of the previous delta into one. This early experiment failed (before 600 BC). The load of silt carried annually by the Yellow River is 1,000,000,000 tonnes, much of which is deposited in its own bed on the flood plain. The continuous elevation of the river makes it very vulnerable to changes in course and flooding when its banks burst. Therefore, Yu had 'caused the channels and canals to be dug

TOP A Han stone relief of officials in their carriage. A more efficient equine collar harness originated in this period.

ABOVE A carriage on a low wooden beam bridge; a Han stone relief.

Kung at work in the
Imperial Workshops; a
late Ch'ing illustration.

and deepened' and Li Ping, the Ch'in engineer, adopted the motto, 'Dig the channel deep, and keep the dykes low'. Because of the size and variation in the flow of China's rivers the usual policy of hydraulics was co-operation with Nature rather than any attempt to contain the rush of water.

The triumph of Ch'in was intimately bound up with technical advance. Although the First Emperor had supported large-scale schemes before his conquest of all the Warring States, they were a matter of urgent necessity after 221 BC. He was left with an enormous army, besides countless prisoners, and the *nung*, now freed from the old feudalism. In order to occupy these idle hands and break up what remained of the previous social structure, the Ch'in Emperor undertook the construction of the Great Wall, the imperial road network, and strategic canals, like the Kuahsien system in the Ordos (215 BC) and the Magic Canal, which joined the Yang-tze to the West River and opened up the far south (219 BC).

Finally, there was the revolution in metal working. Although bronze reached China as late as 1500 BC, the Chinese attained a far higher level of technique than other bronze users. The advanced kilns of the native ceramics industry must have played an important part in this development, just as they facilitated the unprecedented leap forward in iron metallurgy during the period of the Warring States. There are references to sophisticated iron-casting in Ch'i (before 600 BC) and in Wu (before 500 BC), but archaeology points to the sixth century, when the use of iron probably permeated eastwards via the passes of the Tarim Basin. This could account for the state iron industries in Ch'in, though the rich deposits of iron ore in Shu and Pa must have also contributed to such a decisive advance. Iron weapons, or bronze weapons with iron cores, partially explain some of the crushing defeats that Ch'in armies inflicted on their opponents. In agriculture the growth of irrigation schemes, the use of oxen to pull the plough, the improved calendar and the increasing application of animal and human fertilizer, combined with the introduction of iron implements to cause a revolutionary growth in the productivity of labour. The population of China may have grown five-fold to around fifty millions in the Classical Age, an upsurge that was supported by better agricultural methods as much as by an extension of the area of cultivation.

Iron was used for tools, weapons and moulds for casting. Most important of all is the fact that iron-casting was practised almost as soon as iron was known. In the West iron metallurgy was to be limited to the forge until 1350. Steel could have been produced during the period of the Warring States, but the earliest archaeological evidence so far indicates the end of the Han Empire. Possible reasons for this amazing progress in iron and steel technology include the high phosphorus content of Chinese iron ores, which have a low melting-point; good refractory clays, permitting the construction of adequate blast furnaces and crucibles; the invention of the double-acting piston bellows, which gave a strong and continuous blast for furnaces, thus keeping temperatures high; the application of water-power to these bellows during the Han Empire; the use of coal for making very hot piles around crucibles, not later than the fourth century; and the expertise derived from the pottery and bronze industries.

3

Classical Philosophy and Art

The final centuries of turmoil and confusion down to the triumph of the state of Ch'in called forth great intellectual ferment. Men cast about for explanations of contemporary failure. This was the time of the Hundred Schools, when roving philosophers offered advice to any lord who would listen to them or collected followers in order to establish a body of teachings. Ch'i was the first state that encouraged scholars to take up residence in its capital; it was a policy of the first hegemon, Prince Huan. But not every state was so enlightened. Although Lu was then regarded as a repository of ancient culture and ceremonies and this prestige did something to deter other states from invading, Confucius was singularly neglected by his fellow countrymen. Many lords, however, welcomed *shih* at their courts, expecting to obtain from their fertile minds all kinds of ideas and schemes that might be turned to good account. Rewards for useful service included titles and emoluments, though even successful policy-makers like Shang Yang could find that execution awaited them at the end of their careers. A descendant of the princely house of Wei, he had entered the service of Ch'in in 350 BC, acted as chief minister and received a high feudal title, before falling from favour in 338 BC. In spite of such uncertainties and the turbulence of foreign affairs throughout the Warring States period, there emerged a number of fully developed and distinct philosophical systems, two of which, Taoism and Confucianism, were to become the main currents in Chinese thought. Because of the lasting importance of these two mutually opposed philosophies we shall discuss each separately, but before doing so, a look at two other schools that competed for the allegiance of men's minds in the Classical Age will not be out of place. Paradoxically, these now neglected philosophies, Mohism and Legalism, were the most heatedly contested in the debates of the time. The supporters of Mo-tzu (*c.* 479–438 BC) were probably the best organized as an intellectual movement and their firm acknowledgement of the spiritual realm had far greater appeal for the *nung* than did the implicit agnosticism of the Confucians. Strangely enough the ideas of Mo-tzu vanished almost without trace after Ch'in Shih Huang-ti burned the books and imposed Legalist doctrines on the Empire. But the harsh code of the Legalists did not enjoy supremacy for long; Confucianism was made the official ethic during the Former Han period and Taoism, its perennial antagonist, revived sufficiently to develop all the attributes of a major religious belief.

So complete was the disappearance of Mohism that Ssu-ma Ch'ien did not

'A HUNDRED
SCHOOLS
CONTEND'

Lao-tzu, the Old
Philosopher, the founder
of Taoism.

56

even know the approximate dates of its founder Mo-tzu. It is now accepted that he died not long before the birth of Mencius, who spent much energy in refuting his ideas. Mo-tzu was born in Lu, where he ran a school or academy like Confucius before him, and it is believed that he was briefly a minister in Sung. After his death Mohists recognized a Grand Master, held by various individuals in direct succession from the philosopher, and some kind of unity was maintained between the different schools of interpretation that came into existence. Of all Mo-tzu's conceptions the most sublime was universal love. He detested war and argued the brotherhood of all men. 'The man of Ch'u is my brother', he told his followers, lest they restrict affection to family, clan or even the Chinese feudal states. The chief target of Mo-tzu was filial piety, so dear to the Confucians, though he stopped short of the condemnation of feudalism enunciated in Taoism. His vision of a world united through love, without a thought of heaven or hell, rested on practical action, not just wishful thinking. Pacifist in sentiment and opposed to militarism, Mohists were prepared to risk their lives to prevent unnecessary violence. They intervened *en masse* in numerous conflicts, throwing themselves into the relief of beleaguered cities or states. Since the ideas of Mo-tzu found a ready audience among the *kung,* many of whom were engineers and artisans expert in the art of military defence, this chivalrous aid was often timely.

In startling contrast to Mohism and the rest of the Hundred Schools stood the inhuman philosophy of the Legalists. They believed that propriety, *li,* was inadequate for a powerful state; it required the additional support of *fa,* positive law. Only when custom had the sanction of dreadful punishment behind it was there any possibility of effective social organization. We have seen how Shang Yang successfully remodelled Ch'in on an authoritarian pattern. Another leading Legalist was Han Fei, who served Han till his assassination in 233 BC on the orders of Li Ssu, the Ch'in chief minister. Both Li Ssu and Han Fei had been disciples of Hsun-tzu (320–235 BC), a heterodox Confucian philosopher who believed that the nature of man was basically evil. Strictness in application of penalties was therefore the quality most prized in the state official. The story of Prince Chao of Han, quoted with approval by Han Fei, makes this harsh point.

> The prince having got drunk and fallen asleep was exposed to cold, whereupon the crown-keeper put a coat over him. When he awoke he asked who had covered him, and on being informed, punished the coat-keeper but put the crown-keeper to death, on the principle that transgression of the duties of an office was worse than mere negligence.

Obedience to the letter of the law was demanded, whatever the promptings of the heart might suggest. As a consequence the ordinary relations that existed between people were proscribed. An early formulation was the Six Parasitic Functions, or the Six Lice: they were care for old age, guests, beauty, love, ambition and virtuous conduct. Later, most of the ethical concepts of the other schools, particularly Confucianism, were added to the list. It is not surprising, therefore, that Li Ssu made his infamous proposal for the burning of the books to the First Emperor. The chief minister was anxious that throughout the Empire, on pain of death, teaching should be banned and all books except those dealing with technical subjects like agriculture destroyed.

TAOISM   The 'madman of Ch'u', the first of the 'irresponsible hermits', according to the Confucians of the Classical Age was Li Er (born 604 BC), but it has become usual in China to refer to the founder of Taoism as Lao-tzu, the Old Philosopher. He may have been keeper of the royal archives at Loyang, the Chou capital, but few details are known of his life. He was 'a hidden wise man', reluctant to found a school and gather a following.

'When he foresaw the decay of Chou,' Ssu-ma Ch'ien tells us in the oldest biography, 'Lao-tzu departed and came to the frontier. The customs official asked the sage to write a book before he retired from the world. So Lao-tzu wrote a book consisting of more than five thousand words, in which the proper way to live was set forth. Then he went on. No one knows where he died.'

The book mentioned here is the *Tao Teh Ching* (*The Way of Virtue*), a collection of profound sayings, many of which date from earliest times. It is significant that in the legend about the final journey into the West, which Ssu-ma Ch'ien records in his brief life, Lao-tzu was only persuaded to leave a record of his wisdom at the very last moment. Saddened by the short-sightedness of his fellow men, their tragic perversity and their inability to follow natural goodness, the Old Philosopher decided to leave feudal society behind him. Making statements, trying to explain his ideas, would only add to the current confusion of the Hundred Schools because words have an un-pleasant way of limiting what should really be said. Unlike the philosophers of the Confucian school, the Taoists held words in mean respect. The *Tao Teh Ching* begins:

> Existence is beyond the power of words
> To define:
> Terms may be used
> But are none of them absolute.
> In the beginning of heaven and earth there
>   were no words,
> Words came out of the womb of matter;
> And whether a man dispassionately
> Sees to the core of life
> Or passionately
> Sees the surface,
> The core and the surface
> Are essentially the same,
> Words making them seem different
> Only to express appearance.
> From wonder into wonder
> Existence opens.

Although the figure of Lao-tzu is wreathed uncertainly in the mists of legend, the characters in his book stand out with pristine strength. 'Conduct your triumph like a funeral'; this saying has lost nothing since it was first applied to the senseless rivalry of the Warring States. 'He who feels punctured must have been a bubble.' What exercised Lao-tzu's mind most was man's rootedness in Nature, the inner power that made all men wiser than they knew. 'Knowledge studies others; wisdom is self-known.' The artificial demands of feudal society had disturbed the natural abilities of men. Instead of following the Way, the *Tao*, codes of love and honesty were invented to provide the people with a new social ethic. Learning became necessary and charity was prized, since it could no longer be expected from everyone. Above all there was the Confucian emphasis on the family, with the endless talk of benevolent fathers and dutiful sons. To the Taoists social evolution had taken a wrong turn with feudalism. They had no time for the reformist measures advocated by Confucius, but, on the contrary, they urged a return to primitive collectivist society, the organization that was said to have existed before the Hsia dynasty. Their ideal society was naturally cooperative, not acquisitive. It preceded Bronze Age feudalism and had even less in common with the institution of private property that was undermining the remnants of the Chou feudal system. So Lao-tzu wanted men to return to the old, natural way of behaviour:

> As the soft yield of water cleaves obstinate stone,
> So to yield with life solves the insoluable:
> To yield, I have learned, is to come back again.
> But this unworded lesson,
> This easy example,
> Is lost upon men.

This verse may partly explain China's age-long capacity for survival. To yield and then come back again. The conquest of Ch'in was neither the last nor the worst invasion that the Chinese had to suffer. When Marco Polo reached Cathay over fourteen hundred years later the government was in the hands of the Mongols, fierce descendants of Genghiz Khan. Water being a strong element is another interesting thought, so different from firmness of rock praised in the West. The formidable rivers of China were there for everyone with eyes to see, but the humility of water, ever seeking the lowest level, was an appropriate route for the descendants of P'an-ku's fleas to tread.

Taoism had two origins. First there were the philosophers of the Warring States period who withdrew from the courts of feudal princes and spent their lives in the forests or on the mountains meditating upon Nature. Lao-tzu simply quit so-called civilization; the absence of a tomb for the Old Philosopher is a notable omission in an age that placed immense store by the rites of ancestor worship. 'Confucius walks within human society,' said Chuang-tzu (350–275 BC), the most distinguished follower of Lao-tzu, 'whilst I walk outside it.' They felt wisdom 'in their bones', and attacked the 'Confucian scholastic knowledge of the ranks and observances of feudal society, not the true knowledge of the Tao of Nature. Confucian knowledge was masculine and managing: the Taoists condemned it and sought after a feminine and receptive knowledge which could arise only as the fruit of a passive and yielding attitude in the observation of Nature.' This philosophical outlook was important for the development of science in China, since it has been plausibly argued that Taoist observation and experiments in alchemy represent the dim beginnings of scientific method. The other root of Taoism was the primitive magic of the *wu* magicians, whose popularity with the *nung* was first evident during the Shang dynasty. The philosophy of Lao-tzu and his followers eventually combined with *wu* magic to form the Taoist religion.

Taoist philosophy received its classical form in the works of Chuang-tzu, a younger contemporary of Confucius' principal follower, Mencius. By then it was a tradition for Taoist hermits to shun human society in order to contemplate Nature. A story about him illustrates the point.

> The Prince of Ch'u sent two high officials to ask Chuang-tzu to take charge of the government and become chief minister. They found Chuang-tzu fishing in P'u. Intent on what he was doing he listened without turning his head. At last he said: 'I have been told there is in the capital a sacred tortoise which has been dead for three thousand years. And that the Prince keeps this tortoise carefully enclosed in a chest on the altar of his ancestral temple. Now would this tortoise rather be dead but considered holy, or alive and wagging its tail in the mud?' The two officials answered that it would prefer to be alive and wagging its tail in the mud. 'Clear off, then!' shouted Chuang-tzu, 'I, too, will wag my tail in the mud here.'

We can still appreciate a little of the story's original impact. How surprised the two feudal officers must have been! The long and weary journey to the remote valley in which the sage's hut was situated would have been a trial for them, but there was the compensation that they would be the first in the Court to meet the new leader. Yet Chuang-tzu had declined the highest office of state, something a member of the Confucian school would never have done. 'A thief steals a purse and he is hanged,' he wrote later, 'whilst another man steals a state and becomes a prince.' From the Taoists came the conviction that government was a necessary evil. China needed some form of organization, they admitted, but it should be reduced to the minimum, lest the elaborate restrictions of feudalism hinder the natural way of doing things. Chuang-tzu commented on the pre-Hsia period: 'The ancients, in cultivating *Tao*, nourished their knowledge by their calmness. Throughout their lives they refrained from employing that knowledge in any purpose contrary to Nature. Knowledge and calmness mutually sustained each other; harmony and order developed accordingly.'

Behind this attitude to public office was the ancient Taoist concept of *jang*, or yieldingness. In the *Tao Teh Ching* the sign of the sage is his effective non-assertion. 'The wise man keeps to the deed that consists in taking no action and practises the teaching that uses no words.' He gives up in order to get; he relinquishes control in order to understand; he welcomes a relationship that is mutual; he is moved by a sense of profound non-possessiveness. The historical origin of this fundamental Taoist idea could have been the custom of 'potlatch'. In primitive collectivist society the prestige of a leading man depends on the amount of food or other commodities which he can distribute to the community as a whole at periodical or seasonal feasts. Yielding place, seeking to give up the better position, is now entwined in the Chinese custom of 'face', whereby each person tries to allow for the social prestige of another. A cautionary tale about the ruin that the lack of social modesty can bring occurs in the *Book of Lieh-tzu*. Yu, a wealthy man from Wei, lost everything through the chance meeting of a party of rowdies and a rat. It happened that a kite dropped the carcass of a rat on the heads of these passers-by at the very moment a burst of laughter came from Yu's house. Jealous of the rich man's luxurious life and angered by this apparent insult the rowdies took their revenge and attacked his family, killing everyone. Lieh-tzu himself provided a perfect example of obscurity. He 'dwelt on a vegetable plot in Cheng for forty years, and no man knew him for what he was'. Chuang-tzu quotes the cook of Prince Hui as an exponent of *Tao*:

> Prince Hui's cook was cutting up a bullock. Every blow of his hand, every heave of his shoulders, every tread of his foot, every thrust of his knee, every sound of rent flesh, and every note of the chopper, were in perfect harmony – rhythmical like a dance, harmonious like a piece of music.
>
> 'Excellent,' cried the Prince, who was watching him. 'Yours is skill indeed!'
>
> 'My lord,' replied the cook, 'I have devoted myself to *Tao*, which is superior to mere skill. When I first started to cut up oxen, I saw before me only whole carcasses. After three years' practice I saw no more whole animals. And now I work with my mind and not my eyes, because I am attuned to eternal principles. I follow the natural structure, my chopper slipping through existing openings or cavities. I avoid both joints and bones. A good cook changes his chopper once a year, because he cuts. An average cook needs a new chopper every month, because he hacks. But I have used this chopper for nineteen years, and although I have dealt with many thousand carcasses, its edge is as if fresh from the whetstone. For where the parts join there are chinks into which my thin blade can easily slip. A complicated joint requires caution – that's all. I fix my eyes on it. I move slowly, and gently apply my chopper, until it gives and separates like crumbling earth. Then I am satisfied and clean my blade for another day.'
>
> 'Well done!' cried the Prince. 'From the words of this cook I have learnt how to manage my own life.'

From this passage it can be seen that *Tao* was the naturalness, the very structure, of all things. The cook had come to understand this fact in relation to butchery. He had followed the Way. Finally, there is a revealing discussion on Nature between Tung Ko-tzu and Chuang-tzu; its conclusion, that *Tao* informs both the highest and the lowest, is so different from the social focus of the school of Confucius.

> Tung Ko-tzu asked Chuang-tzu, 'Where is *Tao*?'
> 'Everywhere,' Chuang-tzu replied.
> 'Tell me one place where it is,' Tung Ko-tzu said.
> 'It is in the ant,' Chuang-tzu told him.
> 'Why in such a lowly creature?' Tung Ko-tzu asked.
> 'It is in the weed too,' Chuang-tzu added.
> 'Still lower,' Tung Ko-tzu wondered.
> 'It is in the earthenware tile,' Chuang-tzu said.
> 'But no lower than that, surely!' Tung Ko-tzu insisted.
> 'Yes,' Chuang-tzu said, 'it is in dung also.' This silenced the questioner completely.

CONFUCIANISM

Historically younger than Taoism, the school of philosophy that derived from Confucius' ideas was destined to shape the civilization of China for two thousand years. Its doctrine contained neither the mystical nor the anti-social tendencies that were latent in the rival philosophy. From the beginning it was marked by pragmatism and social consciousness. Born in 551 BC, Confucius

Confucius founded a school of philosophy that was to influence the development of Chinese civilization for two thousand years.

felt himself to be an active member of the feudal system, but the abuses prevalent during his lifetime set his mind on a course of reform. He strove for social justice within the framework of the feudal, or feudal-bureaucratic social order. 'I am a transmitter and not a creator,' Confucius said, 'I believe in the past and love it.'

There are plenty of traditions concerning the life of Confucius, but precise details of his ancestry are lacking. Although his family were certainly *shih*, its claim of descent from the royal house of Shang cannot be fully substantiated. It will be recalled that the immediate relations of the defeated Shang dynasty had been awarded Sung by the Duke of Chou. But Confucius did enjoy the patronage of powerful nobles in Lu; his father died soon after he was born and the good education Confucius received is testimony of the interest taken in him as a young man. He held a minor clerical post attached to the state granaries, then another appointment connected with the use of pasture-land, but his real ambition was to play a role in practical politics. Like other members of the impoverished *shih*, Confucius was discontented with the *status quo*. He abhorred the duplicity of leading nobles and the connivance of their ministers, but his constitutional inability to flatter or conduct intrigues debarred him from a successful public career. As an alternative to direct influence on state affairs Confucius devoted his life to teaching and formulating a philosophy of just and harmonious social relationships. He gathered students, rejecting none on grounds of birth. The only criteria for admission to his school were virtuous conduct, intelligence and a willingness to work. Just as he concentrated on the quality of education received rather than the form, his view of public administration was likewise pragmatic. Without questioning feudalism Confucius sought to open up government public service to people with ability, though he lamented on several occasions that it was hard to find one person willing to study for three years without thought of material reward. Many of his students rose to eminent positions in state administrations – their loyalty to principles, not factions, proved an invaluable constant to those in power during those tumultuous times – but, at the age of sixty, tired of the neglect he suffered in Lu, Confucius set out on a series of journeys in search of a ruler who would listen to his teachings and put his philosophy into practice. Honours and material rewards were presented to him; executive power or practical influence he failed to achieve. In 482 BC he returned to Lu, a man disappointed but not disheartened, and spent his remaining three years teaching and writing. The achievement of his life seemed at the time of little consequence, he was the founder of only one of the Hundred Schools. Yet so immense has been the influence of Confucian philosophy on China that he has been dubbed the 'uncrowned Emperor'.

Confucius was a moral philosopher. His this-worldly doctrine was a feudal ethic, which expected the prince to rule with benevolence and sincerity, avoiding the use of force at all costs. Like the Duke of Chou and other great rulers of the past, he had to manage affairs so that justice was enjoyed by every subject. Numerous soldiers and guards were a sign of bad government. Virtue or benevolence, *jen*, consisted of affection for others, and the ruler by the consideration he showed for his people called forth the loyalty and virtuous nature concealed in all men. *Jen* was acquired by self-cultivation and self-denial; *li*, propriety, represented the rules of good behaviour through which the perfection of human personality could only be attained. The character for *li* tells us something of Confucius' original conception. It is a sacrificial vessel in which precious objects have been placed as a sacrifice to the ancestral spirits. The rites of ancestor worship, elevated into a moral code by Confucian philosophy, were the meeting point of two worlds, the spiritual and the temporal. Here the benefits from Heaven were bestowed on the dutiful descendant, the preserver of traditional values. Individual sacrifice in respect of propriety is the fundamental Confucian ideal. In the *Analects* we find, 'Death and life are as decreed, wealth and rank depend upon Heaven; the gentleman is serious and does not fail in his duties. He behaves courteously and accords with *li*.' What Confucius particularly disliked was hypocrisy. He appreciated the educative value of family worship and was short with dissemblers. 'I cannot bear to see the forms of *li* gone through by those who have no reverence in their hearts.'

The attitude of Confucius to religion was practical. 'I stand in awe of the spirits,' he told his students, 'but keep them at a distance.' It was inevitable that his attention was focused on the problems of declining feudal society. Since the sanctions of religion were no longer capable of controlling the relationships between men, they seemed of less concern to him. Confucius did not disbelieve, he simply had too much to do in the temporal world. Among the *shih* there was a growth of scepticism, but it was not so much a denial of the existence of any supreme power as a growing feeling that the celestial realm was far above men's comprehension: something not to be readily plumbed by scapulimancy or star-gazing. Nor could natural phenomena, like eclipses and floods, be so readily interpreted as a specific manifestation of the will of Shang Ti. Yet the reluctance of Confucius to pronounce on religion did help in introducing a sense of balance in the supernatural world as well as on the earthly level. The characteristic kind of good life aimed at in the main stream of Chinese philosophy, 'high though it is', Fung Yu-lan observes, 'is not divorced from the daily functioning of human relations'. The sage attains to the sublime but performs the common tasks. Such a rational detachment from 'the spirits', then, ensured that a certain amount of scepticism was always available during religious crises. The T'ang scholar, Han Yu (768–824), drew strength from this tradition when he presented the emperor with his famous memorial, *On the Bone of Buddha*, a stinging attack on the religious excesses of the Court. Han Yu was exiled, not executed. Confucian disdain for popular religion was taken a stage further by Chu Hs'i (1122–1200), who replaced a personal deity with a moral force which impersonally ruled the universe. 'There is,' he said, 'no man in heaven judging sin.' In Max Weber's memorable phrase, Confucianism was marked by an absence of 'almost all residues of religious anchorage'. Taoism tended to shade too easily into magic. In the Chinese mind, however, there was room for elements from both the philosophies of Confucius and Lao-tzu. This capacity to retain diverse viewpoints at the same time is a notable feature of Chinese thought.

Of all the pre-Han followers of Confucius, Mencius was the greatest. He spent his life (*c.* 390–305 BC) teaching in Ch'i and other eastern states. One of his chief contributions to Confucianism was the development of political theory. Confucius had charged the *shih* with part of the responsibility for public morality. They had to display an independence of mind in the service of the prince. When Confucius was asked how a ruler should be served, he

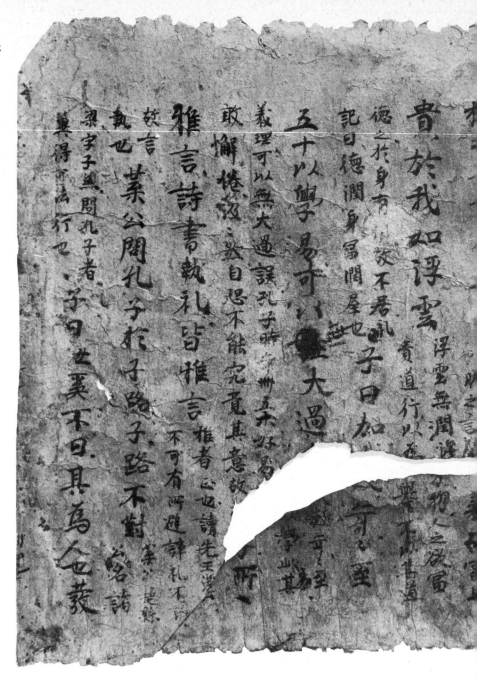

The *Analects* of Confucius; a paper fragment dating from the T'ang period, with a later commentary. The text refers to the delight Confucius took in music; on hearing the music of Ch'i 'for three months he forgot to eat meat'. Found in 1967 at Astana, near Turfan, Sinkiang, this rare copy was preserved by the dry conditions of the area.

answered, 'If it becomes necessary to oppose him, withstand him to his face, and don't try roundabout methods.' This firmness of principle was destined to be the cardinal rule of the later imperial civil service; officials were to perish at the hands of impatient emperors, only to be admired for generations afterwards. Mencius extended this conception of righteous opposition to unjust government into the democratic theory of justified rebellion against wicked rulers. The Mandate of Heaven was withdrawn from a corrupt dynasty whenever a successful rebel arose. This theory, usually called the 'Chinese Consti-

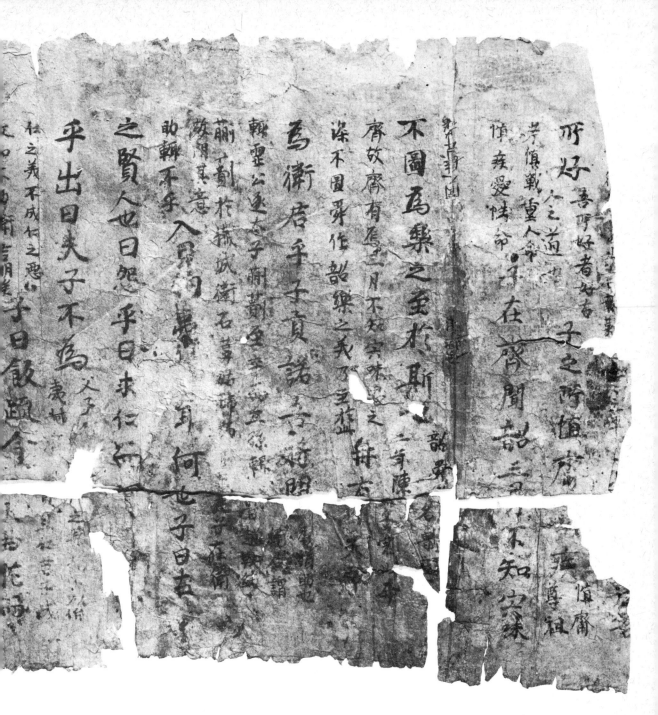

tution', was evolved from the famous saying in the *Shu Ching* that 'Heaven sees according to what the people see, Heaven hears according to what the people hear'. The consent of *nung* was as crucial as the cooperation of the *shih*.

Man, Mencius insisted, was good. 'Human-heartedness is the essential quality of man's mind, and justice is man's essential path.' The sympathetic virtue (*jen*) treasured by Confucius becomes something warmer and more spontaneous in Mencius' teaching. Unfortunately, the majority of men stray from the path of justice and need to be reminded of their true selves, their human-heartedness. This is the duty of the teacher, though the onus for proper upbringing rests with parents. Nurture, not nature, is fundamental, as this popular story about the philosopher's own childhood explains.

> At first they lived in a cottage near some tombs. Finding young Mencius interested in funerals and tomb construction, his mother moved to a house by a market. But the activity in the market attracted the boy so she moved again. Next to a college she was pleased to see Mencius watching the comings and goings of scholars. She said, 'This is the right place for my son'.
>
> Returning from school one day Mencius found his mother weaving on her loom. 'Have you learnt everything now?' she asked. 'Yes,' he replied. 'I know enough.' Immediately she picked up her scissors and ripped across the cloth. Mencius was shocked and worried. 'Your stupidity about learning is like my cutting through this unfinished piece of work. Men only attain fame for their knowledge after hard work and great effort. Wise men possess a breadth of learning, live in peaceful places, and shun bad things. Realize this and you will come to no harm. . . .'

Though the Confucians agreed with the Taoists over the goodness of humanity, their remedy for the times was quite different. They placed great hope in education, particularly within the context of the home. Social deprivation was singled out as the prime cause for wickedness. Young people needed to be nurtured in the ways of virtue – loyalty, respect for elders, decorum, attention to ceremonies and rites. Referring to the Taoists, Confucius had said, 'They dislike me because I want to reform society, but if we are not to live with our fellow men with whom can we live? We cannot live with animals. If society was as it ought to be, I should not be wanting to change it.'

SHANG AND CHOU ART

In the early history of Chinese art two great questions remain unanswered by archaeology. First, there is the explanation of the sudden rise of advanced bronze metallurgy in the Shang period. To some extent evidence is accumulating that would suggest a direct development from the Neolithic pottery industry. The outstanding skills of early Chinese potters, whose advanced kiln construction has already been remarked, could have transferred to bronze working and so account for the absence of archaeological discoveries of any rudimentary stage of Chinese bronze technique. Excavations at Ao, near Cheng-chou, since 1954 have found parallels between pottery and bronzes; certain shapes existed side by side and point to the ceramic origin of several vessels previously thought to be peculiar to bronze. Ao was the cultural centre of the Shang kingdom about 1400 BC, when the dynasty shifted its capital northwards to Anyang. The second uncertainty revolves around the transition from Shang to Chou bronze traditions. A change in styles used for ritual vessels can be observed after 1027 BC, the year that the Shang were defeated by Chou. It appears that the conquerors from the Wei valley introduced their own artistic style. Bronze founding was no longer confined to the capital which, initially, may account for the unsophisticated appearance of some vessels. Possibly the Chou were pastoralists down to a time not far distant from their conquest of Shang. But the relative ease with which the change-over from Shang to Chou styles occurred lends weight to the argument that sees the

An early Chou *fang-yi*, a bronze wine jar of the tenth century BC. The masks on the sides are a Shang influence. The inscription reads: 'For the august deceased Father Sixth Day, a precious ritual vessel to be placed in the ancestral temple, to be treasured in prominent use for a myriad years and in perpetuity by sons and grandsons'. 'Sixth Day' refers to the offering day of the ancestor to whom the vessel was presented.

Chou people in possession of a bronze-using culture entirely contemporary with the Shang kingdom. Their tradition could have been as old as the Shang, though separate and distinct.

Art objects surviving from the Shang and Chou periods are usually associated with the ceremonies of ancestor worship and the fertility rituals practised by the priest-king. Decoration of the ritual vessels must have had a religious significance, but all remains obscure till the Early Chou period; then, long and historically circumstantial inscriptions were made on bronze. Ancestor worship involved the preparation and presentation of both food and wine. The human participants consumed whatever of the 'communal' repast was left over by the spirits. Special bronze vessels were cast for these ceremonies: for food, there was the *ting*, a tripod cauldron with a round shape (one discovered at Anyang stands 1·33 metres high and weighs 900 kilogrammes); the *li*, another tripod cauldron, but with a more bulbous appearance; the *hsien*, a steamer, in which a lower part, like an enlarged *li*, is surmounted by another vessel with a perforated base (we noticed these forms in Yang-shao ceramics, and, indeed, so characteristic of Chinese culture are they that the Shang pictogram for sacrifice is a drawing of a *hsien*); and the *kuei*, a container that recalls a pottery bowl. For wine, there was the *tsun*, a tall jar, sometimes square in shape, and highly decorated during the Chou period; the *lei*, a later version of the *kuei*; the *kuang*, a wine mixer, often cast as a monster, with the blunted

TOP LEFT The bronze bells from the tomb of the Marquis Chao of Ts'ai. The bells have no internal clappers and were intended to be struck on the outside; they date from the fifth century BC.

RIGHT The 'great lute' with twenty-five silk strings; a Ming illustration of this now extinct instrument.

LEFT A green jade *pi* of the Later Han dynasty excavated at Ting-hsien, Hopei, in 1959.

horns of the sacrificial victim; the *yu*, round, with a small base, a lid and a handle; the *fang-yi*, square, with a steep roof-like lid and a knob at the top; the *chueh*, a tripod libation cup, whose beak-like spout and handle make it the most striking of the Shang bronzes; the *ku*, a tall and slender goblet; and the *chia*, a tripod vessel, with a handle. For water, there was the *p'an*, a basin used for ceremonial washing; the *ho*, a kettle-like pourer, with three or four legs and a pronounced spout; and the *yi*, another pourer that rested on either legs or a base.

The inscription on a remarkable *fang-yi*, displayed at the 1973 Chinese Exhibition in London, explained: 'For the august deceased Father Sixth Day, a precious ritual vessel to be placed in the ancestral temple, to be treasured in prominent use for a myriad years and in perpetuity by sons and grandsons.' The 'Sixth Day' refers to the offering day of the ancestor to whom the vessel was dedicated. The *fang-yi* dates from the period of the Early Chou and has monster faces, or masks, on each of its four sides, a decorative style that first appeared at Anyang. Casting may have been achieved by the 'lost-wax' method, whereby complete, engraved moulds of fired clay were prepared to receive directly the molten bronze; a rough clay model of the desired vessel was covered with wax and then surrounded with clay, except for a small hole through which the wax melted and escaped during the firing, leaving behind the mould. Another impressive exhibit in the Chinese Exhibition was the set of

nine bronze bells, tuned in scale, from the tomb of a lord of Ts'ai, at Shou-
hsien on the Huai River. They were recovered with other bronze objects when
the tomb was excavated in 1965. The date of the burial was in the Ch'un Ch'iu
period, the first quarter of the fifth century BC, when Shou-hsien remained a
flourishing city, though Wu had recently been overrun by Yueh (493 BC).
Marquis Chao of Ts'ai was, in fact, a refugee in Shou-hsien because Ts'ai, a
small neighbouring state of Wu, was under the control of Ch'u. The bells were
intended to be hung and struck on the outside, there being no internal clapper.
Music was regarded at this time as 'something essentially magical'. Ceremonial and music were united in Chou ancestor worship. The spirits were
tempted to return to earth not only by the prayers of their descendants, but by
the sweet sounds of musical instruments and the delicious smell which rose
from the sacred bronze cooking vessels. The descending music of Heaven, the
voice of the wind, mingled beneficially with the ascending music of the earth,
the rhythms of bells and drums. That the bell, a Chinese invention, evolved
from the grain scoop should not surprise us when the ancient association of
music and agriculture is remembered. 'Primitive musicians all the world over
used whatever was handy as their earliest instruments. In China the rice pestle-
and-mortar existed in the classical orchestra till modern times as an instrument
of percussion.'

Jade was, and still is, prized as the most valuable of all precious stones. From
earliest times it was used for ritual purposes, though the meaning of jade rings
found in graves of the Lung-shan culture cannot be guessed. In the Shang
period the *pi*, a jade disc pierced in the centre, symbolized Heaven. It may have
been intended to represent the twelve months too. The *tsung*, cylindrical
within and cube-shaped without, has been said to symbolize the earth, though
we do not know the reasons behind this idea. The two *kuei*, one a tablet
pointed along a single side, with a hole bored through the lower half, and the
other rectangular in shape, with pointed single end, are conjectured to be
symbols of royal power. These ceremonial objects must have derived from
Neolithic times, as the pierced *kuei* is very reminiscent of the Yang-shao
polished stone axes. The semi-circular *huang*, usually worked in black jade, is
half a *pi*; it was buried at the foot of a corpse.

These ceremonial jades and others like them were sometimes decorated.
There are geometrical designs as well as animals, like the stag and the dragon.
But, often, the polished magnificence of the stone itself was felt to be sufficient.
No jade occurs in the Yellow River area. Imports must have come some
distance from the outside, and the most likely source would have been the
mountains of southern Siberia. The Chinese belief that jade had magical
properties valuable in death could have been imported too. It was firmly held
in the Han Empire that jade had the power to prevent the putrefaction of
corpses; whilst the well-to-do stopped the orifices of the body with jade, the
Han Princess Tou Wan (died *c*. 125 BC) was encased in a jade funeral suit, knit
together with gold and silk-covered iron wire. The view has been put forward that 'the Shang jade was obtained in the first place from a source lying
in a region where it was already used to manufacture rings. This would point to
Baikalia, whence it might reach Shang China . . . along the Amur valley. . . .
The Shang custom of burying *pi* with the dead was inherited from the Lung-
shan Neolithic, a culture with connections extending far to the north-east.'

A detail of the jade funeral suit of the Han Princess Tou Wan who died in the first century BC. Her tomb at Man-ch'eng, Hopei, was discovered in 1968. Some two thousand pieces of jade are knitted together with gold and silk-covered iron wire.

4

Imperial Unification: the Ch'in and Former Han Empires

221 BC–AD 9

By 221 BC all resistance had ended and Prince Cheng was able to proclaim himself Shih Huang-ti, 'the First Emperor'. Although the Ch'in dynasty was of short duration, such was the energy and determination of its founder that this period represents a turning point in the history of Chinese civilization. In place of the old feudal system of government belonging to the Classical Age a centralized monarchy was established. The bureaucratic type of government that had developed in Ch'in became the model for future Chinese political organization, lasting until the twentieth century. The significance of the revolutionary change that Ch'in Shih Huang-ti began and Liu Pang, the founder of the following purely Chinese dynasty, the Han, completed cannot be underestimated. The early civilization of China *was* the working out of the possibilities offered by imperial unification.

The ruthless determination that had directed the 'Tiger of Ch'in' in his defeat of the Warring States soon became evident in the organization of the Ch'in Empire. In order to unify China he was obliged to become one of the great destroyers of history. Lacking any degree of economic integration, the Ch'in Empire was insecure in two main directions – the east and the north. The deposed aristocracy of the old feudal states posed an internal political threat, especially in the lower valley of the Yellow River, whilst in the north there was danger from the Hsiung Nu nomads, probably the Huns who invaded the Roman Empire in the fourth century. Military control seemed the quickest and most efficient way of bringing stability. Therefore, Ch'in Shih Huang-ti abolished feudal holdings; compelled the nobles to reside at the capital, Hsienyang, where isolated from their supporters they remained without influence; awarded the *nung* greater rights over their land, but made them liable for taxes; and divided the Empire into new administrative areas, under the control of military governors and civil administrators. Everything was reduced 'in a uniform manner': there was standardization of weights and measures, written language, and even vehicle axles, which ended the transfer and reweighing of goods at borders because of differences in ruts made by cartwheels from one state to another. The freer interchange of people and commodities fostered a wider national consciousness, though Ch'in Shih Huang-ti was careful to restrict the benefits that the *shang* derived from the growth of commerce.

Two bronze wrestling figures dating from the fifth or fourth century BC, the Chou dynasty.

Emperor Han Kuang-wu, the founder of the Later Han dynasty. A detail from *The Scroll of the Thirteen Emperors* by Yen Li-pen, a T'ang court painter. The scroll portrays emperors from the Han to Sui dynasties.

The location of the imperial capital in the Wei valley was militarily sound. From Hsienyang, protected on three sides by mountain or desert, Ch'in Shih Huang-ti could sweep down the valley of the Yellow River into the lowlands and retire into an almost impregnable stronghold whenever the forces of the eastern provinces were organized. A network of tree-lined roads radiating from the capital was begun so that imperial orders and troops could be rapidly conveyed to the farthest outposts. Resentment was felt over the geographical location of the imperial capital, tucked away in the north-western corner of the Empire, but the same strategic and economic reasons were to prejudice the Former Han rulers in favour of the Wei valley. The refusal of Ch'in Shih Huang-ti to countenance any survival of feudalism – he would not grant fiefs to his own sons or relatives, lest the old rivalries of the Warring States period return – alienated the more traditional *shih* and caused Li Ssu, the chief minister, to recommend the 'Burning of the Books'. What this statesman feared was an alliance between the old aristocracy and Confucian scholars. Although Confucius had not condemned the Empire, he was unaware of such a possibility, so that his followers during the Ch'in dynasty were opposed to the end of feudalism. By imperial edict all schools of philosophy were required to close, with the exception of the Legalists, and all books were to be destroyed, except the imperial archives and works on medicine, divination and agriculture. This sweeping measure effectively destroyed feudalism; it caused a definite break in consciousness. When, in Han times, the ancient texts were painfully reconstructed from memory and the badly tattered copies that had been hidden at great personal risk, the feudal world seemed historically remote. Education rather than birth appeared as the important social qualification. If Li Ssu broke the power of the nobles, he had weakened the Ch'in dynasty too. The *shih* were united in hatred against the imperial house; the official class of Ch'in alone remained loyal.

It was the measure introduced to deal with the Hsiung Nu, namely the construction of the Great Wall, that spread dissension amongst the *nung*. This project was an immense task. Meng T'ien, the Ch'in general, was ordered to set up a line of fortresses in 214 BC, but, surprisingly, few details of the complex logistics that must have been involved were recorded. He had already driven a road north from Hsienyang and dug the Kuahsien canal system in the Ordos Desert. Literally armies of men toiled on these projects, working and dying in the cold mountains and desert lands of the northern frontier. Through the mobilization of labour on such an unprecedented scale Ch'in Shih Huang-ti hoped to solve the problem of the Hsiung Nu as well as provide employment for the great reservoir of labour made idle by the end of war and the abolition of serfdom. It is therefore certain that the almost continuous use of the corvée in massive public works did much to accelerate social change. But there is no denying that the harsh demands of the Ch'in dynasty on ordinary people led directly to the popular rebellions that arose after the death of Ch'in Shih Huang-ti and dethroned his feeble successors. The terrible lot of the conscripted labourers who built the Great Wall has been recalled in Chinese folk-song ever since.

Another policy of Shih Huang-ti was encouragement of the southward movement of the Chinese people. He was anxious to halt any movement to the north in case the farmers of the northern outposts might abandon agriculture

A Ch'in pottery measure excavated at Tsou-hsien, Shantung, in 1963. The inscription on this 'correct' measure explains how Ch'in Shih Huang-ti used such means to reduce everything 'in a uniform manner' and to bring 'peace to the black-haired people'.

and take up stock raising, so strengthening the nomad economy. Imperial forces conquered Fukien, whose difficult terrain of forests and mountains had previously assured its independence, and reached as far south as what is now North Vietnam. Access to the West River area was obtained by the cutting of the Magic Canal. This waterway connected with the Yang-tze River so that men, equipment and supplies could flow into the West River basin. As an administrator, Ch'in Shih Huang-ti was efficient and hard working; he handled 'one hundred and twenty pounds of reports' daily, and he undertook tours of inspection in the provinces. On the other hand, there was little to militate against the harshness of Legalism. Ch'in governors, backed by permanent garrisons, seemed to enforce an endless series of severe decrees. Rebellion came swiftly once the central authority showed signs of weakness. An intrigue of Li Ssu over the succession gave the opportunity for popular revolt. The chief minister concealed the fact of Ch'in Shih Huang-ti's death in 210 BC long enough to force the crown prince and Meng T'ien, the most capable Ch'in general, to commit suicide by a forged imperial command. Because the crown prince had been prepared to displease his father by protesting at the treatment meted out to the *shih*, Li Ssu feared for his own safety after his master's death, and had the second son declared Er Shih Huang-ti, or 'the Second Emperor'. In the event the second Ch'in ruler could not defeat the rebels. Soldiers deserted and joined the *nung* already armed against the dynasty. A complicated struggle between several rebel leaders and the Ch'in emperor ensued, till Liu Pang gained overall control in 202 BC. A man of obscure origins and illiterate, he may have been forced into active rebellion by the rigour of Ch'in law. One tale relates how Liu Pang, having lost a group of convicts and being doomed to execution for this failure of duty, fled and was made the leader of a band of such fugitives.

Behind the popular rebellions against the Ch'in dynasty was a wish to return to feudal times. 'The Avenging Army of Ch'u' was adopted as the name of the southern rebel force. The measures which Ch'in Shih Huang-ti had introduced to weaken the old order proved so thorough and effective that in the moment of Ch'in's humiliation all attempts to re-establish feudal authority failed. Appreciating the uncertainty of the social situation, Liu Pang, as the Emperor Han Kao-tsu, sought a compromise. Though he realized that Ch'in policy was correct in reducing everything 'in a uniform manner', the need for tact and diplomacy was not lost on him. He decided to reduce feudal institutions to insignificance slowly. Whilst the restored feudal princes were given lands, and fiefs were granted to his own supporters, these holdings were small and contained within the imperial framework of provinces, controlled by governors and magistrates directly responsible to the emperor after the Ch'in pattern. Moreover, he steadily eliminated possible rivals, loyal generals included, so that his successors inherited undisputed sway over the 'Empire of all under Heaven'. The Ch'in practice of concentrating old and powerful families near the capital was revived in 199 BC 'to strengthen the trunk and weaken the branches'. This policy was abandoned as unenforceable around 40 BC, but it may have contributed to the success of the Han dynasty in putting down the so-called Seven States' Rebellion of 154 BC, when the feudal territories of the eastern provinces rose against the encroachment of the throne. Emperor Han Ching-ti (156–141 BC) used the occasion to alter the laws of inheritance: henceforth, all the sons of a lord were co-heirs to their father, and his lands divided between them. This amendment did much to quicken the breakdown of large feudal holdings into little more than substantial country estates. But it was Emperor Han Wu-ti (141–87 BC) who completed the process of demolition. Nobles were dispossessed for misconduct, sometimes without any real justification, whilst *k'u-li*, or harsh officials, were commissioned with the task of destroying powerful families. This was a definite policy of the government, which feared the rise of new sectional interests following the end of feudalism. There is evidence from late in the Former Han period that 'powerful and cunning persons' were in alliance with robbers in several provinces. Such local power bases were to revive in Later Han and became alternative centres of authority as the imperial house lost prestige and influence.

The decision of Liu Pang to retain the administrative structure of the Ch'in Empire made possible the dominance of Confucian philosophy in China. The discredited Legalist officials were identified in the mind of the people with the worst excesses of Ch'in rule, and the first Han emperor needed a civil service, an educated and trained army of officials, to administer effectively his many provinces and 'balance the Yin and the Yang'. The *shih* of Confucian persuasion, then, seemed to be the most reliable alternative, and their interest in education offered a regular means of renewing the official class. Despite his own lack of learning Liu Pang perceived the advantage to his house of allowing the *shih* to reconstruct the ancient texts and reopen their schools. All these developments, of course, did not happen at once. The emperor had to be convinced of the value of Confucianism just as the traditional Confucian *shih* had to be persuaded of the virtue in serving Han. An episode concerning the emperor and his chamberlain, Lu Chia, reveals the civilizing efforts of Confucian scholars.

So often did Lu Chia quote from the *Book of Odes* and the *Book of History* that Emperor Kao-tsu became annoyed and said, 'I conquered the Empire on horseback. What is the good of these *Odes* and *Histories*?' Lu Chia replied, 'That is correct but you won't be able to govern it on horseback. The ancient kings T'ang and Wu rose by violence, but ruled in accordance with the people's will. . . . If Ch'in, having made itself the master of the Empire, had governed it in humanity and righteousness, if it had followed the precepts of the ancient sages, then Han would not have got it.' The Emperor blanched and said, 'Explain to me the reasons for the collapse of Ch'in and the rise of Han as well as what it was that won and lost kingdoms of old.' In obedience to the Emperor's wish Lu Chia wrote a book about state craft, in twelve chapters. When Emperor Kao-tsu listened to Lu Chia reading aloud his book, he praised his ideas strongly.

In a similar manner Confucius' teaching on rites became the pattern for decorum at Court and the emperor himself assumed responsibility for the rituals belonging to the state worship of Heaven. The transformation of the Han Empire into a Confucian model was necessarily a gradual process. The proscription of books and teaching was repealed formally in 191 BC, though it had not been effective for several years before the death of Han Kao-tsu (194 BC). The punishment of the three *tsu* was discarded in 179 BC. This severe and terrible Ch'in punishment for criminal offences extended to the three *tsu* of the guilty person; that is, punishment was inflicted upon the father's clan, mother's clan and wife's clan, so that hundreds bore collective responsibility and were liable to execution for a single crime.

The Emperor Han Wen-ti (179–156 BC) first embraced Confucianism whole-heartedly. The histories tell us he was noted for 'his generous, humane feelings, for his stern economy, and for the unceasing care that he took of his people's interests'. His concern for welfare included famine relief at government expense, pensions for the aged, the freeing of slaves and the abolition of the cruellest Ch'in methods of execution. He also appointed Confucian *shih* to the highest offices of state, assuring the permanent triumph of this school of philosophy. During the long reign of Emperor Han Wu-ti, fifty-four years altogether, not only did the civil service become the accepted basis of organization for the Empire, but the means of selection partly depended upon a candidate's understanding of the books in the Confucian canon – the *I Ching* (*Book of Changes*), the *Shu Ching* (*Book of History*), the *Shih Ching* (*Book of Odes*) and the *Ch'un Ch'iu* (*Spring and Autumn Annals*). To these works were added others that had been rediscovered or re-edited by Han scholars. They were the *Li Chi* (*Book of Rites*), the *Chou Li* (*Book of Ceremonial Usage*) and the *I Li* (another book on ceremony), now thought to be spurious. The ideal candidate for the civil service examinations was distinguished by 'abundant talents', respect for family, moral rectitude and learning. In 124 BC the *Poh Shih Kuan*, or Imperial University, was set up, with a department for each of the books in the canon of the seven *ching*. Many of its students were recruited as government officials, others dispersed to teach in provincial centres of learning. The Han emperors encouraged the development of education for good reasons, not least connected with their own humble origins and lack of noble blood. Promotion based on learning, not on birth, was not inappropriate for a family that had raised a member to the exalted position of Son of Heaven by his own efforts.

Emperor Han Wu-ti (141–87 BC) visits a renowned scholar to seek his opinion.

Ch'in Shih Huang-ti had not destroyed feudalism for the benefit of the forty million *nung*. His object was to attain nothing less than absolute power for his own house, which he expected would endure 'for thousands of Emperors, with no ending whatsoever'. The emancipated peasantry were the source of the state's wealth and manpower; they sustained the Ch'in war machine. In order to preserve this economic basis the activities of the *shang* were restricted. Such a Legalist attitude was adopted by Liu Pang, though the first Han emperor, a man of the people himself, approached the problem from a more humane angle. Seeking firm support for his régime, he favoured an alliance between the *nung* and the *shih*, thereby ensuring agricultural prosperity as well as administrative order. The Ch'in abuse of the corvée was discontinued, and the civilian arm of government was allowed to gain the initiative in the imperial executive. It happened, therefore, that merchants were weakened at the same time as pressure was directed against the old feudal families. The legal status of the *shang* became more unfavourable. An edict of Emperor Han Kao-tsu, obviously intended to hamper and humiliate merchants, prohibited them from wearing brocades, embroideries, silks, and other kinds of fine cloth, from carrying weapons and from riding on horses. Emperor Han Wu-ti levied heavy taxes on their property as well as on their carts and boats. Another of his measures was aimed at stopping land speculation, for he decreed in 119 BC that merchants could not own landed property, but it does seem to have produced the desired result. The blocking of all avenues of social advancement to the *shang* was much more effective because it prevented the sons of successful business men from becoming officials. Doubtless this prohibition faithfully

Diligent peasant-farmers,
nung, at work in the fields.
The availability of iron
implements may have
been responsible for the
lack of a significant slave
class in ancient China. A
rubbing from a Han stone
relief.

reflected the contemporary attitude of *shih*, who were determined that the *shang* should remain in the lower stratum of society. During the Ch'in dynasty merchants had begun to fill the power gaps left in the provinces after the collapse of feudalism, something 'loyal' officials wisely feared since financial aid given to rebel leaders by merchants was to be an important factor in the final disintegration of the Han Empire (AD 220). Liu Pei, founder of Shu, one of the Three Kingdoms that succeeded Later Han, relied on the wealth of a rich man, Mi Chu, whose family had been involved in commerce for generations.

As a consequence of the unfavourable status of the *shang*, those *shih* without official positions, even if impoverished, would avoid trade, lest it spoil any future opportunity of an official career. Farming was accepted as a reasonable alternative to employment in the civil service. Poverty and humble occupations were not a hindrance to the social mobility of *shih*. The first poor scholar to become an Imperial Chancellor in the Han Empire was Hung Kung-sun (125 BC). Emperor Han Wu-ti was impressed with Hung's erudition and demeanour; it was observed that the humble *shih* 'was careful and sincere in behaviour, that he had more than eloquence, and that he was familiar with the documents of the law yet supplemented them with the method of Confucius'. Before this appointment the post of Imperial Chancellor had always been held by marquises, most of whom were military men. These 'meritorious officials' had been ennobled at the beginning of the Han dynasty, largely for military services rendered to Liu Pang during the civil wars that followed the fall of Ch'in. They were not members of the old feudal order, and through the development of the Confucian civil service and the policy of later emperors they formed a temporary class, one that soon disappeared altogether. The nobility in the Han Empire was confined to the imperial household; only a member of the Liu family could ascend the throne, an accepted fact of political life because of the great prestige enjoyed by the family and the succession of excellent rulers it produced.

Political difficulties, however, arose in the imperial palace, with plots and intrigues centred on the consort family, the relations of the empress. With the passing of the feudal kingdoms a China isolated from the rest of the world could not provide royal brides for each new emperor. The advantage of a foreign wife for a ruler, as European kingdoms have discovered, is that she has no relatives in the country and cannot readily become the centre of a faction. Because in China marriage within the same family was strictly forbidden by immemorial custom, the choice of a new empress became a matter of immense concern. As relatives of the One Man her kinsfolk automatically became 'the Second Family'. They expected high offices and rewards, and the empress would wish to see her own people enjoying the status they now deserved. As long as the empress and her family could guarantee the favour of the emperor, they would remain in power; but this relationship, like all others, was liable to change. Conflict became intense when two consort families were struggling for position. This situation usually occurred when the new consort family, the relatives of the emperor's bride, were opposed by the old consort family, the relatives of the emperor's mother. Empress Dowager Lu, the widow of Emperor Han Kao-tsu, tried to secure the influence of her own family, the Lu, but she died before the family had consolidated its position. Such court intrigue, then, was a feature of the Chinese Empire from the Han dynasty

A green-glazed pottery
watch-tower of the Han
period. This model
suggests that the pagoda
may have originated from
such tower structures.

onwards. It was a function of the shift of power from the outer to the inner court of the palace. The creation of the inner court was a device to concentrate power in the hands of the emperor, so reducing the power of the Imperial Chancellors: in 8 BC the three most senior officials were all recognized as Imperial Chancellors. In fact, this attempted transfer of power was of benefit to the consort family, who, unlike the *shih*, had access to the inner court. According to legend, Emperor Han Wu-ti took the desperate course of executing members of his wife's family, but if this did occur it was extraordinary. As a result Wang Mang was able to usurp the throne for fourteen years, from AD 9 to 23. The Wang family was in power for two decades before AD 9, under the protection of Empress Dowager Wang, and Wang Mang's own daughter became empress in AD 4. In the Later Han period eunuchs were used by the throne against the consort families, till they became a dangerous faction in their own right.

Action in the economic sphere was forced upon the Han Emperors by mounting difficulties. Ch'in Shih Huang-ti had done a creditable job in uniting

Acrobats and dancers entertaining courtiers; painted models from the Han period.

the Warring States during his short reign, but the Ch'in Empire overburdened the economic foundation. After its collapse the Emperor Han Kao-tsu was faced with chronic inflation and widespread destitution in the countryside. His measures against the *shang* need to be seen in this light. Private profit could not be permitted at the public expense, though after the first Han emperor's death an official had to memorialize the throne in these terms, 'Now the law despises merchants, but the merchants become rich and noble; it honours farmers, but the farmers have become poor and mean.' The economy deteriorated rapidly in the reign of Emperor Han Wu-ti, whose military expeditions against the Hsiung Nu drained the resources of the Empire. Private minting of money had debased the coinage to such an extent that there were violent fluctuations in face value. The emperor called in much of the 'cash', by issuing treasury notes each worth 400,000 copper coins. The skin of a white stag, a very rare beast, was made into the notes; they were a foot square and bore a special pattern. This remarkable experiment in central banking had only a temporary success, there being a limited supply of white stags, and soon Emperor Han Wu-ti was forced to enlist the aid of the *shang* directly. Besides selling honorary titles to merchants and heavily taxing commercial enterprise, he brought into the civil service leading *shang*. For a moment in Chinese civilization social mobility was granted to merchants – they became officials, though their expertise was used for very revolutionary ends. After 87 BC this kind of mobility was checked again by traditional forces.

The revolutionary purpose that Emperor Han Wu-ti had in mind was nationalization. In 120–19 BC the state declared a monopoly over the iron and salt industries. Tung K'o, a salt boiler, and K'ung Chin, an ironmaster, were put in charge of the new ministry, to the horror of the *shih*. The philosophical reasons for this extension of public control were set forth in the *Discourses on Salt and Iron*:

> Formerly the overbearing and powerful great families, obtaining control of the profits of the mountains and lakes, mined iron ore and smelted it with great bellows, and evaporated brine for salt. A single family would assemble a multitude, sometimes as many as a thousand men or more, for the most part wandering unattached plebians who had travelled far from their own villages, abandoning the tombs (of their ancestors). Thus attaching themselves to the great families, they came together in the midst of mountain fastnesses and desolate marshes, bringing about thereby the fruition of businesses based on selfish intrigue (for profit) and intended to aggrandize the power of particular firms and factions.

The former owners of these industries were employed to run them for the government, which took the largest share of the profits. Another innovation was the 'ever normal' granary. In order to prevent speculation in basic food-stuffs provincial officials were ordered to establish public granaries, to buy grain when prices were low, and to sell in times of shortage. This was known as the *p'ing chang* or 'levelling system', specially designed to prevent any cornering of the market by the *shang*. Even Ssu-ma Ch'ien, a bitter critic of Emperor Han Wu-ti, admitted the value of this measure, recognizing the benefit of reasonably priced food that it afforded the *nung* and *kung*, even when large supplies were required for military ventures. Though these economic policies confirmed the dominant role of the state in production and distribution – they will be seen to recur with modifications throughout the early civilization of China – their effect was insufficient to salvage the economy. The usurpation of Wang Mang was connected with the problems that still beset the Han dynasty, just as his own fall was caused by the even more revolutionary reforms he proposed to deal with them.

IMPERIAL EXPANSION

Foreign policy under the Former Han dynasty hinged almost entirely on the Empire's relations with the Hsiung Nu. The Great Wall of Ch'in Shih Huang-ti, manned by soldiers armed with crossbows, proved an effective barrier against the nomads in the north only when combined with the *ho-ch'in* policy. Emperor Han Kao-tsu adopted this policy of conciliation after the reverse at the battle of P'in-ch'eng, where he almost fell in the hands of the Hsiung Nu (200 BC). The first *ho-ch'in* agreement assured the Hsiung Nu a fixed number of annual gifts as well as the hand of a Han princess to their Shan Yu, the nomad counterpart of the Son of Heaven. In return for this special relationship the Shan Yu undertook to prevent raids on Chinese border areas. The *ho-ch'in* policy remained in favour down till the accession of Emperor Han Wu-ti in 141 BC, but there were *shih* who questioned its long-term value. Chia-i (201–169 BC) had urged Emperor Han Wen-ti to change from a defensive foreign policy to one of expansion by force, thereby ending the *ho-ch'in* agreement and substituting a tributary system. He argued for imperial expansion, but at the same time he appreciated the control over the nomads that the conciliation policy gave to China. The Hsiung Nu appeared 'abandoned by Heaven for being good-for-nothing', according to the Han Chinese, for the main reasons that they possessed neither agriculture nor settled habitation. Certain social customs of the nomads were most abhorrent, like the practice by which a son took into his harem all the wives of his dead father, except his own mother, as well as all the wives of his deceased brothers.

In 133 BC it was finally accepted that the *ho-ch'in* system would have to be abandoned. Nomad raids continued to trouble the northern frontier; Chinese defectors and rebels sought refuge in the lands of the Hsiung Nu, where they plotted against the Han Empire; and, financially, the growing annual gifts expected by the nomads put an insupportable strain on the imperial exchequer. An abortive ambush of the Shan Yu in 135 BC had led to a renewal of hostilities between the Hsiung Nu and the Chinese. This war, Emperor Han Wu-ti insisted, would be decisive and vast resources were allocated for the struggle. To separate the Hsiung Nu from the peoples of Central Asia whom they dominated and, at the same time, to obtain allies for the Han Empire, Chang Ch'ien had been dispatched as an imperial envoy in 138 BC. His mission was the establishment of diplomatic relations between China and the Ta Yueh Chi, nomads living in 'the Western Regions', whose hatred of the Hsiung Nu had become known to the emperor. In spite of being held prisoner by the Hsiung Nu for a decade, Chang Ch'ien eventually located the Ta Yueh Chi far removed from China and uninterested in returning. They had settled in Ta Hsia, now part of Russian Turkestan and Afghanistan, but what had been a few years before the Chinese envoy's arrival the Greek kingdom of Bactria.

Chang Ch'ien was amazed to discover a settled population; his report of the

Large-scale crossbows were used as defensive artillery on city walls; an illustration from a Sung book.

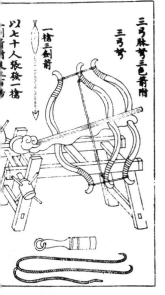

journey speaks of 'cities, mansions and houses as in China'. Here was another civilization, beyond the steppe. The description of what the envoy had seen excited great speculation in the Court at Ch'ang-an, to which he had returned in 126 BC. But, typically, what interested Emperor Han Wu-ti were the fine horses Chang Ch'ien had noticed on his way through Ta Yuan. These large animals could carry heavily armed men against the Hsiung Nu who rode the smaller Mongolian pony. Chang Ch'ien believed that friendly relations and trade could be established with 'the Western Regions', because he had found that the peoples living there were anxious to obtain Han goods. It seems that a supply route of barter exchange through Yunnan was in use. His advice to Emperor Han Wu-ti became the basic policy line towards 'the Western Regions' for the Han Empire. Embassies and military expeditions were sent to Ta Yuan, the incredible distance of three thousand kilometres, until in 102 BC the forceful emperor had enough horses for stud purposes in China as well as an adequate number of 'outer vassal' states in Central Asia.

The struggle between the Chinese and the Hsiung Nu came to a temporary halt in 51 BC, following civil conflict within the nomad nation. When fighting resumed in the Later Han Empire the Chinese exploited this division between the rival nomad tribes, the Southern and the Northern Hsiung Nu. The policy was called *i-i-fa-i*, or 'using the barbarians to attack the barbarians'; it was combined with gifts in order that China should divide and rule. But the significance of the long feud with the Hsiung Nu lay in the era of exploration and conquest that it stimulated. The Han Empire stretched into 'the Western Regions' and discovered the rest of the world. An expedition of seventy thousand men, led by General Pan Ch'ao, reasserted Han influence over Central Asia in AD 97. Though he camped on the shores of the Caspian Sea, the closest point a Chinese army has ever approached Europe, his ambassadors did not succeed in opening up relations with Ta Ts'in, the Roman Empire. The other civilization that was to touch China was India, its powerful influence being channelled through the Buddhist religion.

To finance the war against the Hsiung Nu, Emperor Han Wu-ti was obliged to adopt a new economic policy. Nationalization of the iron and salt industries was expected to offset some of the burden falling on the *nung*, whilst the 'ever normal' granary provided the surpluses needed for the army. There can be little doubt that the *shang* introduced as civil servants did help straighten out imperial finances, but the emperor himself was aware of the economic dangers of the aggressive policy he adopted. In 91 BC he spoke thus to general Wei Ch'ing, a veteran of the nomad wars:

> In the early years of the Han dynasty there was an increasing number of incursions into China by four kinds of barbarians. If I had not changed this, later generations would have been helpless. If I had not sent armies out in punitive expeditions, the Empire would not now be at peace. But, if one does these things, one cannot avoid placing a heavy burden on the people. If later generations repeat what I have done, they will be following in the footsteps of the ruined dynasty of Ch'in.

Imperial expeditions were sent out in directions other than north and west. In 111 BC six Chinese armies reduced Nan Yueh in a brief campaign. This southern kingdom, which was centred on the city of Canton, had been tem-

A bronze horseman armed with a halberd of the Later Han period. It was excavated at Wu-wei, Kansu, in 1969.

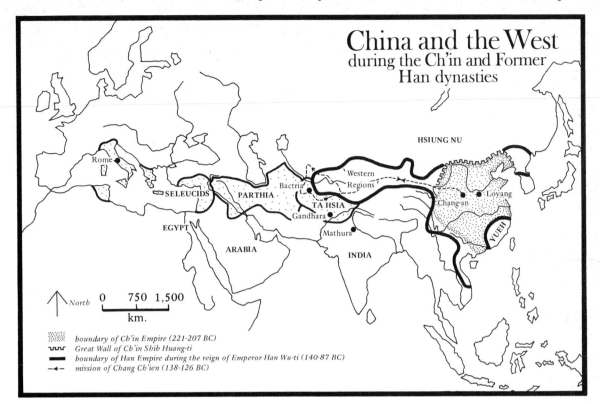

China and the West
during the Ch'in and Former
Han dynasties

HSIUNG NU

Rome

Western
Regions

Bactria

SELEUCIDS   PARTHIA

TA HSIA   Chang-an   Loyang

Gandhara

EGYPT

Mathura   YUEH

ARABIA

INDIA

↑ North   0   750   1,500
km.

boundary of Ch'in Empire (221-207 BC)
Great Wall of Ch'in Shih Huang-ti
boundary of Han Empire during the reign of Emperor Han Wu-ti (140-87 BC)
mission of Chang Ch'ien (138-126 BC)

porarily incorporated into China during the Ch'in dynasty, but had reasserted its independence after 207 BC. This thrust to the far south took the authority of Emperor Han Wu-ti into modern Tongking, then known as the Commandery of Jihnan. Meanwhile Han influence was extended in the south-west, tribes in the border areas of Szechuan and Tibet accepting Chinese supremacy. Only Yunnan, which means 'South of the Clouds', succeeded in resisting imperial pressure; it was not annexed until the thirteenth century, when the Mongol invaders passed through the high plateau in an outflanking manoeuvre against the Southern Sung dynasty. In his southern campaigns Emperor Han Wu-ti was following the policy of Ch'in Shih Huang-ti, who had facilitated the movement south of the Chinese people.

Another direction taken by Han armies was north-east. In 109 BC two expeditionary forces were sent to conquer northern Korea – one sailed from Shantung, the other marched overland through southern Manchuria. Friction between Han and Korean authorities had arisen over the activities of political refugees from China. Resistance was short-lived and the province of Lin-t'un was annexed to the Empire in 108–7 BC.

SSU-MA CH'IEN
AND CHINESE
HISTORIOGRAPHY

The first comprehensive history of China, the *Shih Chi* (*Historical Records*), was written about 100 BC. Its author Ssu-ma Ch'ien was the Imperial Astrologer, an appointment he inherited from his father, Ssu-ma T'an, who may have begun the task of writing the *Shih Chi*. Though the dates of his birth and death are uncertain, the life of Ssu-ma Ch'ien can be said to correspond to the reign of Emperor Han Wu-ti. The Ssu-ma family were of noble origin, their native place having been a part of T'sin state on the upper Yellow River that had fallen to Ch'in. Ssu-ma Ch'ien travelled widely: he explored the Empire from the Great Wall in the north to Yunnan in the south, and this first-hand experience may partially account for his awareness of economic considerations in historiography. The connection of the Chengkuo Canal and the triumph of Ch'in was not lost on him. In his own lifetime the continued importance of this key economic area is recorded in the *Shih Chi*, for 'Kuan-chung occupies one-third of the territory in the Empire with a population three-tenths of the total; but its wealth constitutes six-tenths of all the wealth in the Empire'.

Ssu-ma Ch'ien wrote a history of the entire knowable past. It was his belief that mankind existed long before he began his narrative, but he refrained from speculation or comment on the grounds that the sources to hand were untrustworthy. This reluctance to name a point of creation is characteristic of Chinese historiography, with its emphasis on politics and society rather than other-worldly salvation. 'Unlike Hebrew, Christian, or Japanese historians, Ssu-ma Ch'ien and his countrymen recognize no dateable beginning to human history. Their conception of time is astronomical. . . .' Another characteristic that deserves sober notice is the unofficial nature of the *Shih Chi*. Ssu-ma Ch'ien – and perhaps his father – 'seems to have compiled his history as a private person, in spite of the fact that as a court astrologer it must also have been his official task to note and co-ordinate acts of his ruler and the phenomena of nature, particularly those in the sky, which was the duty of the ancient astrologer-recorders as exemplified in the early annalistic works'. The *Shih Chi* was the result of an individual historian's desire to record the achievements of the age in which he lived, despite his own critical attitude to Emperor Han Wu-ti. In 99 BC a memorial about the nomad wars was misunderstood by the throne and manipulated by his opponents; the result was the charge of attempting to deceive the emperor, a perfunctory trial, and castration. The humiliation of this punishment was never forgotten by Ssu-ma Ch'ien, whose chapter on Emperor Han Wu-ti himself is missing from the *Shih Chi*, no doubt because it contained all the hostility the historian harboured against the ruler for his unjust sentence.

Nevertheless, Ssu-ma Ch'ien 'stands as a watershed, gathering together and summing up the traditions of the past, and in his great history of China down to his own day, the *Records of the Historian* providing the unsurpassed model for the long line of Standard Histories which has stretched after him in an unbroken line to the twentieth century'. It would seem appropriate to let Ssu-ma Ch'ien give his explanation of the great transformations of China down to the establishment of the Han Empire, before we end this chapter on the Former Han. Discussing the first three Chinese dynasties, the Hsia, Shang and Chou, he explains that they all started well, each founded by a man of extraordinary virtue and wisdom, but after a number of generations they declined, till at the end of each dynasty a cruel and incapable ruler sat on the throne. This is 'one of the most persistent patterns of Chinese historical writing. . . . The cycle begins again when a new hero-sage overthrows the worthless tyrant of the old house and sets up a new rule.' The Hsia dynasty, according to Ssu-ma Ch'ien, was distinguished by good faith at first, but towards the close of its period of rule,

The gilded bronze figure of a kneeling girl with a lamp; from the tomb of the Princess Tou Wan.

there was a retreat to a more primitive cultural phase. With the foundation of the Shang an age of piety was inaugurated though this degenerated into superstition at last. The Chou kingdom, the feudal system at its most developed stage, was characterized by ceremonial, which from the Ch'un Ch'iu period began to deteriorate into little more than a sham. To Ssu-ma Ch'ien, of course, the Ch'in dynasty was a rude, semi-barbarian intrusion that failed to hold the Middle Kingdom because it relied on the harsh philosophy of the Legalist School, an ethical code that the successful Han dynasty had wisely rejected. The triumph of Confucianism during the Former Han was a return to the good faith of the Hsia.

5

The Later Han Empire

AD 25–220

The Han dynasty was divided into two parts, the Former Han and the Later Han, by the so-called 'usurpation of Wang Mang', otherwise styled the first and last Hsin emperor. Today, he remains a controversial figure; some would argue that his far-reaching reforms were socialist in intent, others holding that he was concerned to strengthen the bureaucratic Empire. Whatever final judgment is reached on Wang Mang there can be little doubt that his reign represented the culmination of attempts made by the early Empire to hinder the growth of large estates.

At the centre of his programme for reform was a redistribution of land. It is debatable whether he took the 'well-field' system of Chou times as the ideal agrarian model, one in which a communal-feudal arrangement for land tenure prevailed, but he did seek to ameliorate the desperate plight of the *nung*. The process of land concentration had started during the Ch'in dynasty; great landlords came to dominate agriculture, buying out smaller farmers who could not compete. Increased agricultural productivity, the result of the enclosure of smallholdings, helped provide foodstuffs for a growing population, but speculation was encouraged and landowners became an influential group in society. It was inevitable that many *shih* should have taken advantage of this situation because landed property was considered to be the most secure investment and family wealth could best be handed down to the future generations if it was in the form of land. The most fertile land was in demand; the area irrigated by the Chengkuo Canal was known as 'earth fat'. Whilst the big landowners got richer and enjoyed a luxurious life, the small farmer was hard put to retain his holding. A bad harvest, higher taxation, an imperial requisition, the corvée, rebellion, a nomad incursion – any of these events could mean debt and ruin for the *nung*, who lacked financial reserves.

The edict of the Hsin emperor that forbad both the buying or selling of land, and the traffic in slaves was a bold attempt to protect the small against the big. Henceforth the land in the Empire was to be designated 'the emperor's land', and families with large holdings were required to pass their surplus fields to those without land. This nationalization of land and the re-allocation of fields according to the needs of the cultivator failed. Like most of the other revolutionary measures devised by Wang Mang, the reform was introduced without adequate planning. There was no means of implementation; the civil service was reluctant to involve itself so closely in economic affairs, and the *shang*, when recruited as officials, seized the chance for personal enrichment.

The Duke of Chou directing the building of the new city of Lo, near modern Loyang. An illustration from the *Shu Ching*.

92

作邑東國圖

周公

Before looking at the other policies of the Hsin emperor it is necessary to consider the political situation. Wang Mang derived his strength from two sources – his relatives, the consort family, and the antiquarian wing of the Confucian *shih*. As regent to the child Emperor Han P'ing-ti, in whose name he administered the affairs of state, Wang Mang was referred to as 'the second Duke of Chou'. Once in power himself, the reforms he sponsored were justified in terms of high antiquity, the world revealed in the newly recovered *Rituals of the Chou Dynasty*. Archaic titles and dignities were revived alongside the nationalization of land. The combination proved unworkable; the new measure proved impossible to enforce. The Hsin dynasty lasted only fourteen years because, unlike the Later Han, it was prepared to take drastic action in social and economic affairs. Against Wang Mang were ranged the landowners, the uneasy *shih*, the *shang* and, at last, the *nung*, who were suffering as much as anyone from the reforms intended to help them.

Apart from the prohibition on the buying and selling of land, other measures to support the *nung* were introduced. The *p'ing chang* or 'levelling system', first employed by Emperor Han Wu-ti, was brought back to deal with activities of the *shang*. Idle land was made subject to triple taxation and encouragement was given to those *nung* who would open up new areas for cultivation. The government offered small loans to farmers at a low rate of interest. This was to enable the poorest *nung* to obtain seed and proper tools. Finance for the loan scheme was made available from the state monopolies on salt, iron and liquor. For the benefit of the entire economy Wang Mang attempted to standardize coinage. He called in gold coins in exchange for bronze, his new coins being minted in a number of denominations. Again, he lacked a competent and willing civil service to carry through this fiscal reform successfully. To add to the difficulties faced by the Hsin emperor an expedition of 300,000 men against the Hsiung Nu was deemed necessary. Some of the famines that broke out towards the end of his reign 'were in part the result of this diversion of manpower from production'. A contemporary shift in the course of the Yellow River and successive droughts served to exacerbate the economic problem, which eventually drove both big and small farmers into open rebellion. One rebel group, the 'Red Eyebrows', was a secret society, an organization that attracted very wide popular support in times of distress in China. But the landowners backed Liu Hsiu, a collateral member of the imperial house of Han, and this young noble defeated Wang Mang on the battlefield, so ending the Hsin dynasty. The head of 'the Usurper', exhibited in the market-place at Ch'ang-an, was stoned by the crowd.

IMPERIAL DECLINE

The debt that Emperor Han Kuang-wu (AD 25–58) owed to the landed gentry made it difficult for the state to interfere again with land tenure. The proprietors of the great estates had been largely responsible for the restoration of the imperial house, and their continued support seemed the best guarantee for the stability of the Empire. As a direct result of the throne's enforced neutrality on the land question a number of social developments took place during the Later Han. The *nung* lost most of their freedom, becoming dependant farmers on large estates. The economic condition of those whose land was less than one hundred *mou*, the mass of the 'poor and humble', became intolerable. Debt forced them to sell their holdings. Two methods of livelihood then remained: they could stay on their land as share-croppers, paying fifty per cent of the harvest to their landlord, or, still worse, accept employment as wage labourers. The lot of the oppressed tenant was misery: they usually 'wore the coverings of oxen and horses and ate the food of dogs and pigs'. The corollary of this social downgrading of the *nung* was the formation of a quasi-feudal system. Powerful families acquired economic and military influence, their great estates acting as 'states within the state', especially in times of civil discord. Large family groups appeared; the extended family, which included three generations or more at the same residence, became typical. Kinsmen drew together for mutual protection at the end of the Later Han and the period of the Three Kingdoms, when the government was unable to control soldiers or bandits. How different the new social order was can be glimpsed from this description:

> The houses of the powerful are compounds where several hundreds of ridgebeams are linked together. Their fertile fields fill the countryside. Their slaves throng in thousands, and their military dependents can be counted in tens of thousands. Their boats, carts and merchants are spread throughout the four quarters. Their stocks of goods are held back for speculation in the principal cities. Their great mansions cannot contain their precious stones and treasure. The upland valleys cannot hold their horses, cattle, sheep and swine. Their elegant apartments are full of seductive lads and lovely concubines. Singing-girls and courtesans are lined up in their deep halls.

There is a clear military function implied. The landowning families could back their demands for political power with both economic and military pressure.

The civil service gradually filled up with members of the landlord class. The system of recommendation, by which the 'virtuous and wise', the 'upright' and the 'filially pious and incorrupt' were proposed as gentlemen in the Court by officials, developed into a regular quota from each province. The *jen-tzu*, the parallel system under which a relative of a 2,000 *picul* official was given the privilege of being appointed a gentleman automatically too, only served to strengthen vested interests in the imperial administration. Both of these avenues of advancement had been open in Former Han but in Later Han they greatly contributed to the rise of the powerful families. This domination of government ensured that such reforms as proposed by Wang Mang were never mooted again. Furthermore the disappearance of a free peasantry caused a serious reduction in the money and manpower available to the emperor. In AD 46 conscription was abandoned, making the central government dependant on regular troops and the 'myriad retainers' of the powerful families. At the same time pounded earth and brick fortifications were built, even in areas unlikely to suffer nomad incursion. Where powerful families organized themselves militarily and constructed fortresses, they were joined by small and weaker families in search of adequate protection.

All these changes in domestic politics and administration indicate a decline from the imperial pattern established during Former Han. That there was less social and economic cohesion in the Empire was a fact that was not missed by the barbarians who had been brought into the tributary system by Emperor Han Wu-ti. The civil war at the fall of the Hsin dynasty offered a pretext for the 'outer vassals' in Central Asia to forget about their tributary status to China as well as allowing the Hsiung Nu almost unopposed pillage in the border areas along the Great Wall. It was the good fortune of the Later Han Empire that internal conflict within the Hsiung Nu nation hampered the nomad assault. The Southern Hsiung Nu became allies of the Empire and together with Chinese forces they inflicted heavy defeats on the Northern Hsiung Nu in AD 73 and 88. The 'outer vassals' were restored by General Pan Ch'ao in AD 97, when overland contact between Rome and China was blocked by the interposing power of Parthia. But Chinese influence in Central Asia waned after the middle of the second century. These advances were less substantial than the imperial expansion achieved in Former Han for the very reason that victories over hostile barbarians were obtained through the aid of friendly barbarians. In adopting the *i-i-fa-i* policy China came to depend on those who had been its enemies. Later, the Tsin dynasty was unable to resist pressure from barbarian peoples who had been allies in civil disturbances. By 316 everything to the north of the Yang-tze watershed had fallen to the Tartars.

Other factors, too, were involved in the disintegration of the first Chinese Empire. After Liu Hsiu had regained the throne for the house of Han, he decided to move the imperial capital downstream from Ch'ang-an, in the Wei River valley, to Loyang, in the lower Yellow River valley. This change was very significant, for it followed the movement of the key economic area. Though Kuan-chung was economically still very important, the lower Yellow River valley and the Huai River valley were acquiring an even greater status. The further economic development of areas south of the Huai River led to the period of the Three Kingdoms (221–80). It was, as Chi Ch'ao-Ting explains:

a typical case of division generated by the internal forces of Chinese society. The material and fundamental factor responsible for such division was the rise of rival economic areas, whose productivity and location enabled them to serve as bases for a sustained challenge of the authority of the overlord who commanded the central or main key economic area. In this case it was the increasing maturity of Shu, or the Szechuan Red Earth Basin, and the adolescent exuberance of Wu, the lower Yang-tze valley, that produced the balance of power politically represented by the Three Kingdoms.

Another contributory factor was the political conflict between rival factions in the Court. A new element had been introduced into the situation when Emperor Han Kuang-wu began to replace ordinary officials with eunuchs in all posts within the palace, though the first dispute between the consort family and the eunuchs did not break out till AD 92. On this occasion Emperor Han Ho-ti enlisted a eunuch, Cheng Chung, in a plot successfully aimed at the Tou family. Against powerful families the Later Han emperors were tempted to use the eunuchs, but these conflicts tended to make them increasingly powerful in affairs of state. Several emperors were effectively under the control of their eunuchs, and the overthrow of the Han dynasty was a direct result of this disastrous influence in the palace. On the death of Emperor Han Ling-ti, in whose reign the eunuchs had ceased to bother disguising their power, a final struggle between the eunuchs and the army occurred (189). The assassination of general Ho Tsin in the palace was the signal for a wholesale slaughter of the eunuchs by the infuriated soldiery. The ensuing civil war destroyed the Han Empire and split China into the Three Kingdoms.

An ornamental brick house in the form of a gateway. Dating from the Han period, it was found near K'ai Feng.

LIFE IN TOWN AND
COUNTRYSIDE

In AD 1–2 an official census of the Han Empire recorded the existence of 12,233,062 households, or 59,594,978 individuals. The greater part of this population was engaged in agriculture, and it is thought that between six and ten million people were urban dwellers. The shortage of accurate historical data makes general conclusions difficult, but the old tradition of the walled-city-in-the-country should lead us to expect a considerable population living in cities and towns. In each of the 1587 prefectures of the Empire at least one town would be needed as an administrative centre, while the more populous prefectures of North China must have included several major settlements. The

太保相宅圖

太保

two imperial capitals of the Han Empire, Ch'ang-an and Loyang, had populations of 246,000 and 195,500 respectively.

The site of Ch'ang-an, it will be recalled, was chosen for strategic and economic reasons. Political considerations also determined the layout of the city's ground-plan. A rectangular grid of streets divided the area within the fifteen-mile-long city walls into a number of quarters, which contained smaller *li*, or wards. Each of the one hundred and sixty wards of Ch'ang-an was surrounded with a wall controlled by a single gate. Each household in turn had the equivalent of a wall with a gate. Near neighbours in adjoining wards could visit each other only through the wards gates, which were closed and guarded at night. Drums were sounded in the evening to give warning of closure. Visitors from distant wards were often obliged to stay overnight because their far from direct journey home through the different gates was impossible between the drum call and the night watch. The central and southern parts of Ch'ang-an were occupied by the imperial palace, the secretariat and the houses of the noble and official classes. To the north and west was the service quarter, where the *kung* lived and worked. The rest of the population was concentrated in the east. The nine markets that served the city were all located along the main north–south thoroughfare. At the beginning of the Han period the *shang* were segregated; their houses had to be built outside the walls of the capital.

Behind the town planning of Han cities was a set of ancient ideas and practices, which can be termed *feng-shui*, or 'wind and water'. The initial siting of a settlement involved complex calculations by geomancers, whose occult and practical knowledge ensured that evil spirits or influences would not trouble the inhabitants. The Chinese chose to ally themselves with Nature rather than oppose it. A square, the basic shape of the classical settlement, found a parallel in the belief that heaven was round and the earth square. But in terms of everyday life the people who lived in towns were effectively under the control of the authorities. The rigidity of the Han town planning was relaxed later, as a result of population expansion, less centralized régimes, the growth of commercial activity and the enforced movement of large numbers to less typically Chinese cities in the south through the barbarian invasions of the north. Nevertheless, the cities in China have never been centres of social change. Unlike those in the West, they did not develop wealth through trade and industry; their independence was never sufficient to reject established political, legal and religious ideals. As university centres they have acted to support centralization by preparing students for entry examinations to the civil service. The *shang* has never become a socially significant class because 'the Chinese town . . . was not a spontaneous accumulation of population, nor of capital or facilities of production, nor was it only or essentially a market-centre; it was above all a political nucleus, a node in the administrative network, and the seat of the bureaucrat who had replaced the ancient feudal lord'.

The density of population was high in the city. Even the wealthy had a rather restricted living area, though every courtyard, no matter how small, became something of a garden by the use of plants and small trees in pots. The sense of seclusion was preserved by the design of the traditional Chinese house, which centred on the courtyard, referred to as the 'Well of Heaven'. A substantial family dwelling would have two such courtyards. Just inside the gate to the street there was the 'public' yard, which might have contained shrubs and a goldfish pond; here traders and persons unconnected with the household would be received. The 'private' yard, at the centre of the house, was reserved for members of the family and close friends; rooms for in-laws, relatives and, possibly, concubines were ranged along the sides, whilst the main building for the head of the household and his wife stood at the far end. Directly behind this were the kitchens and the servants' quarters. A small garden might surround the building within the outer wall. The architecture was enhanced by 'a lavish use of colour, not only in roof tiles, but on painted columns, lintels and beams, richly bracketed cornices, and broad expanses of plastered walls'.

Loess cave dwellings in Shansi province.

The daily management of a household was the responsibility of the elder members of the family. Servants or slaves would be sent out to purchase whatever was needed to feed and clothe the family. Cleaning would be accomplished under the direction of the senior women. The amount of domestic work involved would depend on the affluence of the family. Poor households were satisfied with simple furnishings: beds made from wooden planks and covered with rush-mats, and blankets stuffed with silk floss. The richer families however, covered their floors with embroidered cushions, woollen rugs or rush-mats and possessed beds carved from the finest wood and hung with beautifully worked drapes. Various *shih* railed against the extravagance and luxury of the capital – silk-lined slippers, fur-trimmed coats, the profusion of jewellery, splendid carriages with well-fed horses, the musicians and singing girls, banquets, drinking parties and gambling – and reminded their readers of the unremitting toil of the 'diligent farmer'.

Lessons for Women, written by Pan Chao, the sister of Pan Ku the historian (AD 32–92), offers an insight into marriage during the Later Han dynasty. The age for a man to marry was thought to be between sixteen and thirty and for a woman, between fourteen and twenty. Marriage between persons of the same surname was strictly prohibited, lest the couple have a common ancestor; this rule originated in Chou times, and its influence has not entirely disappeared from China today. There were seven grounds for divorce of a wife, namely disobedience to parents-in-law, barrenness, adultery, jealousy, incurable disease, loquacity and theft. Pan Chao wrote that 'the way of respect and compliance is the woman's great *li*', or proper rule of conduct. A daughter-in-law who cared for her marriage should never displease her husband's parents. Remarriage for women, the *Lessons for Women* states plainly, cannot be acceptable to the devoted wife, but in this view Pan Chao was not in accord with contemporary behaviour. It was, however, a society in which a man could have only one wife. Concubines were not regarded as full members of the family and the status of a concubine was inferior to that of a wife. The children of concubines could not expect to have the same rights of inheritance as the children of the wife. Concubinage was always the preserve of the wealthy.

Before turning to the countryside a word needs to be said about slaves, or *nu*, a class which formed the lowest social stratum. Exactly how many slaves existed in the Han Empire is impossible to calculate from the surviving evidence, but all historians are agreed about the relative smallness of this inferior class. In AD 44 there were one hundred thousand government slaves, the majority of whom were engaged in looking after government-owned animals. Only convicts, *t'u*, are mentioned as working in iron mining and manufacture.

A modern example of land reclamation through the terracing and irrigation of loess hillsides in Shansi province. From early times the *nung* were expert in such large-scale agricultural projects through the corvée.

Convicts, unlike slaves, were sentenced to servitude for a definite period of time. The corvée provided the manpower needed for hydraulic engineering and grain transportation, as there were hundreds of thousands of wandering labourers who could be mobilized without too much disturbance of the rural economy. The *shih* frequently complained about the uselessness of government slaves who 'idle with folded hands' in contrast to the hard-working *nung*. Private slaves were kept too. In striking contrast to Rome, the civil rights of household slaves were considerable. Han law did not permit a master to kill a

slave of his own free will; two princes were disinherited for ordering the execution of slaves and Wang Mang made his middle son, Ho, commit suicide for the murder of a male slave. 'In all Chinese history there is no parallel to the slave-manned oared war-galley of the Mediterranean. . . . When the water-mill appeared early in the first century for blowing metallurgical bellows, the records distinctly say that it was considered important as being more humane and cheaper than man-power or animal-power.'

In 111 BC Emperor Han Wu-ti had issued the following edict:

Agriculture is the basic occupation of the world. Springs and rivers make possible the cultivation of the five grains. . . . There are numerous mountains and rivers in the domain, with whose use the ordinary people are not acquainted. Hence the government must cut canals and ditches, drain the rivers and build dikes and water tanks to prevent drought.

Dominating life in the countryside was the problem of the proper use and regulation of water. Family solidarity was the effective basis of co-operation amongst the *nung*, upon whose diligence the success of harvests has always depended. Not surprisingly then, the maintenance of irrigation ditches and the repair of terraces was a village responsibility shared by all of its working members, whereas large-scale improvements were organized periodically by government officials. In North China the landscape featured long, narrow fields of wheat or millet on terraces winding round the loess hillsides; the 'endless chain' and other human-powered devices were used to raise water from canals and wells. In South China the landscape was to become an intricate patchwork of terraced and flooded paddy fields, once the primitive system of slash and burn gave way to a more settled approach to cultivation. This transformation started during the so-called Six Dynasties (220–580), when refugees from the northern provinces fled to the Yang-tze River valley, and it converted South China into the key economic area for the Sui and T'ang Empires (581–907). Though rice had been introduced north of the Yang-tze River by the first century, it could be grown only in summer and with very careful irrigation. Its cultivation remained the chief agricultural activity of the Yang-tze River valley, though the exceptional productivity of rice led to its adoption as far north as the southern part of the flood plain of the Yellow River. The skill of the northern *nung* in water regulation made this adoption possible.

An advance in land use for the northern *nung* had come from a proposal made in 100 BC by Chao Kuo, an agricultural adviser to Emperor Han Wu-ti. He devised a system of ploughing that aided planting, irrigation and soil renewal. The standard field measured one *mou*; it was two hundred and forty paces long and six paces wide. Chao Kuo recommended that at the start of the farming year the field should be split into three shallow furrows, separated from each other by ridges; furrow and ridge each measured 0.3 metre in width, and their relative positions were changed annually. The gains were immediate: seed previously sown broadcast was now efficiently concentrated into the furrows; farmers could work more easily, as they stood on the ridges and dealt with the growing plants below; weeding the ridges loosened and transferred soil to the furrows, where it strengthened the new stalks; watering the crop was simpler; and, not least, the movement of the ridge and furrow ensured a rotation of sown and fallow. As a result the annual yield could now be the same from one year to the next, providing there were no drastic variations in climate. Great attention was paid to fertilizers too. Poor soil would be carried to the village, for composting with organic refuse, and then replaced on the fields. Ashes, manure, organic debris and human waste were all converted into fertilizer. And river silt as well as canal mud had been spread over the surface of fields from earliest times.

Although oxen and water-buffalo, introduced from the far south, were yoked to plough the land, the lot of the *nung* was hard. On large farms all kinds of new equipment could be found – improved ploughshares and moulding

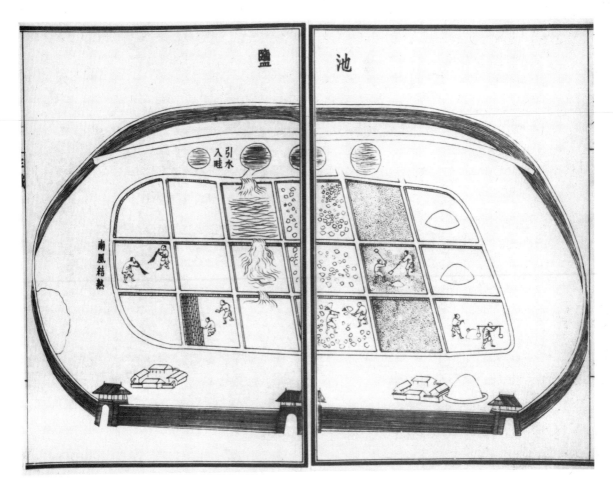

鹽　池

Salt mining became a
nationalized industry in
120 BC; a Ming
illustration of a saltern.

boards, water- and animal-powered milling of grain by tilt-hammers or circular stone grinding wheels, water raising machinery and better crop strains – but the small farmer was forced to retain the ancient methods and crops, depending on the hoe, the manually-operated grain mill and the transport of water by yoke and bucket. The Chinese farmer, however, is a 'time economiser beyond any other'. By careful use of the calendar and his spare time, he avoids the need to rush into over-hasty action in any season. For instance, in the essential task of ploughing he was exhorted to attend to it during a drizzle or after rain, thus conserving moisture that could be invaluable in the summer. Frugality and foresight were the fundamental qualities of the best *nung*. The general pattern of the rural family was self-support; most of the food, clothing and utensils used by a family would be home-produced.

While the rich vied with each other in extravagance, the Jen abstained, were frugal, and worked hard at farming and stock-breeding. While other people strove for land and cattle at low prices, the Jen were the only ones to take the dear and the best. The family remained rich for several generations. However, the family regulations of Mr Jen were that nothing that was not produced from their own fields or cattle should be used for clothing or food; and that until the common work was done, no one could drink wine or eat meat. Because of this, they became the model in their rural community.

LEFT A Sung cast-iron
pagoda erected in 1061.

The 'wooden ox' or wheelbarrow, a Chinese invention dating from the third century AD.

Because of the fundamental role of Nature in early Chinese civilization – that ancient intimacy of man and environment which found philosophical expression in the Yin-Yang theory – specialists such as astronomers, astrologers, engineers and magicians were absorbed into the central bureaucracy. Science and sorcery were able to coexist together because of the old idea that natural phenomena, like flooding, earthquakes or eclipses, were connected with supernatural powers. The benevolence of Shang Ti was entreated by the sacrifices of the priest-king; hence the attention paid to astronomy, whose predictive function in respect of heavenly movements was regarded as a state secret. An imperial edict of the later T'ang dynasty indicates the security-mindedness of the throne in 840. The officials in the imperial observatory were addressed thus:

> If we hear of any intercourse between the astronomical officials or their subordinates and officials of other government departments or miscellaneous common people, it will be regarded as a violation of security regulations which should be strictly adhered to. From now onwards, therefore, the astronomical officials are on no account to mix with civil servants and common people in general. Let the Censorate look to it.

Chinese astronomers have amassed long series of observations on things which were not studied elsewhere, for example novae and supernovae, so important in current cosmological speculation. A Shang oracle-bone of 1300 BC bears the oldest record of a nova in any civilization. The inscription reads: 'On the seventh day of the month . . . a great new star appeared in company with Anatres.' Systematic records of sun-spots were kept from 28 BC; imperial astronomers must have observed through thin slices of jade or some similar

TECHNICAL
ADVANCE AND
THE BEGINNINGS
OF SCIENCE

Water-powered trip hammers; just one invention that aided the improvement of agricultural techniques on the large estates while the *nung* were forced to maintain the ancient methods. A Ming illustration.

水碓

盖利
用芽

取繭

Sericulture; feeding of the
silk worms. A Ming
illustration.

translucent material. Possibly the chief task of the Bureau of Astronomy was the regulation of the calendar. Not only did the agricultural cycle depend upon its accuracy but even more it was an immemorial custom that acceptance of the calendar promulgated by a ruler was a symbol of submission on the part of the subject. The lack of an accurate calendar could prove a tactical disadvantage for a rebel leader because celestial portents were liable to political interpretation. Four Han officials handled the sensitive area of 'explaining' natural phenomena: they were the Imperial Astronomer, who attended to observations and the calendar; the Imperial Astrologer, whose task was observation and the prediction of fortune; the Imperial Meteorologist, who dealt with the weather conditions, records of which have also been found on Shang oracle-bones; and the Imperial Clock Official, who was charged with the supervision of clepsydras, or water clocks.

It should not cause surprise to learn that inventors and scientists in Chinese civilization were even members of the ruling classes, either heads of bureaux or minor officials; otherwise they tended to be *kung* or near-slaves in government employ. Chang Heng (78–139) was an inventor, mathematician, astronomer, cartographer and poet. His seismograph was one of the wonders of the imperial observatory, which he ran as Imperial Astronomer. It could locate earth tremors at a distance of several hundred miles. North China was subject to earthquakes from earliest times; Loyang suffered considerable damage in 133 and 135. Chang Heng's 'earthquake weathercock', as it was called, could not furnish a scientific explanation of seismic disturbance, but it did give the One Man immediate notice of a natural disaster. Other inventions to his credit were an improved armillary sphere to trace the paths of planets and the first known application of motive power to the rotation of astronomical instruments. Although astronomy was an 'official' science and its study was a concern of the civil service, no lack of speculation about the nature of the universe existed among contemporary philosophers. A strikingly modern point of view was known as the Hsuan Yeh, or 'Infinite Empty Space Teaching'. Here is an account of its later spokesman, Ch'i Meng:

> The books of the Hsuan Yeh school were all lost, but Ch'i Meng, one of the librarians, remembered what its masters before his time had taught concerning it. They said that the heavens were empty and void of substance. When we look up at it we can see that it is immensely high and far away, having no bounds. . . . The sun, the moon, and the company of stars float in the empty space, moving or standing still. All are condensed vapour. . . .

By the end of the Later Han dynasty, China had made a number of significant technical advances, accumulated a mass of information, formulated some fundamental principles of science and anticipated many discoveries traditionally attributed to the West. Until quite recently it has been fashionable to refer to Chinese civilization as other-wordly, unscientific and anti-technological. At best it has been hinted the Chinese were practical rather than theoretical, because their advances were unscientific in their methodology. This view has had to be thoroughly reassessed in the light of contemporary historical research. Indeed, it has been realized that technology and the beginnings of scientific understanding were inevitably intertwined. Technology produced the instruments that were necessary for scientific measurement; Han craftsmen had use of sliding callipers graduated in decimals. There is not space here to discuss in detail every object of scientific or technological interest; only the chief items can be mentioned.

A high provincial official, Tu Shih, then Prefect of Nanyang, is said to have introduced a water-powered metallurgical blowing-engine in AD 31. The continuous blast thus afforded was of inestimable value to the state-owned iron industry and may have led directly to the production of steel. From this time onwards there is mention of 'the harmony of the hard and the soft', which could mean steel made by a 'co-fusion' process; that is, 'the piling up together and heating of billets of wrought iron and cast iron, with the object of obtaining a material, steel, which we now know has an intermediate carbon content'. But there is no doubt that steel was being produced during the sixth century by a method that foreshadowed the Siemens-Martin process of combining cast and wrought iron. Another invention of the imperial workshops was paper-making, announced in 105 by the director, Ts'ai Lung, who was a eunuch. Previous to this appointment, he had been confidential secretary to the emperor. Paper, when combined with block-printing in the T'ang Empire, brought about a revolution in communications. The earliest known printed book, the *Diamond Sutra*, dates from 868 and was found in the immense complex of Buddhist temple-caves at Tun-huang. Older than this scroll is a block-printed Buddhist charm (770). The advance in printing came from the fusion of two skills; for centuries the Chinese had used ink and paper besides being expert in stone engraving. During the early part of the tenth century block-printed editions of the Classical Books became generally available. The growing number of *shih* were the immediate beneficiaries but during the Two Sungs the illiterate *nung* were able to listen to someone reading them aloud. To be a Chinese came to mean belonging to a great cultural tradition as well as to an Empire. Paper-making assisted the spreading of hygienic habits throughout society too. Before the T'ang dynasty the use of paper in lavatories was general.

The state-controlled salt industry was able to exploit wells in Szechuan from the Former Han dynasty. Deep bore-holes were achieved with iron or steel bits; extraction of underground brine was permitted to a depth of two thousand feet. A long bamboo tube with a valve was sent down as a bucket, and the raised brine evaporated in large iron pans, with the aid of natural gas collected from other bore-holes. The ability to tap this source of salt so far from the sea has been invaluable in times of national crisis, the last such occasion being the Japanese invasion during World War II. An advantage for early Chinese technology was the abundance of natural piping in the form of bamboo. Besides its usefulness in salt mining, split bamboos and wooden constructions could be arranged as irrigation flumes, thereby providing a means of overcoming unsatisfactory surfaces for water. Such technical advances in hydraulic engineering were to be expected, given the age-old connection between centralized government and 'water benefits'. But irrigation, though important, had 'to share its prominence with an unceasing struggle for river-control and a constant preoccupation with inland water transport'. Grain-tribute was the fundamental source of supply for the centralized state; by 110 BC Ch'ang-an already required an annual quota of 6,000,000 *tan* from the lower Yellow River valley. Emperor Han Wu-ti had the Ch'ang-an Canal cut in 131–129 BC in order to connect the capital with the lower Yellow River;

Acupuncture, as a method of healing, originated in the Chou period, 1027–256 BC. This bronze model, made in 1443, indicates 365 points where acupuncture may be applied.

it shortened the distance that grain tribute had to be transported by two-thirds. After all, 'for nearly twenty centuries the Chinese alone appreciated the great mechanical advantage which artificial navigable waterways could offer the systematic transportation of heavy goods, anticipating in this the industrial revolution of the eighteenth century and dazzling all foreign observers who visited their works prior to that time'.

A nautical invention of supreme interest is the stern-post rudder, whose prototype has been discovered in a pottery model of a ship lately recovered from a Former Han tomb. The steering oar, general in the West until the thirteenth century, put a severe limitation on the size of vessel that could be safely constructed, besides giving the steersman a hazardous task of control in stormy seas. The development of the stern-post rudder and the watertight compartment allowed junks to become large deep-ocean craft. The Ming fleet that was to cruise down the eastern coast of Africa under Admiral Cheng Ho, nearly sixty years before Vasco da Gama rounded the Cape of Good Hope in 1497, comprised vessels of more than 1,500 tonnes. The Portuguese ships of da Gama did not exceed 300 tonnes fully laden.

On land several technical advances in transportation deserve attention. First, the wheelbarrow is reputed to have been invented by a Shu general in the Three Kingdoms period, but it seems likely that the 'wooden ox' was known in the Later Han dynasty, over eleven centuries before it reached Europe. In China labour-saving devices have never been rejected because of the fear of technological unemployment. A second improvement concerned the equine harness, now transformed into the highly efficient collar harness. This further advance on the Warring States model increased effective traction enormously. The Chinese wagon was much larger than its counterpart in other parts of the world till the Middle Ages in the West. Lastly, there was the foot-stirrup, the first certain evidence of which has been found in a Ts'in tomb (300). This kind of stirrup had a profound influence on world history, outside China.

It effected nothing less than the application of animal-power to shock combat. The cavalryman was welded into a unity with his steed in a way which none of the Asian mounted archers had ever been, so that he had only to guide, rather than to deliver, the blow. Horsemen fighting in this manner with the Carolingian wing-spear, and gradually more and more enveloped in protective metal armour, came in fact to constitute the familiar feudal chivalry of nearly ten European medieval centuries. It may thus be said that just as Chinese gunpowder helped to shatter European feudalism at the end of this period, Chinese stirrups had originally helped to set it up. [But] nothing of this kind happened in China. Once again, [Joseph Needham concludes] we face the astonishing stability of that civilization.

In agriculture the appearance of the water-powered cereal trip-hammer stamp-mill and the rotary winnowing fan, worked by a crank handle, facilitated the handling of the harvests grown on large estates. For sericulture the continuous driving belt may have been invented. Silk was the only long-staple textile fibre of antiquity; each thread could stretch to several hundred yards in length. The potter, too, experimented with early glazes and stoneware, whilst finely-decorated bricks and tiles became a part of building construction.

A pottery vase, *hu*, decorated in unfired pigments. It dates from the Former Han period, the second or first century BC, and was excavated at Loyang.

OVERLEAF A detail from the *Admonitions of the Instructress to the Court Ladies* attributed to Ku K'ai-chih (*c*. 334–406).

人咸知飾其容
而莫知飾其性
性之不飾
或愆禮正
斯乃
同衾以疑

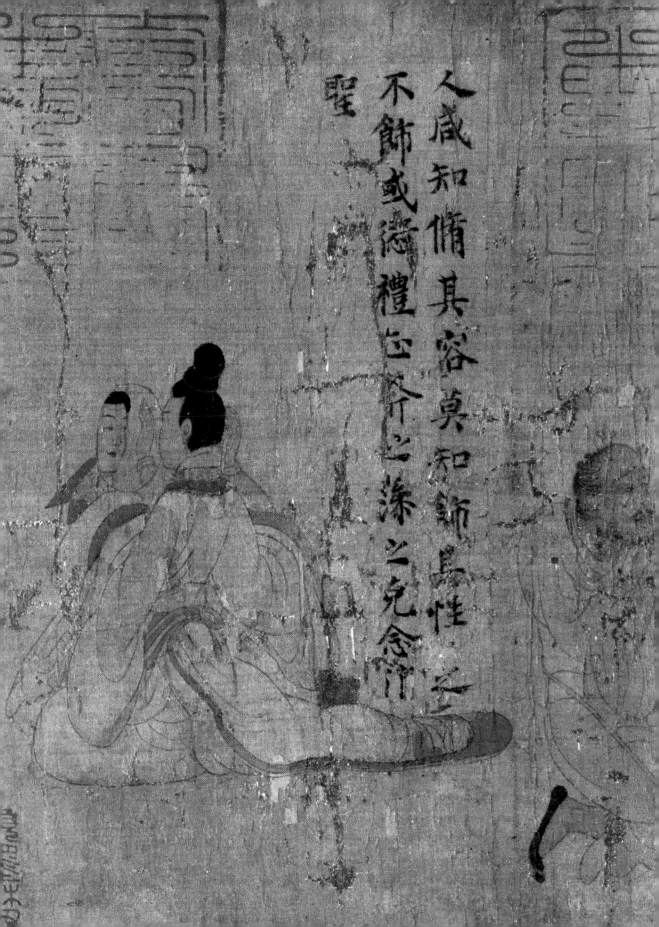

人咸知備其容莫知飾其性性之不飾或愆禮正斧之藻之克念作聖

The 'unofficial' sciences, alchemy and chemistry, always associated with
Taoism, were involved in the beginnings of science, albeit indirectly. An off-
shoot of divination was magnetism, 'the greatest Chinese contribution to
physics'. Taoist geomancy was concerned to adapt the residences of the living
and the dead so as to be in harmony with local currents of the cosmic force. A
part of the geomancer's equipment was the loadstone spoon. A passage
written in AD 83 states, 'But when the south-controlling spoon is thrown upon
the ground, it comes to rest pointing at the south.' This is the earliest record of
magnetism anywhere, yet by T'ang times a compass was in use. The magnetic
compass was 'the first and oldest representative of all these dials and pointer
readings which play so great a part in modern scientific observation'. It was, in
fact, the original self-registering instrument.

Though the functions of the magician and the doctor had been separated in
the Chou dynasty, the study and practice of medicine was still a Taoist science,
because the essential problem was seen as the balance of the forces of the Yin
and the Yang within the body's main organs. Not till the T'ang dynasty does
one find that the doctor was accorded the status of *shih*; in 758 the examination
of medical students in general literature and the philosophical classics was
instituted, but the earliest example of qualifying medical examinations at the
Imperial University dates from only the fifth century. At the assembly of
scientific experts called together by Wang Mang in AD 4 there were present
those skilled 'in magical and medical techniques'.

The holistic character of traditional Chinese diagnosis had been encouraged
originally by the work of Pien Ch'io. In 501 BC he insisted that judgement
should take account of the history and condition of the patient as a whole. At
this period acupuncture was appreciated as a method of healing. The system
consists of a large number of points on the surface of the body in which needles
of varying length and thickness are inserted. In Later Han there were 360
recognized points, ninety less than are used today. Examination of the pulse
was systematized in the *Mo Ching* (*Pulse Book*), written by Wang Shu-ho
(265–317). He expounded the six pulses that could be checked in order to
discover the condition of each of the twelve internal organs. Pulse types could
be superficial, deep, slow or fast. Altogether fifty-two chief varieties were
recorded, including seven that signify impending death. Perhaps more important in his future influence was Chang Chun-ching (*c.* 152–219), whose
Shang Han Lun (*Treatise on Febrile Diseases*), was composed about 200. He was
exceptional in his belief in clinical treatment, eschewing the supernatural and
magical cures; his work on typhoid remained standard for centuries. Finally,
Hua T'o (190–265) developed massage and physiotherapy. He was both a
physician and a surgeon of distinction, in spite of pressure from the *shih* who
were against dissection of bodies. It is uncertain whether his knowledge of
anaesthetics and surgery survived his own death.

6

The Age of Disunity: the So-Called Six Dynasties
220–587

The four hundred years of disunity between the Han and the Sui Empires is known as the Six Dynasties because of the habit of Chinese historians in tracing a 'legitimate' succession for ruling houses, irrespective of the territorial area each might control. This traditional practice does not imply any political blindness on the part of historical commentators but rather a preference for dynastic chronology. There were, in fact, upwards of two dozen royal houses and states during the so-called Six Dynasties. The Later Han dynasty can be said to have lasted till 220 in name only. Ts'ao Ts'ao, the soldier-poet, took command of the Empire shortly after the coup of 189, when the bitter conflict between the eunuchs and the consort family, then the Ho, ended in the mutual ruin of the rival factions. Though it was convenient for Ts'ao Ts'ao to maintain the fiction that he was a servant of the Han, the emperor was his prisoner and official policy and appointments emanated from the general. In 220 Ts'ao Ts'ao's son, Ts'ao Pi, was strong enough to compel the puppet emperor to abdicate in his favour. This new dynasty, titled the Wei, was short lived. It was not a real continuation of the Chinese Empire, following on naturally from the Later Han, nor was it the result of any social consensus, the usual basis for a transfer of the Mandate of Heaven; rather it was an expression of the extent to which the imperial system had disintegrated. Two other leading families took immediate advantage of this artificial situation; the Sun, having repulsed the forces of Ts'ao Ts'ao at the naval battle of Ch'i-pi on the Yang-tze River (208), established themselves as the royal house of Wu, and the Liu, originally allies of the Sun, proclaimed a third power in Shu, or Shu-Han.

The prolonged struggle between the Three Kingdoms of Wei, Wu and Shu was ended in 280 by the Western Tsin dynasty, which had overthrown the house of Wei fifteen years earlier. The first emperor, Ssu-ma Yen, like Ts'ao Ts'ao, was another general from the North, but he outdid his soldier-poet predecessor by briefly achieving the reunification of the whole country. Under the Western Tsin, Wei, the older 'core area' of China, the Middle Kingdom, reasserted its control over the western and southern regions, two newly developing areas of economic activity. What stood behind the victory of Wei was its greater concentration on agricultural productivity and water transport as means of strengthening military power. Ts'ao Ts'ao's system of military agricultural colonies was expanded. From 241 fifty thousand men were

The Buddha at the cave temples of Yunkang, near Ta-t'ung, the capital of the Toba Wei. This Buddhist cave complex was begun in the early fifth century AD.

permanently settled in the Huai valley as state colonists, to defend the most accessible frontier with Wu and to contribute grain for stockpiling against future campaigns. Land under cultivation was much extended, canals were cut and transportation facilitated; and, there was a large accumulation of grain. By avoiding pitched battles and waging an economic war of attrition Wei was able to reduce Shu (264) and Wu (280). Perhaps this conflict can be attributed to something other than economic rivalry. The Ch'in Empire had been regarded as an alien imposition throughout China, but the people who lived in the old state of Ch'u had more reason to dislike its north-western austerity. They were heirs to a quite different cultural tradition, one that contained strong maritime and southern elements. Though the compromise of the Han Empire had worked for centuries, the possibility of economic independence in the South may have been seized not so much by an ambitious family as by a southern people in cultural reaction to the North.

A combination of pressures along the northern frontier provided the Western Tsin dynasty with a problem that it could handle for less than fifty years. Encroachment from nomadic peoples was long standing, but in the Later Han a new approach, the *i-i-fa-i* policy, had led to the settlement of large numbers of allied barbarians within the Great Wall itself. These people posed an internal threat that was not fully appreciated, though Ts'ao Ts'ao had contrived to disperse the largest tribes into smaller groups, each under the supervision of a Chinese official. Periods of civil strife were the most dangerous times, since opposing camps were tempted to call upon friendly barbarians for support. This happened in 304. The Hsiung Nu backed one prince and the Hsien Pei, Tartar tribesmen, were enlisted by another. Soon the northern provinces were overrun with barbarian and Chinese armies. In 311 Loyang was sacked by the Hsiung Nu and the emperor captured; then in 316 the next, and last, emperor of the Western Tsin was also taken prisoner on the fall of Ch'ang-an. Resistance to the barbarians, now reinforced from the steppes, collapsed in North China and the survivors of the defeated imperial house fled to Nanking, formerly the capital of Wu; from there, the Eastern Tsin dynasty managed to hold on to the lands south of the Yang-tze River watershed.

Pressure from the steppe was irresistible because of the presence of numerous barbarian tribes in North China. Once these warlike people were embroiled in the civil wars they proved impossible to expel or control. A fatal political error made by Ssu-ma Yen tended to weaken the unity of the restored Empire. He had decided that his sons should govern separate principalities. Since he had twenty-five sons, these semi-feudal holdings were hopelessly at odds after his death, hindering centralized government and acting as an encouragement for intrigue with the various barbarian groups. 'It is a mistake to believe that it was simply unsoftened native vigour that made the barbarians a menace. They became really dangerous to the extent that they became civilized, and versed in the arts of organization, production and war.'

At the same time as the Eastern Tsin dynasty was consolidating its position in the Yang-tze River valley, not without some opposition from the southern inhabitants who looked askance at the flood of refugees pouring into their lands, North China became the battle-ground of competing barbarian kings.

THE TARTAR PARTITION OF CHINA (317–589)

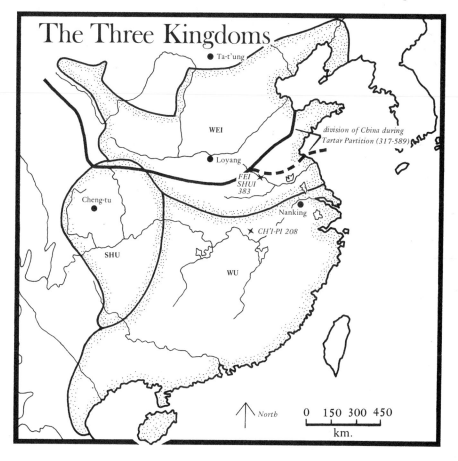

These warring tribesmen made one concerted effort to invade the South in 383, but their army, reputed to have comprised 270,000 cavalry and twice as many infantry, was beaten back at the battle of Fei Shui. The superior discipline of the smaller Tsin force told in the engagement with the loosely arranged barbarian troops. But the frontier between the Tartar dynasties of the North and the Chinese dynasties in the South was almost identical to the northern boundary of the wet-rice growing area, countryside unsuited to the military tactics of nomad cavalry. The failure of this southern expedition disturbed the balance of power in North China, which succumbed to a fresh barbarian invasion by the Toba Tartars, a branch of the Hsien Pei that was already urbanized. These people founded a new dynasty, the Toba Wei, which through a succession of able rulers annexed all the northern kingdoms (439). The Toba kingdom soon modelled itself on Chinese principles of government and inter-marriage with the native inhabitants led to the sinicization of the barbarian conquerors. In 500 the Toba Wei emperor issued a decree prohibiting the use of the Tartar language, costume and customs. Everyone had become Chinese.

This astounding instance of the integrative and absorptive power of Chinese culture needs discussion. After the end of the Western Tsin dynasty, there was nothing like a mass exodus from North China. Large numbers did journey southwards, yet very many more remained where they lived and worked. Alternative social arrangements to the centralized state had existed in embryo during the Later Han. On the large estates could be found an organization for production and defence, with a corresponding quasi-feudal social order that was capable of filling the power vacuum caused by the decline of central government, particularly from 316 to 439. The powerful family, which controlled the locality with fortified encampments, offered security to the *nung*, *kung* and *shih*, whose Confucian scholarship remained useful, albeit on a smaller scale. These local barons, as it were, often fought among themselves and often became allies of one or another of the barbarian tribes. Yet they were accepted by the invaders as a permanent feature in the political scene, an admission that ultimately produced the sino-barbarian synthesis in North China under the Toba Wei dynasty. What these Chinese lords had to contribute, above all else, was a framework for settled government, something the recently nomadic Toba Wei needed as the initial foundation for their own state. Moreover, the scholar-gentry had to be called in as administrators, for they alone 'possessed the necessary mastery of the written language, of official procedures and of essential techniques such as hydraulic engineering'. It should be recalled that it normally took about twenty years to reach full literate proficiency in Chinese. In theory from the Han Empire onwards talented candidates for the civil service could rise from the *nung*, for some of whom village education was available to a level below that required of *shih* intending to enter the bureaucracy, but the length of the learning process for the would-be official ensured that such recruitment was numerically small and that these new *shih* were trained to conform strictly to the *mores* of the scholar class. 'China, therefore, stands an extreme example of how, when a virtually non-phonetic system of writing becomes sufficiently developed to express a large number of meanings explicitly, only a small and specially trained professional group in the total society can master it, and partake of the literate culture.'

The Tartar partition of China, then, stands in marked contrast to the contemporary barbarian invasion of the Roman Empire by Germanic tribes. In the West, these inroads destroyed the ancient civilization, except where remnants of it had taken refuge behind monastery walls. There was a definite lowering of social conditions, in which the Germanic peoples forfeited both their own culture and that of the world they had won. But the western provinces of the Roman Empire were not populated by working people who partook of the cultural tradition; and, besides, there was an enormous slave class. 'The old civilization ... was never very deeply rooted.' In North China on the contrary, the *nung*, steeped in Taoist and Confucian conceptions, constituted a huge cultural reservoir not easily drained of Chinese traditions.

The first rulers of the Toba Wei used forcible removals of population to pacify their barbarian neighbours as well as to increase the agricultural output of the environs of their capital, Ta-t'ung, in northern Shensi. They were persuaded of the need to promote agriculture by the Chinese officials in their administration. The accession to the throne of Emperor Hsiao-wen-ti in 471 was the moment of decision in the history of the Toba Wei and, by implication, of China. The taxation system was reformed, the payment of salaries to

A Taoist temple. Although the guardian deities were always supposed to protect and favour 'the children' (the people) these devotees may well be more concerned with having children themselves. One of the roots of Taoism was the fertility gods of the countryside.

officials started and the land-tenure system revised. In the latter policy Emperor Hsiao-wen-ti achieved a rare success, when compared with the difficulties encountered by Wang Mang. The tendency to over-concentration of ownership and waste was arrested as the central government reasserted its authority to be true custodian of the soil. An imperial decree announced, 'We are now sending commissioners to the provinces and commanderies who will, in co-operation with local officials, allot the land of the Empire in an equitable fashion. The reversion and allocation of the land will be on a lifetime basis.' The rural scene was not suddenly changed, nor did the *nung* immediately benefit, but, once again, notice had been given that in China feudalism could never be accepted as the social pattern. After 550 the disappearance of professional soldiery and the restoration of conscription (farmer-soldiers organized as divisional militia, not unlike Ts'ao Ts'ao's colonists), brought conditions in North China almost back to normal, apart from equipping the military leaders of the Northern Ch'i dynasty (557–581) with the means of reuniting the whole country. General Yang Chien, a man with Hsien Pei blood in his ancestry, seized the throne, defeated the Ch'en dynasty in South China, and reunited Empire under the dynastic title of Sui in 589.

Though it was the northern provinces that formed the basis for eventual re-unification, militarily and administratively, a brief word about the Chinese dynasties that controlled the South is required, before we look at the intellectual and religious climate of the time. The battle of Fei Shui left the southern provinces safe from barbarian attack, but it did not give rise to stable government. After the Eastern Tsin fell in 420, no dynasty endured longer than fifty-nine years. The early friction between the northern refugees and the southern people gave place to the rise of powerful families, a faction no less disruptive to centralized government, as we have already seen in Later Han. A stronger tendency towards hereditary power appeared here than in the North, which was reflected in the renewed independence movement in Szechuan. Nothing approaching a civil service based on scholarship developed, nor were there any social or political events of lasting importance. The only ruler who is remembered, Emperor Liang Wu-ti (502–49), attained this signal honour through his exceptional enthusiasm and fervour for Buddhism.

In Later Han the supremacy of Confucianism was unchallenged. Emperor Han Kuang-wu appointed Confucian *shih* and sought to promote Confucian learning. By the end of his reign it had become customary to offer sacrifices to the Sage of Lu, as one 'who had given good laws to the people'. The following emperor, Han Ming-ti (AD 58–75), enjoyed expositions of Confucian doctrine, in which discussions he was sufficiently learned to take a leading part, and he even visited the shrine of Confucius at Ch'u-fu in AD 72, an event that marked the state adoption of the cult of Confucius. Confucian philosophy had become a moral code, a yardstick for measuring correctness of behaviour, something ideally suited to the administration of 'the Empire of all under Heaven'. Yet a leading thinker, Wang Ch'ung (AD 27–97), was sceptical of the subtle interpretation of the Confucian classics, then in vogue, and maintained that it was unnecessary to elaborate social distinctions into a universal theory. Established conventions and common sense were sufficient. He held similar views to the Hsuan Yeh school concerning the nature of the universe, insisting that Heaven was no more than a blind force and that there was no observable relationship between the movement of celestial bodies and human events. But the appeal of Confucian theory and the scepticism of Wang Ch'ung was confined primarily to the *shih*, the scholar-gentry and the officials. Though the mass of people agreed with Confucius about the importance of the family and respect for ancestors, they wanted something less austere and clung to Taoism, at this time absorbing the magical rites and practices of the countryside. The local gods of ancient tradition found room under the spreading umbrella of Taoism; the followers of Confucius respected Heaven, but showered the chill water of ridicule over the spirits and lesser deities. What completed the transformation of Taoist philosophy into a popular religion was competition with a new faith from India, Buddhism, during the centuries of confusion that succeeded the dissolution of the Han Empire.

Taoism had been a reaction to the feudal religion of the Chou kings, whose interest in ceremonial was remarked by Ssu-ma Ch'ien. The priest-king was the One Man who officiated at sacrifices; worship was conducted in the feudal palace, excluding the people from participation in the rites. Hence was it not

TAOIST RELIGION

A bronze vessel of the third century BC with the Taoist symbol of the 'Mountain of the Immortals'.

natural that the *nung* should continue to look to the *wu* magicians and the dissident *shih* find consolation in the philosophy of Lao-tzu? Confucianism adapted the rites of ancestor worship and the official sacrifices to Heaven into an ethical system, pertinent to the social conditions of a stable empire, but lacking in the kind of religious and emotional appeal that a bewildered people needed after 220. Taoism responded to the national crisis and became the indigenous religion of individual salvation. It developed at two distinct levels, the philosophical speculation so prized by the *shih*, and the magico-religious rites demanded by the *nung*; but it was the popular response that proved the decisive factor.

Chang Tao-ling, reputed to have lived from AD 34 till 156, a span of one hundred and twenty-two years, was the first *T'ien Shih*, or Heavenly Teacher, of the Taoist church. For a time he was able to set up a small, semi-independent state on the borders of Szechuan and Shensi. His organization of the *nung* there into a quasi-religious, quasi-military movement was the first of many

such rural ventures. In 184 the rebellion of the 'Yellow Turbans', a popular
uprising against the Later Han dynasty, had strong Taoist associations. But
Chang Tao-ling was a precursor in another way too. In his mountain fastness
he studied alchemy and sought the elixir of life, a drug capable of bestowing
immortality. The Taoist adept was expected to be a magician, versed in the
secret arts of this world and the next. Longevity had always been appreciated
by the Chinese, as the ancient ideal of 'five generations in one hall' indicates,
but interest in earthly immortality was linked with the belief that Lao-tzu
never died after he crossed the border into the west. Later, the Taoist church
was to claim that Buddhism was a diluted and debased form of Taoism on the
grounds that Lao-tzu had journeyed westwards in order to convert the barbarians. Alchemical theory received comprehensive statement in the writings
of Ko Hung (third century).

Whilst Taoism evolved into a popular religion, with a liturgy and a
pseudo-science of its own, equally fascinating the northern and southern
provinces of China, there was a brief flowering of Taoist philosophy during
the Three Kingdoms and the Western Tsin periods. Wang Pi (AD 226–49)
wrote commentaries on the *I Ching*, the *Tao Teh Ching* and the *Chuang-tzu*.
His analysis of these texts, like those of his later colleagues in the Hsuan Hsueh,
or the 'Mystical School', reflected the general direction taken by the Taoist
religion. There is an emphasis on the interpretation of the mysteries of the Tao,
which involved the clearing-up of a number of earlier inconsistencies, those
marvellously wild statements so beloved by Chuang-tzu. Wang Pi himself

was essentially a Confucian, since he acknowledged Confucius as superior to Lao-tzu, but the 'Seven Sages of the Bamboo Grove', a group formed in 262, pursued Taoist speculation with less orthodoxy. It would appear that they made personal eccentricity something of a virtue and were notorious for their absurd behaviour. There was much attraction in the study of Taoist philosophy at this time. Retirement from the troubled world, noble non-action, seemed a sage policy. As Lao-tzu had said,

> Who will prefer the jingle of jade pendants if
> He once heard stones growing in a cliff!

Yet there was a divide between these Taoist speculators and the Taoist philosophers of the Classical Age. Their approach to the 'mysterious learning' was less creative, less spontaneous, and exemplified a basic indifference to the scientific elements originally incorporated in the Taoist observation of Nature, which boded ill for the further development of science in China. Intellectually, it was the Ch'an Tsung, or the 'Inner-light School' of Buddhism, that derived most from Taoism, though this borrowing too did not accord entirely with the original Taoist spirit.

THE COMING OF BUDDHISM

Towards the end of the Later Han there was an increase in the prestige of Taoism at Court, in 165 imperial sacrifices being for the first time offered to Lao-tzu; but we have seen how this did not really endanger the Confucian orthodoxy. Buddhism, on the contrary, made a serious and sustained bid to become the dominant philosophy of the *shih* as well as the religion of the *nung*. At every level in Chinese society the teachings of the Buddha have had a profound effect. Until the modern period, only India, 'the Holy Land of the East', has influenced China. Yet that singular Chinese capacity to absorb alien peoples, whether Tartar, Mongol or Manchu conquerors, was active in the development of Buddhism too. At last the Buddhist faith was modified to suit Chinese society, rather than China modified by the new religion.

Buddhism was already several centuries old on its arrival in China. Gautama Siddhartha (*c.* 563–479 BC), the North Indian prince who became the Buddha, 'the Enlightened One', had required his followers to isolate themselves from the worldly life. The saffron robe worn by Buddhist monks was a badge which showed ordinary society that they had elected to leave its toils; the colour of this garment was the same as that used to dress condemned men on the day of execution. What was demanded from the individual believer was nothing less than the extinction of the ego, freedom from aversion and desire. A hard and lonely path to tread, for the Buddha had said, 'no man can purify another'. The history of Indian thought during the period just preceding the birth and mission of the Buddha, Heinrich Zimmer has said, 'reveals a gradual intensification of this problem of the rediscovery and assimilation of the Self.... A process of withdrawal from the normally known world was taking place.... Men were turning all their attention inward, striving to attain and hold themselves in a state of unmitigated self-awareness through sheer thinking, systematic self-analysis, breath control and the stern psychological disciplines of yoga.' In the story of Siddhartha's own quest for release, *moksa*, the inwardness of the vision is fundamental. As an infant prince it was prophesied that he would not be a great king, but a great sage, if he became aware of the sufferings of the world. The king, his father, did his utmost to prevent him from having any contact with the outside world; a special palace was built in which all possible pleasures were offered to beguile the young prince's mind. However, one day Siddhartha saw a sick person, and later a tottering old man. These experiences troubled him considerably, but it was an encounter with a corpse on route to the cremation ground that jolted him into active discontent with his luxurious surroundings. The serene calm of a hermit suggested a course for him and, abandoning throne, family and offspring, he became a wandering ascetic, bent on discovering the true nature of things. Having tried the way of self-mortification for a number of years without success, Siddhartha resolved to sit in meditation till he completed his quest. His Enlightenment followed, whereby he became the Buddha, the One who was released from the overwhelming consciousness of suffering.

According to some traditions, the Buddha encountered setbacks when he attempted to communicate his new understanding of the bondage of individualized existence, the endless round of birth, suffering, decay, death and rebirth. He soon realized that men were not prepared to accept his doctrine in its fullness. His vision of the universal void, *sunyata*, frightened them.

> Therefore, he committed the deeper interpretation of reality to an audience of *nagas* (serpent-genii), who were to hold it in trust until mankind should be made ready to understand. Then to his human disciples he offered, as a kind of preliminary training and approach to the paradoxical truth, the comparatively rational and realistic doctrine of the so-called Hinayana division of Buddhism. Not till some seven centuries had passed was the great sage Nagarjuna, 'Arjuna of the Nagas', initiated by the serpent kings into the truth that all is void (*sunya*). And so it was he who brought to man the full-fledged Buddhist teachings of Mahayana.

This legend of the origin of the two great 'vehicles', the primitive Hinayana and the developed Mahayana, is an attempt to rationalize the split in the Buddhist faith that occurred after the Buddha had passed into *nirvana*, or the unconditioned world of non-being, that obscures the true extent of the diversity in belief. At the congress called by King Kanishka (78–123), a gathering known as the Fourth Buddhist Council, the representatives of no less than eighteen Buddhist sects were in attendance. These differences in doctrinal interpretation must have sprung directly from the paradoxical position in which the Buddha found himself as a teacher. He alone understood Enlightenment, because it was an internal experience, yet he wished to point others along the way to self-realization. Enlightenment, like the *Tao* of Lao-tzu, could not be adequately explained in words or represented visually. It was ineffable. Perhaps this block in communication explains the reluctance of the Buddha to sanction pictorial representation of his life and deeds. Instead, an empty seat or a footprint were adopted as symbols of the way he had discovered and taught. But, as the Buddha is supposed to have foreseen, his teachings became an organized religion over the centuries, till in its final stage in India Buddhism was merged with Brahmanic Hinduism.

Many Western students of Buddhism have disparaged the Mahayana school as an unfortunate lapse, almost a vulgar popularization of the Buddha's

A Buddhist temple in Canton.

teaching. This unjustified prejudice may be connected with contemporary occidental admiration of speed, causing some people to feel an affinity with the technique of instantaneous self-realization in Zen Buddhism rather than the slower method of adjustment favoured by the Mahayanists. Though in matters of religion it does appear easy to mistake the finger for the moon, towards which the finger is pointing, there can be no doubt that the Mahayana doctrines that began to reach China from the first century contained a subtle metaphysics, which forced Confucianism on to the defensive, and a religious power, whose strength was sufficient to churn the souls of the *nung*. When the Chinese pilgrim Fa-hsien reached India around 400 there were four mature Buddhist philosophical systems – two of these were of the Mahayana school.

In contrast with the Hinayana school, which placed emphasis on individual release, the lonely path trodden by the Buddha, the Mahayana school was less austere and evolved a complex iconography. Siddhartha became one reincarnation of an apparently endless series of Buddhas, who have lived and preached in the myriad worlds that compose the universe. The present world will have passed away before the next Buddha, Maitreya or Mi-lo, is born. The highest ideal of Mahayana Buddhism was the bodhisattva Avalokitesvara, who renounced *nirvana* out of compassion for the sufferings of all created things. The bodhisattva, sublimely indifferent, yet filled with pity, remains in the world until all shall enter eternal bliss. 'The fierce will and the struggle for superhuman power of the old ascetics of the hermit groves thus attain, in the bodhisattva ideal, to their most benign transfiguration.' We need to remind ourselves that Buddhism was never the preserve of the monk-community, the *sangha*. Monasteries and wandering monks were looked upon as the instrument for teaching the *dhamma*, the way of self-cultivation that brought about the cessation of rebirth, by throwing off *karma*, the cycle of conditioned action.

Physical isolation from the world was not a basic tenet of Buddhist monasticism. The Christian monastic system was born of the eremite's aloofness, a trait of the solitary desert dweller that has remained dominant ever since.

The exact date of the coming of Buddhism to China is uncertain. In AD 65 Emperor Han Ming-ti addressed his nephew, Prince Liu Ying, as one who 'recites the subtle words of Huang-lao, and respectfully performs the gentle sacrifices of the Buddha'. There is also reference to *sang-men*, monks. Thus, in the first record of a monastic community we find that characteristic mixture of Taoist and Buddhist elements. Eclecticism was forced upon early Chinese Buddhism by a number of related circumstances. There was a lack of texts; those that had travelled down 'the Silk Road' belonged to foreign believers, and the few that were available could not be translated by a Chinese before the late fourth century. Though a number of missionaries were well versed in the Chinese language, ignorance of Sanskrit and Indian culture prevented Chinese believers from understanding every aspect of Buddhism. Also, the doctrines of various sects reached the country at different times. To overcome these unresolved questions Chinese pilgrims like Fa-hsien (left 399, returned 414), and later Hsuan-tsang (between 629 and 640), travelled to India in order to receive instruction and collect manuscripts. Energetic drive was added to the Buddhist mission by a Parthian monk, An Shih-kao, who settled in the White Horse Monastery at Loyang in 148. He inaugurated the translation of Buddhist texts by establishing the first translation team. His work marks the beginning of 'a form of literary activity which . . . must be regarded as one of the most impressive achievements of Chinese culture'. Opposition to imperial interest in the teachings of the Buddha was voiced by the *shih* in a couple of memorials to the throne in 166. The new faith was attacked as unfilial. But the *shih* themselves were not immune from Buddhist speculation, once translations of high literary quality came into general circulation. An Indo-scythian, Chih Ch'ien, and a Sogdian, K'ang Seng-hui, both born in Chinese territory and both recipients of a Chinese education, made a considerable impression by their teaching and translations. The ruler of Wu, one of the Three Kingdoms, appointed Chih Ch'ien as a scholar of wide learning, *po-shih*, and charged him with the instruction of his son. But the increase in activity in North China under the Western Tsin was a result of renewed contacts with Central Asia; the line of communication followed 'the Silk Road', for 'early Chinese Buddhism was from the outset a distinctly urban phenomenon'. The subsequent push westwards by the Toba Wei had similar effects. Kamarajiva (343–413) was brought back to the capital, Ta-t'ung, at the specific request of the Toba Wei ruler. This Indian monk was living in Kucha, annexed in 384, but his fame had spread to China. He improved translations, personally supervising the rendering of three hundred texts, and expounded the doctrines of Buddhist sects hitherto unknown there.

By 500 the Buddhist faith had penetrated all parts of China. In the southern provinces the *shih* were drawn into the fold by such eclectic thinkers as Chu Tao-ch'ien (286–374). Having studied at Ch'ang-an before the city was fired by the Hsiung Nu, most of his life was spent with his numerous followers in the Shan mountains of Chekiang. Honours were showered on him by the southern Court, but he preferred to teach the harmony of Buddhist doctrine and Taoist philosophy. The greatest patron of Buddhism was Emperor Liang Wu-ti, who

The bell terrace of the Temple of Confucius, Peking.

was persuaded with difficulty to reassume the throne after becoming a monk. Two famous Indian teachers visited his Court. Paramartha (498–569) was sent from Magadha by the reigning Gupta king in response to a mission of Emperor Liang Wu-ti, who had asked for Buddhist texts. He undertook translations and sponsored doctrines belonging to the Hinayana as well as the Mahayana school. Bodhidharma reached Nanking from Conjeevaram in South India around 527. Legend has been thickly woven around this enigmatic man, credited with the inauguration of the Ch'an Tsung, or 'Inner-light School'. Yet the account of his interview with the emperor is worth repeating, because it gives an inkling of the unease that must have troubled the Confucian *shih*. The audience was brief and abrupt, for when the emperor described all that he had done to promote the faith, such as founding monasteries, support-ing translators and undertaking charitable deeds, and asked what merit he had acquired in so doing, a reasonable question in terms of gradualist Mahayana doctrine, Bodhidharma replied, 'No merit whatever!' Amazed, the emperor asked his visitor about the first principle of Buddhism. 'There isn't one,' was the answer, 'since where all is emptiness, nothing can be called holy.' 'Who, then are you?' the emperor asked. 'I don't know,' replied Bodhidharma. Leaving Nanking, he went northwards and settled in a monastery where he spent the rest of his life in meditation – 'gazing at a wall'.

Apart from the elaborate palace and tomb of 'the First Emperor' at Hsienyang – both were devastated in the civil wars which broke out in 207 BC – the Ch'in dynasty was notable for its indifference to art. With the establishment of the Han Empire the situation completely changed. The lifting of the imperial prohibition on intellectual activities not directly related to the needs of the government led to an upsurge in creativity, as much in the visual arts as in the practice of letters. Civil strife at the end of the Later Han dynasty and subse-quent barbarian invasions have destroyed by far the greater part of the art objects produced during the Han Empire. When in 470 the Toba Tartars, having conquered North China, decided to establish their own capital on the Chinese model, they had to send people to survey the ruins of Loyang. What we know of the Han period today results from archaeological investigation of tombs, largely carried out under the People's Republic of China. Unlike the surviving Chou works of art, valuable finds have been made from the tombs of minor officials as well as the Han nobility. Art had ceased to be purely religious, and its appreciation was no longer restricted to a feudal hierarchy.

ART IN THE HAN EMPIRE AND THE SIX DYNASTIES

During the Former Han dynasty art continued the late style of the Warring States period, the result possibly of the initial compromise of Liu Pang which encouraged men to reconsider the age of feudalism. The finest work is found on inlaid bronzes. The *hu*, a round wine-jar with a base, a lid and two rings at the sides for handles, was often inlaid with gold and silver. Designs include clouds and dragons, decorative script and scroll and geometrical shapes. In the first century the *kung* invented fire-gilding, a process whereby gold and mercury were painted on the bronze, the mercury being dispersed by heat once the gold had been satisfactorily applied. Another ritual object was the censer in the shape of a cosmic mountain, *po-shan-lu*, depicted as the home of mankind, wild beasts and sacred animals. But the central attraction of the recent Chinese Exhibition in London was undoubtedly the jade funeral suit of the Han princess, Tou Wan. It was found in her tomb at Man-ch'eng, Hopei, in 1968. Princess Tou's suit consists of 2,160 pieces of jade, wired together with gold and silk-wound iron. This archaeological exhibit reflects the preoccupation of the imperial house with Taoist magicians, whose 'superstitious practices' appalled the Confucian *shih*. Princess Tou Wan was buried in the middle of the long reign of Emperor Han Wu-ti (140–87 BC), a ruler who expanded the scope of imperial sacrifices and magico-religious rites, and spent a great deal of time in trying to establish better relations with supernatural beings. The costly jade suit was but a Han extension of the primitive Lung-shan belief in the efficacy of grave furniture: significantly, this kind of funeral attire became a fashion at a time when Taoism was in the ascendant in Court circles.

The abundance of art objects buried with nobles and officials during the Han Empire reflects the prosperity of China at this time. Tombs constructed in the Later Han dynasty have been discovered to hold numerous pieces of fine quality, even where the occupants held relatively minor appointments in the imperial administration. Such officials were, of course, not the traditional *shih* of Former Han but rather the representatives of the wealthy landowning class, all-powerful after the fall of Wang Mang. The growth of this new patronage may not be unconnected with the change in artistic tradition that occurred in the second half of the first century BC, when the old, formal, non-realistic style gave way to an interest in realism. This realistic approach is evident in the choice of subjects from everyday life in bas-reliefs as well as the introduction of

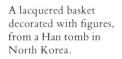

A lacquered basket decorated with figures, from a Han tomb in North Korea.

figurines and models. The Wu-wei tomb, excavated in 1969 in Kansu, contained one hundred and seventy-seven bronze objects in spite of two robberies. Many of these bronze figurines were horses, accompanied by chariots and carts. The so-called 'flying horse' of this collection is one of the Western breed that Emperor Han Wu-ti obtained from Central Asia after so much effort.

Two other highly developed skills of the *kung* during the Han Empire were the manufacture of textiles and of lacquer ornaments. Our knowledge of both of these crafts remains fragmentary, because of the perishable nature of silk and wood, but an inkling of their magnificence can be gained from the few archaeological finds we do have. At the site of Lo-lang, a military colony planted in North Korea by Emperor Han Wu-ti in 108 BC, a number of lacquer objects have been saved, including a splendid box, decorated with filial sons, ancient worthies and famous princes. Again with silk, archaeological finds have been made outside the eighteen provinces of China proper. Central Asia and the area of the western terminus of the Great Wall, both of which straddle 'the Silk Road', provide most impressive examples of silken garments and hangings, their unique preservation being due to the dry, sandy soils there. Silk worms were evident in China from the Shang period, but international trade along the caravan routes of Central Asia can be said to have become a major economic activity only in the Former Han.

Though the pottery industry stagnated, or even went into temporary decline, the other arts continued to progress during the chaotic conditions of the Six Dynasties. By the time of reunification under the Sui dynasty, art as well as literature had asserted itself and won autonomy. In China a work of art came to be accepted as something that was beautiful, something that possessed significance without direct reference to religion or Confucian morality. This momentous step forward, which freed the artist from conventional restraints and encouraged him to explore new possibilities, can be seen as a parallel to the development of personal belief in Taoist religion and Buddhism. The individual artist has emerged. From the fifth century there were private collections of painting and calligraphy and to the house was added the designed garden, that remarkable Chinese initiative in applied art.

Painting and calligraphy were intimately connected from the beginning. The Ch'in general, Meng T'ien, is credited with the invention of the brush, which replaced the stylus, but whatever the truth of this still unsubstantiated claim, there can be no reservation concerning the shaping influence that this new instrument for writing had on painting. Unlike any other civilization, China has used the same instrument, the brush, in literature and painting; hence, the naturalness of the Chinese 'poem-painting', where brush-writing could match the pictorial content in meaning, style and form. The oldest surviving painting, *The Admonitions of the Instructress to the Court Ladies*, now in the British Museum, is a portion of a hand scroll which dates from the fourth century, although it may be a ninth century copy of the original. The painter, Ku K'ai-chih, lived under the Tsin dynasty. We cannot be sure that it is by the hand of Ku, since it has been subject to damage and restoration, but there is everything to suggest that the ultimate source is a master of the Six Dynasties period. Ku himself was a Taoist and renowned for his portraiture. *The Admonitions* and contemporary tomb paintings serve to remind us that there already existed a long-established Chinese tradition of figure and landscape

A general view of Yunkang, Shansi. The colossal statue is of the Buddha Amitabha who presides over the Western Paradise or Pure Land. The *Pure Land Sutra* was the most popular Buddhist scripture after the *Lotus of the Good Law*.

painting closely related to calligraphy, though the active agent within the creative ferment in painting and sculpture during the Six Dynasties was Buddhism.

The foreign religion brought 'outside' artistic attitudes as well as religious concepts to China. The caves near the oasis town of Tun-huang reveal this process at work on one wall after another. In 366 the first cave was dedicated as a Buddhist temple. Paintings executed during the Wei domination of North China – these Tartars controlled 'the Western Regions' as far as Kucha – represent a striking mixture of Central Asian and Chinese influences. There is a tension between the formal, hierarchical positioning of the figures and the supporting use of landscape and other realistic features like the folds of robes. At Tun-huang, however, the predominant influence was Chinese and the 469 caves in the monastery complex bear witness to the gradual absorption of Buddhist iconographic representation into the native tradition of painting from which Ku K'ai-chih drew his strength. But in sculpture the impact of Buddhist art was more profound, because this branch of art had been the least developed in China. Monumental sculpture in stone began in the Han Empire, yet it remained limited to the needs of tomb architecture. At Gandhara and Mathura in north-west India a Greco-Indian school of sculpture had arisen in the second century and it was this style that was transmitted to China, via the great Buddhist centre at Bamiyan, in present-day Afghanistan. The antecedents of the immense rock carvings to be found in China are situated in this valley, with its mile-long procession of cave temples and colossal standing figures of the Buddha. At Yunkang, south-west of their capital at Ta-t'ung, the Toba Wei were persuaded by a monk to carve shrines and Buddha figures, so as to translate the splendours of Bamiyan to China (*c.* 400). From this time onwards the growing involvement of the ruling class with Buddhism, whether Tartar dynasties in North China or native ones in the South, led to the construction of similar monuments as 'good works' deserving merit.

唐太宗像

7
Reunification:
the Sui and T'ang Empires
581–906

THE SUI DYNASTY
(581–618)

Reunification came from a movement starting yet again in the northern region of China. Having toppled the Northern Ch'i dynasty in 581, Yang Chien, a Chinese-Hsien Pei general, marched south and defeated Ch'en, the last of the Six Dynasties: he became Emperor Sui Wen-ti and brought China under a single administration for the first time in two-and-a-half centuries. If the brief rule of the Western Tsin is discounted, then three-and-a-half centuries of disunity can be said to separate the Later Han and the Sui Empires. Though the Sui dynasty itself was short-lived, its successor, the T'ang, successfully consolidated the position it inherited and ensured that the Chinese would in the future always prefer unification. Henceforth, the country was united for far longer than it was divided either by internal conflict or external conquest. The Sui prelude to the T'ang has been likened by many Chinese historians to the relationship between Ch'in and Former Han. Of Yang-ti, the second and last Sui emperor, a Ming scholar wrote, 'He shortened the life of his dynasty by a number of years through his extravagance in public works, but benefited posterity unto ten thousand generations. He ruled without benevolence, but his rule is to be credited with enduring accomplishments.' Just as the construction of the Great Wall was the last straw that broke the backs of the *nung* during the Ch'in Empire, so the digging of the Grand Canal became the most specific reason to hate the house of Sui.

Emperor Sui Wen-ti transplanted the two distinctive institutions that had developed in North China during the Tartar Partition, namely the equitable field system and the divisional militia, and together they formed the foundation of the restored Empire. The system of the divisional militia was not formally wound up till 749, a significant date in Chinese history because it left the T'ang emperor dangerously exposed to the whims of military leaders at the head of professional forces. The disastrous rebellion of the barbarian general An Lu-shan in 755 was a consequence of imperial reliance on professional soldiers. In 590 Emperor Sui Wen-ti had decreed that all soldiers should be attached to a prefecture and cultivate the land like the *nung*. This militia suffered during the rebellion that overthrew the Sui, but the system was continued by the early T'ang rulers who had risen to power as commanders of local contingents. With such forces Emperor Sui Wen-ti inflicted defeats on the Mongols in the north, the Turks in the north-west and the Tibetans in the

Emperor T'ang
T'ai-tsung (627–650).

west. After reuniting the country and dealing with external enemies, he turned to domestic reconstruction. 'Ever-normal' granaries were established through-out the Empire, thus introducing them to the Yang-tze valley for the first time. By 605, the year that Emperor Sui Wen-ti died, the state reserves of cereals were reputed to have reached record levels.

Within little more than a decade Emperor Sui Yang-ti, Wen-ti's son, managed to provoke a rebellion as widespread and violent as the one that destroyed the Ch'in dynasty. There can be no reply to the charge that this ruler overstretched his people, although, along with the Ming commentator quoted above, we must recognize the strategic and economic logic behind his grand water schemes. During the Tartar Partition of China the Yang-tze valley had begun to be exploited seriously by the Chinese dynasties ruling there, with the result that agricultural production increased and the key economic area shifted to the south. In order to supply the central administration at Loyang and to maintain the armies operating along the northern frontiers, Emperor Sui Yang-ti decided to build an integrated system of canals. The central part of this network was the Grand Canal, which stretched from Che, on the Yellow River near present-day Peking, to Hangchow, via Loyang, where it met a branch that led upstream to Ch'ang-an. In its final form, under the Yuan dynasty in the fourteenth century, the length attained was almost 1,800 kilometres. The Sui Grand Canal, dug between 605 and 610, effectively joined the northern and southern provinces of the Empire. Construction involved the re-opening of older sections of existing but derelict water courses as well as the cutting of extensive lengths of new canal. Over three million labourers were put to work on this vast project, an engineering feat whose only parallel can be the building of the Great Wall. Decapitation, flogging, neck weights and the confiscation of property awaited those people who dared to shirk the corvée.

The burden of such public works pressed hardest on the *nung*, who were also conscripted for a campaign in Korea. One million three hundred thousand men were mobilized by Emperor Sui Yang-ti in 612, when it was decided that the border attacks of the Koreans could be tolerated no longer. But the logistics of this campaign proved too complex, and the walled cities of Korea were able to resist the besiegers until their supplies of food ran out. Failure abroad and severity at home combined to produce conditions suited to popular rebellion. The bankruptcy of the 'ever-normal' granaries, emptied by the numerous conscripted armies of labourers and soldiers, gave the Sui dynasty no room to manoeuvre once the uprising started. When famine acted as the spur to rebellion, it was the genius of Li Shih-min, the future Emperor T'ang T'ai-tsung, that made certain of the change of imperial house in 619.

The man instrumental in the preservation of the reunified Empire was Li Shih-min. After the fall of Sui the sectional interests that had grown up during the Tartar Partition could easily have reasserted themselves and caused another period of fragmentation. In contrast with the history of the West, the T'ang rulers were able to restore the glories of Han as well as make their own contribution to the advance of early Chinese civilization. Byzantium not only failed to reunite permanently the Mediterranean provinces of the former

A block-printed prayer
sheet, dated August 947.

Roman Empire but even lost control of Egypt to Islam in 642. The later
attempt to restore Roman power made by Charlemagne (768–814) proved
equally transitory. In China, however, the T'ang dynasty presided over a
Golden Age. Yet the restored Empire was not the same as the Han. Internally,
the re-establishment of the examination system for entrance to the civil service
on a more regular basis than the largely oral test used since the Han period led
to an enormous expansion of education. The invention of block printing sometime in the eighth century met the demand for text-books as well as encouraging the spread of literacy. The hereditary privilege and recommendation
continued as an advantage for the relatives of powerful families, but it became
a familiar event for a group of *nung* to club together and pay for the education
of a promising village boy in order to launch him on an official career. Literary
achievement was the hallmark of the T'ang Empire, with such diverse writers
as the Confucian essayist, Han Yu, and the Taoist poet, Li Po. The Empire
evolved a bureaucratic system in place of the lesser aristocratic one that had
replaced feudalism during the Han period. Externally too, a more flexible
attitude was evident in the ready acceptance of foreign peoples and their ideas.
In the capital, Ch'ang-an, there were priests from India and South-East Asia,
merchants from Central Asia and Arabia, and travellers from Persia, Korea
and Japan. These people made their influence felt in the fashions and amusements of the Court. The second T'ang emperor, T'ai-tsung, gave a personal
interview to the famous Buddhist monk, Tripitaka, or Hsuan-tsang, on his
return from India with scriptures in 645. Although the emperor was inclined
to Taoism, he supported the Confucians for the sake of the civil service, besides

welcoming Buddhism and other foreign faiths. This distinction between the Han and T'ang Empires is expressed today in two common forms of address for the Chinese people. 'Men of Han' embodies a sense of exclusiveness, Chinese as opposed to Hsiung Nu or barbarian, whilst 'Men of T'ang' incorporates the diversity of a China stretching from the steppes to the tropics on one hand and from land-locked mountains to the sea on the other.

The reign of Emperor T'ang T'ai-tsung (627–650) secured the Empire. This ruler had a personal magnetism that attracted the best minds of the day and, not less important, he possessed a self-control and a sense of duty that allowed his Censors to speak frankly on matters of policy or conduct. The Empire, for the first time, was divided into provinces and a regular census instituted. A strong civil service, recruited almost entirely by examination, was the foundation of the century of peace and prosperity that Emperor T'ang T'ai-tsung bequeathed China. It shifted the power centre from the military to the civil. During the Tartar Partition a military aristocracy had grown in strength at the expense of the old alliance between the ruling house and the *shih*. The Li, T'ai-tsung's own family, had belonged to this class, so that as emperor he was well aware of dangers from this quarter. Indeed, he insisted on personally instructing his militia soldiers in the finer points of shooting the crossbow. The divisional militia, properly trained and equipped, formed a reliable core element in the early T'ang armies, thereby avoiding the dangers of using barbarian mercenaries or standing armies of professionals. These seasonal soldiers were not found wanting till the beginning of the eighth century. Farming and fighting ceased to be a practical combination during the long campaigns of Empress Wu; regular forces of professionals or of long-term conscripts were raised. Coupled with this concern for the maintenance of divisional militia was Emperor T'ang T'ai-tsung's protection of the smaller landholder, the *nung*, from whose number peasant soldiers were drawn. The equitable field system was generally enforced, though it was found unsuited to the Yang-tze valley, where the sophisticated methods of rice cultivation tended to be disrupted by periodic redistribution of land. Kiangnan, as the South was now called, retained a system of land tenure whereby paddy fields, with their complicated irrigation network, could be passed down through generations.

The expansionist policies of Emperor T'ang T'ai-tsung were followed by his immediate successors. The nomadic tribesmen beyond the Great Wall had already acknowledged the sovereignty of the Chinese 'khan'. Tibet, independent and powerful, had compromised to the extent that its king had taken to wife a Chinese princess, whose influence on that country was not inconsiderable. Therefore, the way was open for a reassertion of China's authority in Central Asia, the north-east and the far south. Chinese arms had brought practically the whole of Korea and Manchuria under T'ang rule by 668; consolidation of the Sui conquest of northern Vietnam permitted the naming of this province as Annam, or the 'Pacified South'; in the 'Western Regions' the Han *imperium* was more than regained. Before 751, the year in which the Chinese armies in Central Asia were routed by the Arabs at the Battle of Talas River, the T'ang ruled all the territories between Tun-huang and the Aral Sea. Despite our ignorance of this military encounter in the West, it ranks as one of the decisive battles in world history, on a par with Salamis, Tours or Waterloo. The Arabs, having crushed the Sassanid Empire in Persia (642), initially formed

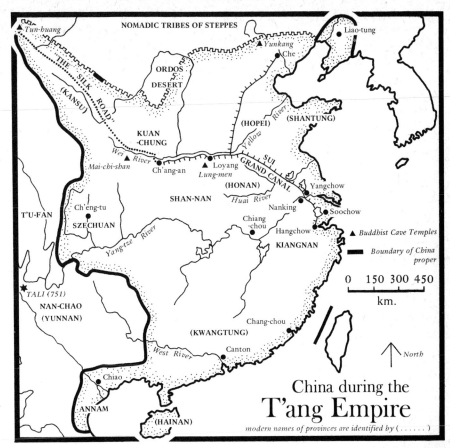

China during the
T'ang Empire

modern names of provinces are identified by (. . . . . .)

NOMADIC TRIBES OF STEPPES

Tun-huang

Liao-tung

Yunkang

Che

ORDOS
DESERT

(HOPEI)

(SHANTUNG)

"THE SILK ROAD" (KANSU)

KUAN-
CHUNG

Yellow River

Wei River

SUI

Mai-chi-shan

Ch'ang-an

Loyang
Lung-men

GRAND CANAL

Yangchow

(HONAN)

Huai River

T'U-FAN

Ch'eng-tu

SHAN-NAN

Nanking

Soochow

SZECHUAN

Chiang-chou

Hangchow

Yangtze River

KIANGNAN

▲ Buddhist Cave Temples

━━ Boundary of China
proper

0   150 300 450

TALI (751)

NAN-CHAO
(YUNNAN)

Chang-chou

km.

(KWANGTUNG)

West River

Canton

North

Chiao

ANNAM

(HAINAN)

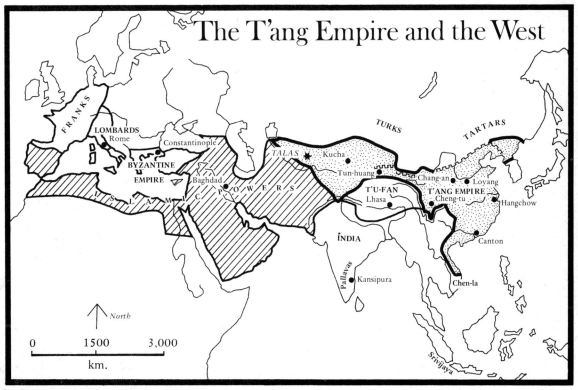

The T'ang Empire and the West

FRANKS

LOMBARDS
Rome

Constantinople

TURKS

TARTARS

BYZANTINE
EMPIRE

TALAS ★ Kucha

Tun-huang

Chang-an

Loyang

Baghdad

I S L A M I C   P O W E R S

T'U-FAN
Lhasa

T'ANG EMPIRE
Cheng-tu

Hangchow

ÍNDIA

Canton

Pallavas

Kansipura

Chen-la

North

0   1500   3,000

km.

Srivijaya

This stone panel from the tomb of Emperor T'ang T'ai-tsung shows his famous charger, Rushing Wind.

an alliance with the Chinese, but they soon began to absorb the weaker states in Western Turkestan. At Talas River they wrestled Central Asia from the Chinese sphere of influence; the region ceased to be Buddhist and was incorporated into the Moslem world. There was no Chinese Charles Martel to turn back the flood of militant Islam, as there had been at the Battle of Tours nineteen years earlier.

Another defeat of 751 occurred on the Tali plain, in Yunnan. A Chinese army of 60,000 men was annihilated by the forces of Nanchao, an independent kingdom. These reverses were symptoms of internal dislocation; the T'ang Empire had overreached itself. The shifting of the key economic area to the Yang-tze valley complicated the supply of foodstuffs to the central administration and the northern armies. By 742 Ch'ang-an and its satellites had a population approaching two millions. The annual cereal transport had increased from 10,000 tonnes to 160,000 tonnes between 627 and 742. Moreover, the far-flung border was easy neither to defend nor to supply. Under Emperor T'ang Kao-tsung (650–83) and Empress Wu (683–705) soldiers were first encamped on the frontiers, and the divisional militia was worn out with fighting. The development of Kiangnan as the ricebowl of the Empire encouraged the tendency towards a permanent military establishment, since the divisional militia had originally sprung up at a time when it was impossible for the central government to command large quantities of supplies. Frontier armies under permanent commanders could not be expected to see every issue in exactly the same manner as the civil service. Such differences of opinion were very dangerous. From An Lu-shan's revolt the T'ang dynasty never recovered and in spite of temporary revivals the Empire contracted, at last disintegrating in the Five Dynasties period (907–60).

To the horror of traditional Chinese historians, all members of the *shih* class, the continued success of the T'ang was in large measure due to an ex-concubine who finally usurped the throne itself. That Wu Chao, concubine to T'ang T'ai-tsung, could escape the Buddhist convent where the concubines of a deceased emperor were required to live, win the favour of the new emperor, T'ang Kao-tsung, and then dominate the government for over fifty years, tells us a lot about the power-structure of the early T'ang Empire. It reveals that the Court, supported by an efficient civil service, was supreme.

Emperor T'ang Kao-tsung was an indifferent ruler but he had the sense to let his consort, now Empress Wu, deal with affairs of state. Though she was ruthless towards her enemies, the period of her ascendency was a good one for China. Government was sound, no rebellions occurred, abuses in the army and the administration were stamped out and Korea was annexed, an achievement no previous Chinese had ever managed. In order to form a party devoted to her rule, Empress Wu made use of the examination system. She selected her own men for key civil service appointments and repressed opposition from the powerful families of Kuan-chung. Not till the rise of Li Lin-fu in 733 did the aristocratic and privileged class recover its position at Court. One of the few favourable comments on her reign pinpoints her desire to find new blood for the Empire. We are told that the empress 'wished to cage the bold and enterprising spirits of all regions'. This policy of favouring less privileged families introduced to official rank many men of humble origin but great talent. But the insecurity felt by Empress Wu led her to rely also on spies and informants, unusual practice for the time. She was fifty-eight when Emperor T'ang Kao-tsung died in 684. Two of her sons acted briefly as figure-heads, till in 690 she assumed the imperial title herself. A new dynasty, the Chou, was proclaimed and she became emperor. Before the death of Emperor T'ang Kao-tsung, Empress Wu seems to have been faithful to him. Thereafter, salacious stories abounded. Young men of unusual sexual abilities were openly recommended to her. One of the first of these associates, Hsueh Huai-i, a peddlar of cosmetics from Loyang, was passed on by a friendly and impressed princess. To facilitate his coming and going in the palace, he was appointed abbot of White Horse Monastery, the same retreat that An Shih-kao had chosen as a centre for the translation of Buddhist texts. Yet Hsueh Huai-i was not protected by the throne on every occasion. In the inner palace his personal services may have been superlative, but in his dealings with senior officials he was obliged to observe the rules of decorum. With advancing years she exercised less restraint on her favourites and a clash between the notorious Chang brothers and Wei Yuan-chung, one of the Imperial Chancellors, set in motion a chain of events that forced her abdication in 705. The alienation of the *shih* and her own illness was the context for the palace coup. Within a year the only Chinese woman to have worn the yellow robe was dead and in 713, after further turmoil in the palace, the third great ruler of the T'ang emerged, Emperor T'ang Hsuan-tsung, her grandson, also known as Ming Huang, 'the Brilliant Emperor'.

This appellation refers as much to his Court and the cultural life of Ch'ang-an during his reign than any specific quality in him as a ruler. Poets, painters and musicians thronged the palace; architects were commissioned to enhance the beauty of the capital; and, in the eyes of later generations, the tragic love of Ming Huang and Yang Kuei-fei has lent a romantic glamour to the age. Writers have made the sad events of An Lu-shan's rebellion famous. Every Chinese knows how the aging emperor fell deeply in love with a beautiful concubine, Yang Kuei-fei, who beguiled his mind. Through her persuasion Ming Huang bestowed undeserved honours on An Lu-shan, a barbarian general serving on the north-eastern frontier. He was eventually appointed commander-in-chief of the northern armies and exploited this position as well as the idleness of the Court to make a bid for supreme power. Almost un-opposed, he captured Ch'ang-an in 755; the emperor fled westwards to Szechuan. When the disheartened troops of the imperial bodyguard de-manded that Yang Kuei-fei should be executed, and backed their demand with a threatened mutiny, Ming Huang was obliged to consent. Below these dramatic episodes there may have been an economic conflict. For An Lu-shan, though born of a Sogdian father and a Turkish mother, received support from Hopei. Like a structure at high pressure, we can see the stresses and strains of the T'ang Empire most clearly as we watch the differing impact of the revolt on the provinces.

In the first place, the rebellion arose and reached its peak in the eastern provinces, whose ancient separatist aspirations had reappeared during the Northern Ch'i (550–77). Hopei had become more prosperous than Kuan-chung and its powerful families resented the domination of Ch'ang-an. Resistance to the T'ang dynasty had been strongest there. The creation of large armies on the frontiers consisting of professional soldiers did have profound effects on government policy. To meet the growing cost of the military estab-

The calligraphy of Ming Huang, 'the Brilliant Emperor'. An ink-rubbing of his comments on the *Hsiao Ching* (*Book of Filial Piety*), a Confucian text dating from the Han Empire. This detail is about two-thirds the actual size.

Pottery figure of a tomb guardian, probably an earth spirit; from the T'ang period.

lishment Emperor T'ang Hsuan-tsung adopted a policy of financial centralization. Since this was disliked by the *shih* in eastern and southern provinces, the difference of view provided the old Kuan-chung families with an opportunity to recover the political ground they had lost in the previous reigns. In 733 Emperor T'ang Hsuan-tsung turned to Li Lin-fu, a member of the imperial clan and a Kuan-chung noble; and, whilst Lin was not uneducated, he had little time for the literary official. From 736 to 752 Lin controlled the central administration, removing from office, sometimes by force, those who spoke on behalf of interests 'outside the passes', and, worse, he appointed barbarians like An Lu-shan to high positions, because they seemed to lack a way of challenging his own personal influence at Court.

Furthermore, the new military situation that had arisen since the beginning of the dynasty made the throne more vulnerable, so that the recruitment of leading officials from solely Kuan-chung divided the *shih* at the most crucial moment for the Empire. The troops of An Lu-shan were veterans, many of them non-Chinese. Not surprisingly the *nung* were unenthusiastic about the rebellion at first, but the ten-year struggle drew in the people of the east, especially after the rapid fall of Ch'ang-an.

In Kiangnan, by contrast, sentiment was unaroused, and fighting did not spread to the Yang-tze valley. Although this part of China escaped the devastation suffered elsewhere, the T'ang Empire had lost its dynamic force. The restoration of Emperor T'ang Hsuan-tsung was due to military commanders backed by barbarian forces, not the divisional militia, with the result that the civil administration forfeited its pre-eminence. Whilst sadness and grief at the death of Yang Kuei-fei consumed the emperor, a weakened China had to relinquish its hold on many outlying territories. From T'u-fan the Tibetans were able to descend and sack even Ch'ang-an.

The T'ang Empire, much reduced, enjoyed another century of peace, before popular revolts arose, those tell-tale signs of impending dynastic change. At Court the eunuchs became a power again; in the provinces military leaders were more independent; the decline of central government caused a neglect of hydraulic works, the traditional unifying force in Chinese history; without, pressure was mounting from the steppes. When the last T'ang ruler was deposed in 906, the country fragmented into nearly a dozen separate states. Perhaps new methods of warfare accounted for the unusual extent of this disunity too. Reference is made to the use of gunpowder in the tenth century.

ECONOMY AND SOCIETY

The T'ang Empire was the largest and most populous state in the world. In re-unification China made itself the exception in the pre-modern world to the rule that political units of such magnitude are unable to survive over long periods of time. Census figures for 754 indicate that there were 9,069,154 families living in over 300 prefectures. This gives for the Empire a total population of 53,000,000. We need to remember that these figures refer to the tax-paying population only. It is likely that the actual total was several millions greater. In addition, there were the so-called 'migrant families', groups of people who had moved from one area to another in order to avoid taxation or to find better land for cultivation. In his attempt to increase government revenue Emperor T'ang Hsuan-tsung appointed special commissioners to register them. During an amnesty in 724 as many as 800,000 unregistered families reported their position to the authorities. Then, the census returns from the less accessible areas of the Empire would have been less accurate. The overall measurements of the Empire should easily persuade us of this fact. From the Great Wall to Annam the distance was nine thousand kilometres, from Tibet to the Pacific it was five thousand kilometres. To this has still to be added 'the Western Regions'. Lastly, landless labourers and other persons exempt from taxation on land were excluded from the census. The latter might be officials, monks or nuns, and foreigners.

The Golden Age of the T'ang came as much from the institutions devised to run the Empire as from the personalities of individual rulers. Everything, one is tempted to suggest, depended upon the civil service, now established in a form that was to last, with modifications, right down to the twentieth century. The conception of the *carrière ouverte aux talents* was a Chinese invention; the T'ang transformed the examination system of the Han, the *k'o-chu*, into a means of advancement for the gifted. Into the central administration were recruited the learned, the *shih*, whose scale of values differed profoundly from that of the *shang*. As a result the central government retained its oversight of the economy: many new water-works were undertaken; the 'ever-normal' granaries eased the situation of the *nung*, as did periodic enforcements of the 'equal field' system; and, fearing the accumulation of capital in private hands, the export of tea was nationalized.

The civil service was organized under three main departments – State Affairs, Chancellery and Secretariat. The head of the State Affairs Department was the senior official in the government, because the function of this department included the examination system and supervision of the civil service; taxation, land tenure and state granaries; rites, ceremonies and foreign relations; defence; criminal law; and public works. The Chancellery dealt with the transmission and execution of imperial decrees. Records were kept by the Secretariat. Within its scope of operation was historiography, the compiling of data for the dynastic history. Separate from these three departments was the Censorate, the *Yu Shih Pu*, whose officials were charged with the duty of reporting all irregularities directly to the throne. The practice of attaching censors to important provincial officials, particularly military commanders, was mistakenly discontinued in the years prior to the rebellion of An Lu-shan.

Although no longer feudal, China still supported a small aristocracy connected with the ruling house. Princes were entitled to the taxes of 10,000 or 5,000 families, according to their status; lesser nobles enjoyed revenues which ranged from 3,000 to 300 families. With these aristocrats, senior officials and scholars of the Imperial University were exempt from land revenue tax. Officials were, of course, salaried.

The *shih* identified themselves with the task of administration, their loyalty being directed towards the Empire itself as much as any individual ruler. The capacity of the T'ang dynasty to make even a partial recovery from the destruction wrought by An Lu-shan was a testimony of this disposition even more than it was the legacy of Emperor T'ang T'ai-tsung's shrewd settlement. Socially, the T'ang Empire was marked by its lack of rigid divisions. Except for the old social stigma attached to commerce, the road to power and influence was open to all classes. This is not to pretend the official class was

A silk fragment dating from the T'ang dynasty.

A T'ang bronze mirror.

'classless'. Obviously, the student from the richer home had considerable advantages – library facilities, expert tuition and freedom to study. The off-spring of an official was automatically initiated into the language of the ruling class: such early linguistic opportunity, as we have come to appreciate recently ourselves, gives the recipient immense intellectual advantage. But the *nung* were able to reinforce the intelligence and stamina of the *shih* through education, and, conversely, the official establishment could shed conveniently those families which had ceased to produce suitable candidates for office.

Nevertheless, the sophistication of the T'ang Empire brought prosperity to both the *kung* and *shang*. Luxury industries were sited in the capital and other large cities. Populous Ch'ang-an was virtually another world. International trade flowed through 'the Western Region' and the capital was decked out with all kinds of fineries. This economic boom rested on access to the rice of Kiangnan that the Grand Canal afforded. A reaction set in after 755, when powerful families in league with the military commanders of the provinces exploited the comparative weakness of the central government. They attempted to build up the position of local independence and prosperity gained by previous magnates in the Later Han.

The most significant economic change of the T'ang period was the rise of Kiangnan. From this point onwards the productivity of the southern provinces outstripped all other areas. This final shift in the key economic area was matched by an alteration in population. Only in the South was there a great increase. The course of events that determined the history of the Sung Empire, with its capitals in K'ai Feng (960) and Hangchow (1127), needs to be considered against this development. In addition to agriculture, the southern provinces became more active in overseas trade. It has been estimated that at the end of the ninth century there were more than 120,000 Moslems, Jews and Persians resident in Canton.

THE BUDDHIST CHALLENGE

T'ang culture, like T'ang society, was tolerant. New ideas were taken up with such alacrity that the Buddhist faith almost submerged Taoist religion and Confucian philosophy. In the next chapter we shall consider in detail the reaction of the literary officials of Confucian persuasion: intellectuals like Han Yu reshaped Chinese prose in order to grapple with what they held to be the religious follies of their age. Yet it needs to be noted that the strength of this resistance derived from a rational, sceptical tradition of thought, which through Wang Ch'ung stemmed from Confucius himself. The Chinese mind has always shown a marked tendency to disbelieve in asceticism and contempt for the world, notwithstanding the Taoist ideal of the hermit. The enlightened atmosphere of the period can be gauged from the following edict of Emperor T'ang T'ai-tsung:

> The Way has more than one name. There is more than one Sage. Though doctrines vary in different lands, they benefit all mankind. O Lo Pen, a man of great virtue has brought his images and books from afar to present them in the capital. After examining his teachings, we find that they are profound and pacific, stressing what is good and important. This religion does good to all men. Let it be preached freely in our Empire.

The Mosque of Soucou-Ta at Turfan, Sinkiang. After the defeat of Chinese forces at the battle of Talas River in 751, 'the Western Regions' ceased to be Buddhist and were incorporated into the Moslem world.

The religion mentioned here is Christianity. O Lo Pen, a Nestorian monk, hailed from the Byzantine Empire. In Ch'ang-an there were Nestorian churches, Zoroastrian fire-temples and Buddhist shrines, besides places for worship of Taoist dieties and the ancestral sacrifices associated with Confucianism. Communities of Moslems, Manicheans and Jews existed in the commercial centres, too. But the exclusive religions of West Asia, creeds with a single deity, like Christianity and Islam, have never made much headway in China. The inclusive habit of mind, coupled with Confucian scepticism, has tended to keep religion and the priesthood as minor elements in Chinese civilization. 'Holy wars' have been conspicuous by their absence. The severe, though short, repression of foreign faiths after 841 was a symptom of national unease and uncertainty connected with the decline of the T'ang dynasty. Nestorian Christianity did not survive this proscription; Buddhism, the chief target, did, though in a form showing that sinicization was complete.

The Buddhist challenge for the minds and hearts of the Chinese was the most potent external force brought to bear on the early civilization of China. So fundamental was this intellectual and spiritual contest that, in one sense, the Neo-Confucianism of the Sung period, that impressive revival of Chinese thought, might be looked upon as a joint Confucian–Taoist reaction to Buddhism. From the outset the unfilial nature of the Buddhist faith raised the hackles of the *shih*. To deal with this Confucian criticism, An Shih-kao had translated *sutras* that dealt with family life. One of these texts entitled *Parental love is difficult to be repaid* told how a *bodhisattva* chose to be reborn as the son of a childless, blind couple who wanted to retire into the forest to lead the life of a recluse. Though the propagandists of Buddhism were quick to realize that they needed to respect the traditional values of the Chinese, this accommodation could not happen without some adjustment of the tenets belonging to the new faith. A religion of individual salvation had to be made relevant to a society which prized family and clan harmony, lest the saffron robe seem quite incongruous. Whereas the introduction of Buddhism into Ceylon, Burma and Thailand was an easy process for the very reason that it exercised a civilizing influence, the situation was different in China, a country already in possession of an ancient and distinct civilization of its own. During the Tartar Partition the spread of Buddhism was general in both the northern and the southern provinces, but in the T'ang dynasty, what may be called the native spirit of the

An octagonal wooden
pagoda of nine storeys,
some 200 feet in height, at
Ying-hsien, Shansi. It was
built in 1056, the
Northern Sung period.

Chinese started to modify and adapt it so that the Indian faith was transformed
into an adjunct of local culture. This amazing transformation, a supreme
example of the absorptive ability of Chinese civilization, was an intriguing
historical process, whose outstanding events we shall briefly trace. 'The deeply
moral nature of the Chinese people,' S. Radhakrishnan has written, 'was stirred
by the Buddhist emphasis on salvation through moral effort and the law of
moral causation or *karma*. . . . It is a great comfort to the rational-minded to be
told that the universe is orderly and man free to shape his own destiny in it.'
Though there is truth in this observation, the purpose to which the Chinese put
the concept of *karma* is the crucial issue. By the early T'ang it was argued that
the Buddha had left home to repay the love and affection of his parents; his gift
was Enlightenment. Only after he had visited heaven and preached the law to
his mother, did he return to the world and resume his mission among men.
This was the filial duty of the Buddha. Ancestor worship, the epitome of filial
piety, had found a place in Buddhist ceremonial. Not only were monks
expected to participate in family sacrifices on memorial days but more so in the
state services arranged for departed rulers. In 838 some five hundred monks
took part in a memorial for an emperor held at the K'ai-yuan temple in
Ch'ang-an.

In India, the *sangha*, the Buddhist monk-community, regarded itself as beyond the authority of secular rulers. Its members claimed to have with-drawn from the distractions of everyday life. During the reign of Chandra-gupta II (*c.* 375–415) Fa-hsien discovered the prosperous condition of the monasteries in the Gupta Empire. He noted the extensive property and assets held by them, as well as the obligation laid upon society to maintain the *sangha* thus:

> Down from the Buddha's *nirvana*, the kings of these countries, the chief men and householders, have raised *viharas* for the priests and provided for their support by bestowing on them fields, houses and gardens with men and oxen. Engraved title-deeds were prepared and handed down from one reign to another; no one has ventured to withdraw them, so that till now there has been no interruption. All the resident priests have their beds, mats, food, drink and clothes provided without stint; in all places this is the case.

A clear line of demarcation was evident. Through membership of an institution apart from the temporal realm, the Buddhist monk was not bound by the norms of political and social conduct that governed the lives of ordinary people. Instead of paying homage to the secular ruler of the state, the *sangha* often received recognition of its superior status from the throne itself. The tyranny of kings could not be accepted.

On arrival in China, Buddhism encountered a political tradition that took for granted a strong central authority, embodied in the person of the Son of Heaven. In as far as an individual religion of salvation could be said to exist, the mystical and magical practices of Taoism acted as an alternative to official rites. No question of supplanting the authority of the One Man had ever arisen. Lao-tzu had simply disappeared into the west. Therefore, the request of the *sangha* for a special place in Chinese society fell on deaf ears amongst the *shih*. The central administration was not prepared to allow the formation of a state within the state; Buddhist monks in China were to be regulated by secular and monastic law. Adherents of the new faith made strenuous efforts to resist this arrangement but, in the T'ang Empire, the *sangha* was compelled to adjust to the Confucian idea of the state.

In 662 an imperial edict proposed that Taoist priests and priestesses and Buddhist monks and nuns should pay homage to the emperor, the empress and the crown prince, as well as to their parents, and asked the officials to discuss the matter. A delegation of three hundred Buddhist monks led by Tao-hsuan participated in a conference attended by over one thousand civil and military officials. Tao-hsuan presented the case for the *sangha* in these words:

> In his manner of living, the monk has no regard for wealth and sensuous beauty and is not shackled by honours and emoluments. He considers mundane matters as floating clouds, and his form and life as a bright flame. Therefore he is proclaimed as one who has left the household life. One who has done so no longer embraces the rites of one who remains in the family, one who has forsaken the world is no longer immersed in the practices of the world. Such a principle is self-evident, and is the unchanging model for a hundred generations.

The Confucian party amongst the officials countered with the argument that all inhabitants of the Empire were the subjects of the Son of Heaven; all

Sericulture; one of the tasks in silk production was the collection of mulberry leaves to feed the silk worms. The Chinese monopoly of sericulture ended in the second century AD when silkworm eggs were smuggled to Korea.

桑田雨足葉蕃滋
怡是蠶大起時頁
喜筐攜笥紛嗔譪
戴儐飛上最高枝
·

采桑

吳兒歌採桑～下
青春深陌里讙歡
好過畦無欺侵深
籃各自攜層梯高
倍尋黃鸝龍慤檻
嘎咤鳴綠陰

Prabhutaratna and
Sakyamuni, the Buddhas
of the Lotus *sutra*. A gilt
bronze stele of the Toba
Wei dynasty. The
Saddharmapundarika or
Lotus of the Good Law was
translated by Kamarajiva
in 410 and was the most
popular of all Buddhist
scriptures in China.

enjoyed the benevolent rule of the emperor and, for that reason, homage was
due from everyone. At the close of the debate a vote was taken and the
majority of the officials present agreed with Tao-hsuan. Accordingly,
Emperor T'ang Kao-tsung decreed that there was no need for monks to
reverence the throne, but they must pay homage to their parents. This partial
victory for the *sangha* gave the new faith a respite for half a century, though in
657 it was decreed that Buddhist and Taoist priests should not receive homage
from their parents and seniors.

After the death of Empress Wu the situation began to change rapidly. In 729
Emperor T'ang Hsuan-tsung ordered the registration of monks and nuns. The
survey revealed that there were 75,524 monks and 50,576 nuns, and 5,358
temples and monasteries. The Buddhists were unable to avoid registration, a
part of that emperor's determined attempt to clarify the financial basis of the
central government. Religious foundations were exempted from land tax and
officials wanted to be certain that only people with a genuine calling were
classified as clergy. Moreover, ordination came under official scrutiny. Only
monks or nuns who had been issued with a certificate by the Bureau of
National Sacrifice, a department set up in 694, could claim exemption from
secular duties. Eligibility for official ordination was achieved by the recitation
of a certain number of leaves from sacred texts – 'three baskets of canon'. A
loosening of these requirements happened during the rebellion of An Lu-shan,
when a hard-pressed administration tried to recoup its finances by selling
ordination certificates. The *sangha*, then, failed to preserve itself as an entity
separate from the apparatus of the state. The firmly based T'ang Empire had
brought it within the scope of the civil service, exercising the right to ordain
and defrock monks and nuns. When Emperor T'ang Hui-ch'ang decided that
the religious establishment had grown too large in 845, his course of action was
straightforward enough. All the monks and nuns in the Empire, numbering
some 260,500, were laicized: thereafter, strong control was exercised over the
affairs of religious orders, extending to the recruitment of personnel and
ownership of property. In 956 an imperial edict of the Later Chou, one of the
Five Dynasties, nationalized some of the large statues of Buddha, the bronze
of which was melted down and made into coins.

In direct contrast to this struggle between the Buddhist church and the
Confucian state, stood the Ch'an Tsung, or 'Inner-light School', the way of
the isolate. Every tie of human society, whether expressed in secular or
monastic regulations, vanished like dust in achievement of Buddhahood.
There, in contemplation, was the world of unconditioned being. Everyone
had this potential Enlightenment in them, the Ch'an Tsung taught, but most
people failed to realize it. Without detriment to the contribution made by
Bodhidharma, there are obvious parallels with early Taoism, particularly in
the lack of formal organization thought necessary for the pursuit of wisdom.
Han-shan, the ninth century monk-poet, was very like a Taoist hermit, keeping the clouds company on his rocky mountainside. There he read both Taoist
and Buddhist texts, living out his life of secluded contemplation. But the
'Inner-light School' was not in the mainstream of Chinese Buddhism, despite
its formulative influence on landscape painters during the Five Dynasties and
the Sung Empire. Its culmination as Zen Buddhism came to pass in Japan, the
Sicily of East Asia.

8

The T'ang Renaissance

Whilst the Han dynasty was distinguished for prose, particularly in the un-ornamented and penetrating style of its historians, and the Sung dynasty was to be the great era of painting, whose apotheosis we shall recognize shortly as the landscape, the T'ang dynasty acted as patron for China's finest poets. Literary activity was central to the T'ang renaissance for a number of inter-connected reasons. There was a general concentration of intellectual forces, chiefly brought about by the restoration and development of the civil service examinations. In the Literary Examination, one of the papers taken by would-be officials, candidates were expected to compose poems. Because of his talent for writing verse, Po Chu-i obtained a First Class in this examination in 800, and thereby opened up for himself considerable prospects for advancement. Although authors were not rewarded for their compositions on a commercial basis, except when asked to compose commemorative inscriptions, such was the esteem in which literature was held that the emperor was obliged to offer those with literary gifts some form of employment. Po Chu-i was appointed as a Collator of Texts in the Palace Library, a sinecure for the 'bright' young man whose future career had yet to be decided. In many respects the T'ang Empire was China's romantic age. Confucianism was less overbearing, and the tolerant atmosphere at the Court militated against the inherent educational conservatism of the civil service. By the middle of the T'ang dynasty Taoism was accepted into the civil service examinations: in 742 it was decreed that the *Chuang-tzu* and other Taoist works should be regarded as classics. The poetical impulse responded to this loosening of cultural restraint, not least during the long reign of Ming Huang, a ruler who consciously sought to make Ch'ang-an the capital of refinement as well as that of an empire.

The *Complete T'ang Poems* comprises over forty-eight thousand poems by no less than two thousand two hundred authors. This prodigious output, a singular achievement by any standard, becomes even more impressive when we appreciate that it includes the great names of Chinese poetry, Wang Wei (699–761), Li Po (699–762), Tu Fu (712–70) and Po Chu-i (772–846). Though accomplished poetry is found in the earliest extant anthology, the *Shih Ching*, whose odes celebrate the feudal society of Early Chou, and rulers like Han Wu-ti took an active interest in verse composition, even inventing the seven character line, the poet did not overtake the writer of prose until the T'ang Empire. Preparations for this cultural advance were made during the Six Dynasties, when the *lu-shih*, the modern or 'patterned' poem, was evolved. Shen Yueh (441–513) both wrote in this new fashion, which paid more atten-tion to the balance of tonal harmony, and investigated the theory of the four

The running script of Emperor Sung Li-tsung. The couplet by the T'ang poet Wang Wei reads: 'I walk to where the water ends, and sit there to watch when clouds arise'. It is written in ink on a round silk fan mounted on an album leaf, with imperial seals on the left.

156

行到水窮處

坐看雲起時

馬仲珪

tones used in the Chinese language. The *lu-shih* has eight lines of five or seven characters, each two lines of which make a couplet, and the third and fourth couplets are required to present an exact parallelism, in terms of grammar and meaning. In translation these subtleties are naturally lost, but this complicated verse form did provide an admirable vehicle of expression for the T'ang poets.

On the death of Wang Wei in 761, his poems were collected, on imperial order, by his brother Wang Chin, then an Imperial Chancellor. These two men had followed quite different careers – one achieved the highest office in the civil service, the other was acclaimed as a famous poet and painter, though he had had an undistinguished and fitful official life. The distance that Wang Wei felt to exist between the affairs of Ch'ang-an and himself recurs throughout his poetry, his disposition towards withdrawal from worldly struggles receiving most poignant expression in the sequence about his country estate on the Wang River, written with his friend P'ei Ti. Frankly, he tells us:

Lacquer Garden

No proud official that man of the past –
Incompetent for secular concerns
The small post he achieved only obliged
His wandering among some such trees.

His rural retreat, about thirty miles south of the capital, was a constant solace to him, but it cannot be separated from the growing belief he developed in Buddhism. After his wife died in 734, he refused to remarry and chose to remain celibate like a monk. Then the death of his mother, a fervent Buddhist herself, served to strengthen this faith. He petitioned the throne for permission to convert his villa and garden into a monastery. This was granted about 750 or 751. Various poems recall his identification of personal solitude with the remoteness from daily life of the recluse.

Wang Wei was also a painter, extraordinary for a poet before the Sung dynasty, and his contemporaries remarked the visual quality of his verse and the poetical aspects of his paintings. None of his scrolls survive, but we know that he influenced poetry and painting in such a way that he encouraged the process by which these two forms of art eventually became inseparable in Chinese culture. Here is a treatment of twilight.

In the hills at nightfall in autumn

In the empty hills just after rain
The evening air is autumn now
Bright moons shining between pines
Clear stream flowing over stones
Bamboos clatter – the washerwoman goes home
Lotuses shift – the fisherman's boat floats down
Of course spring scents must fail
But you, my friend, you must stay.

Another outsider was Li Po. Born in the same year as Wang Wei, his ancestry may have had something to do with Li Po's indifference to Confucian scholarship and the possibilities of an official career. There is a strong likelihood that some of the recent forbears of the poet were Turkish in origin. To his

The Chi Ch'ang garden, near Wu-hsi, Kiangsi. A Ming garden renowned for its rock mountains and the quality of its water for making tea. The garden contained a pond with bridges joining its islands together; an impressive array of gnarled rocks, some very large in size; a dwelling area; and a rich and varied wood, of pines, deciduous trees and clumps of bamboos.

contemporaries, Li Po was certainly a Chinese; he hailed from 'the Western Regions' of the T'ang Empire and was literate in Chinese; but the atmosphere of his home and upbringing must have given him cause to hesitate over complete identification with T'ang civilization. Instead of studying the Confucian Classics and proceeding to the civil service examinations during his youth, Li Po was inclined to Taoism and eclectic philosophy. He dwelt for a couple of years with a Taoist recluse before taking to a wandering life on the road. Though his verse is not colloquial like Han-shan's unusual style of composition, Li Po had a similar longing for the wilder aspects of Nature, vast mist-filled valleys, tumbling waterfalls, bare mountains, deep gorges, jagged cliffs and the piercing cries of wild animals. The rural idyll of the Wang River sequence is never expressed in Li Po's poetry.

Imperial notice of Li Po came with a summons to Ch'ang-an in 742. Taoism was in fashion at the time and the attention of the Ming Huang had been directed to the poet by the emperor's youngest sister, Princess Yu-chen, a Taoist nun since 711. For two years he was one of the group of poets attached to the Court; their duties were the composition of verse about special events or festivities. The post that Li Po enjoyed was a sinecure. He was free to sample the pleasures of the capital, which he did to excess as a member of a group called the 'Eight Immortals of the Wine Cup'. By 744 Li Po considered that he had outstayed his welcome and, resigning his poetical post, he set off on his travels again. The specific cause of his departure was the blocking of an appointment through Court intrigue. 'An artful minister', Li Po claimed, prevented him from joining the official establishment as a regular civil servant. This failure has been attributed to indiscreet talk about an official communication he was once asked to write. He was supposed to have divulged sensitive information at a party. More likely a reason for the circumspection of senior

A detail of *Wang-Ch'uan Villa*, a painting on silk, after Wang Wei.

officials was Li Po's heavy drinking. In China wine often was, and still is, an integral part of creativity for the calligrapher, poet and painter. The long years of training and discipline necessary for accomplished brushwork – twenty years would not be considered as much more than a moderate period of training – tended to induce self-consciousness. The wine cup relaxed the 'heart-mind' and the hand. A philosophical justification for drunkenness was that it placed the individual in a state of perfect, unconditioned receptivity. Chuang-tzu had cited the security of the drunken man, whose lack of consciousness saved him from injury when he was pitched headlong out of a cart. With Li Po, though, drunkenness was habitual and, even if the carousing of the 'Drunken Immortal' did not become an imposition in polite society, it must have been thought that public office would only get him into serious trouble.

The following poem brings into focus the conflict Li Po must have known so well during his sojourn at Ch'ang-an. It is informed by that ancient dispute between Taoism and Confucianism concerning the naturalness of urban life.

Waking from drunkenness on a spring day

'Life in the world is but a big dream;
I will not spoil it by any labour or care.'
So saying, I was drunk all day,
Lying helpless at the porch in front of my door.
When I woke up I looked into the garden court;
A single bird was singing amid the flowers.
I asked myself, what season is this?
Restless the oriole chatters in the spring breeze.
Moved by its song I soon began to sigh
And as wine was there, I filled my own cup.
Noisily singing I waited for the moon to rise;
When my song was over, all my senses had gone.

Ch'ing Yen garden, belonging to Lin Ch'ing, a water conservancy official in the nineteenth century. A long zigzag bridge connects the Pavilion for the Contemplation of the Moon, in the lotus pond, to the shore.

In his later poems there is an increased awareness of the times being 'out of joint'. *Fighting South of the Ramparts*, which has been well translated by Arthur Waley, balances Li Po's belief in the Taoist concept of non-action against his own world-weariness. The poem was written before the rebellion of An Lu-shan. Possibly the poet had in mind the two great reverses suffered by Chinese arms in 751, namely the engagement on the Talas River in Central Asia and the defeat at Tali in Yunnan. But it was the civil war started by An Lu-shan that shattered the life of Li Po, who, like Wang Wei, became entangled with rebel groups. Neither poet was in any way politically motivated, but their eminence made them prestige ornaments for the retinues of rival contenders for the throne. After the restoration of Ming Huang, Wang Wei was pardoned at the behest of Wang Chin, and the intercession of General Kuo Tzu-i, whom Li Po had once befriended in poorer days, changed his punishment to exile in the South. Several years later a general amnesty allowed Li Po to return along the Yang-tze River, in which he is supposed to have drowned in 762. Not far from Nanking a temple dedicated to the poet marks the spot where legend says he drowned when trying to embrace the reflection of the moon in the water.

In 744 or 745 Li Po and Tu Fu first met and began their famous friendship. Having failed a civil service examination nine years earlier, Tu Fu was untied and able to follow the interests of the already famous Li Po. It should be realized that lack of family influence, not lack of talent, had ploughed Tu Fu. The two friends remained close to one another throughout their lives and they exchanged poems on different occasions. After further attempts to obtain an official appointment Tu Fu managed to secure a junior post in 755, but most of his life was a hard struggle for existence. Ironically, it is the neglected Tu Fu whom posterity regards as the greatest of all Chinese poets. From the Sung poets onwards Tu Fu was accepted as the 'Sage of Poetry'.

If the poetry of Li Po can be said to depend on an uncertain tension between romantic exuberance and artistic restraint, then the achievement of Tu Fu represents the combination of technical mastery with utter frankness in observation. None of Li Po's romantic egoism intrudes in his much admired *Autumn Meditation*, from which these three stanzas are taken.

> Gems of dew wilt and wound the maple trees in the wood:
> From Wu mountains, from Wu gorges, the air blows desolate.
> The waves between the river-banks merge in the seething sky,
> Clouds in the wind above the passes meet their shadows on the ground.
> Clustered chrysanthemums have opened twice, in tears of other days;
> The forlorn boat, once and for all, tethers my homeward thoughts.
> In the houses winter clothes speed scissors and ruler;
> The washing-blocks pound, faster each evening, in Pai Ti high on the
>   hill . . .
>
> The thousand houses, the circling mountains, are quiet in the morning
>   light;
> Day by day in the house by the river I sit in the blue of the hills.
> Two nights gone the fisher boats once more come bobbing on the waves,
> Belated swallows in cooling autumn still flutter to and fro.
> K'uang Heng writing state papers, which earned me no credit,
> Liu Hsiang editing classics, my hopes elsewhere . . .
> Yet many of my school friends have risen in the world.
> By the Five Tombs in light cloaks they ride their sleek horses.
>
> Well said, Ch'ang-an looks like a chessboard –
> Won and lost for a hundred years, sad beyond all telling.
> The mansions of princes and nobles all have new lords,
> And another generation wears the caps and robes of office.

Due north on the mountain passes the gongs and drums shake,
To the chariots and horses campaigning in the west the winged dispatches
   hasten.
While the fish and dragons fall asleep and the autumn river turns cold
My native country, untroubled times, are always in my thoughts . . .

Through such poems the image of the T'ang Empire has been recreated and
fixed in the minds of succeeding generations. Tu Fu spent the winter of 756 and
the summer of 757 in occupied Ch'ang-an, but political violence under the
regime of Li Lin-fu had already brushed him. Li Ying, an author and friend,
had been struck down by assassins in 747. Li Lin-fu claimed to have discovered
Li Ying's implication in a plot aimed at the throne, though the Imperial
Chancellor's motive for the writer's execution was partisan. Out of the normal
pattern of Chinese politics were Li Lin-fu's weapons of false charges of sedi-
tion and assassination by special envoys. A Confucian outlook was at the
bottom of Tu Fu's distress over the running-down of social organization,
though his own sense of impotence and isolation deepened this sadness. This
short piece exactly sums up his position.

> *Thoughts on a night journey*
>
> Reeds by the bank bending, stirred by the breeze,
> High-masted boat advancing alone in the night,
> Stars drawn low by the vastness of the plain,
> The moon rushing forward in the river's flow.
> How should I look for fame to what I have written?
> In age and sickness, how continue to serve?
> Wandering, drifting, what can I take for likeness?
> – A gull that wheels alone between earth and sky.

Po Chu-i, the son of a minor provincial official, had a distinguished career in
the civil service and rose to high rank. In 822 he was appointed governor of
Hangchow, the greatest city of the South. When his friend Yuan Chen (779–
831) came to visit him in that city, huge crowds lined the streets to gaze at these
two celebrated poets, whose friendship, like that of Li Po and Tu Fu, had given
rise to an exchange of poems much enjoyed by the general public. Po Chu-i
had plenty of work to do as an administrator, but he found time to compose
verse and visit the Ling-yin Monastery near Hangchow. Buddhism was important to Po Chu-i – he was buried at Lung-men, a Buddhist shrine, on the
outskirts of Loyang; yet he was also a loyal *shih*, profoundly concerned for the
well-being of China. He thought he had something to say to his contemporaries, as this satire shows.

> *The Chancellor's Gravel Drive*
> *(A Satire on the Maltreatment of Subordinates)*
>
> A Government-bull yoked to a Government-cart!
> Moored by the bank of Ch'an River, a barge loaded with gravel.
> A single load of gravel,
> How many pounds it weighs!
> Carrying at dawn, carrying at dusk, what is it all for?
> They are carrying it towards the Five Gates,

Interior of a cave at
Lung-men, a Buddhist
shrine of the Toba Wei
dynasty.

To the West of the Main Road.
Under the shadow of green laurels they are making a gravel-drive.
For yesterday arrived, newly appointed,
The Assistant Chancellor of the Realm,
And was terribly afraid that the wet and mud
Would dirty his horse's hoofs.
The Chancellor's horse's hoofs
Stepped on the gravel and remained perfectly clean;
But the bull employed in dragging the cart
Was almost sweating blood.
The Assistant Chancellor's business
Is to 'save men, govern the country
And Harmonize Yin and Yang'.
Whether the bull's neck is sore
Need not trouble him at all.

As a Censor, he tells us in another poem, his 'bluntness did not suit the times'. Firm memorials to the throne had caused his banishment on more than one occasion. As a poet, too, he favoured content to form; his style is deliberately simple and direct. But to the annoyance of Po Chu-i it was his lighter pieces rather than his ballads that had a serious political or social intention that enjoyed popularity. 'One found them everywhere,' Yuan Chen tells us, 'on the walls of palace buildings, Taoist and Buddhist monasteries and posting-stations. Everyone recited them, princes, and nobles, concubines and wives, ox-herds and grooms. They were even copied out, printed and sold in the market and brought to give in exchange for wine and tea. This happened in many different places.' Such widespread acceptance of his compositions should not cause surprise; his personal poems still communicate today, like this reflection on old age.

On His Baldness

At dawn I sighed to see my hairs fall;
At dusk I sighed to see my hairs fall,
For I dreaded the time when the last lock should go. . . .
They are all gone and I do not mind at all!
I have done with that cumbrous washing and getting dry;
My tiresome comb for ever is laid aside
Best of all, when the weather is hot and wet,
To have no top-knot weighing down on one's head!
I put aside my messy cloth wrap;
I have got rid of my dusty tasselled fringe.
In a silver jar I have stored a cold stream,
On my bald pate I trickle a ladle full.
Like one baptized with the Water of Buddha's Law,
I sit and receive this cool, cleansing joy.
Now I know why the priest who seeks Repose
Frees his heart by first shaving his head.

HAN YU AND THE CLASSICAL PROSE MOVEMENT

The arch-Confucianist of the T'ang Empire was Han Yu (768–824). He was respected as a poet by his contemporaries and by the Sung poets, but his outstanding contribution to Chinese literature was the reform of prose style. We have already referred to the determined opposition of Han Yu to Buddhism and, indeed, his leadership of the Classical Prose Movement needs to be seen in the context of this struggle, which was a reassertion of Confucian orthodoxy in the face of mass religious hysteria.

The limpid style of Han prose did not endure long after the fall of that dynasty. The tendency towards balanced and parallel construction of sentences became general. Artifice seemed as important as meaning. A distinction was made for the first time between practical writing, *pi*, and purely literary composition, *wen*, which was concerned with pleasing expression. Thus, the works of Confucius and Ssu-ma Ch'ien were *pi*. Despite protests from one or two distinguished *shih* the *wen* style came into vogue, very often obscuring sense in communications of administrative importance. Emperor Sui Wen-ti went so far as to punish a governor for writing reports in a flowery style, but the fashion for elaborate prose was not so easily checked. Yet Confucian scholars were worried by the excrescence of ornament because they feared it would confound social terms. In the reign of Emperor T'ang Hsuan-tsung one of them wrote that literary compositions should be founded upon the teachings of the past for the reason that 'the trends of literature decidedly influence the order of society and the customs of the people'. What was urgently required was the elevation of the Confucian Classics and a revival of the classical prose of Han. From this basic rejection of literary composition as an end in itself, Han Yu and his supporters set out to create in *ku wen*, or classical prose, an instrument capable of exposing the stupidities of the age. With the advantage of hindsight, Su Tung-po (1036–1101) could claim that the Classical Prose Movement easily regenerated serious literature, but the issue was by no means certain during the life of Han Yu himself.

In 819 the emperor arranged for the finger of Buddha to be brought to the capital. The mass excitement occasioned by the arrival of this relic shocked Han Yu profoundly. A weeping emperor and an overwrought people thronged the streets of Ch'ang-an to glimpse the sacred relic. At such a time, an eye-witness records, 'a soldier cut off his left arm in front of the Buddha's relic, and while holding it with his hand, he reverenced the relic each time he took a step, his blood sprinkling the ground all the while. As for those who walked on their elbows and knees, biting off their fingers or cutting off their hair, their numbers could not be counted.' In Han Yu's famous memorial to the throne, *On the Bone of Buddha*, the rational, sceptical outlook of Confucian philosophy emerged in explicit opposition to imperial patronage of the new faith. In lucid *ku wen* style Han Yu wrote:

> I humbly submit that Buddhism is a barbarian doctrine. From the time of the Yellow Emperor till the Chou dynasty, the ancient kings had long reigns and the people enjoyed peace. This happened before the arrival of the Buddhist faith.
>
> It was not until the time of Emperor Han Ming-ti that Buddhism first appeared. From then onwards the times changed; there was no peace but only a series of disturbances. . . .
>
> The Buddha was born a barbarian; he knew neither of the duty of minister to prince nor the relationship of son to father. Suppose, your majesty, he were still alive today, and had come to the Court. You would grant him a brief interview, a ceremonial banquet, and make a present of a suit of clothes; then, at once you send him back to the frontier under guard before he could stir up any trouble amongst the people. Therefore, no reason at all can be found for according respect to a decayed and rotten bone that used to belong to this long deceased person. . . .
>
> I beg that this bone be handed over to the authorities to cast into water or fire, that Buddhist superstition be outlawed, that the uncertainties of your people be settled once and for all and their descendants protected from confusion. . . .
>
> If the Buddha should possess the power to harm us, let everything descend on me. I shall not complain . . .!

The emperor was furious. But Han Yu was saved by the Confucian scholars of the day; they rallied behind him and his sentence was commuted to banishment.

Han Yu had behaved responsibly. That is, it was in the classical mould of the Confucian *shih*. His outspokenness may have been dangerous in terms of personal safety and his own career, but it should be remembered that the Censorate was a unique Chinese invention. The officials of this department had the onerous duty of reporting to the emperor all cases of maladministration. Opposition to a Court favourite, a member of a powerful family, or a headstrong ruler called for moral courage. Censors, Chinese ombudsmen, often perished. After his recall to Ch'ang-an, Han Yu used his ethical resoluteness for the benefit of the tottering T'ang dynasty. As an official of the War Office, he was sent by a harassed ruler to persuade a rebellious governor in Hopei against plunging the Empire into another civil war. With only a token bodyguard Han Yu visited the rebel camp and spoke his mind. The officers wavered when they listened to what the elder statesman had to say. As a result the rebel commander, unsure of the strength of his support, was obliged to accept terms and the would-be revolt was over. There was a definite amelioration in military discipline. As one common soldier commented on the fierceness of Han Yu's supervision, 'A person who is prepared to burn the holy finger of the Lord Buddha will not hesitate to chop off the heads of mere soldiers.'

In 583 Emperor Sui Wen-ti commanded that a temple be erected at the foot of every sacred mountain. Over a hundred temples and pagodas were built throughout the Empire before the dynasty was overthrown by the T'ang. At Mai-chi-shan, a sacred mountain just off 'the Silk Road' in Kansu, there was extensive activity, including the carving of new caves, the construction of colossal images and the restoration of earlier work from the period of the Tartar Partition. On the south-east cliff face of Mai-chi-shan, or 'Corn Rick Mountain', three colossi, over fifteen metres high, represent Mi-lo, the coming Buddha, flanked by two *bodhisattvas*, one of whom can be identified as Kwan-yin. These figures, built up in clay plaster over a core of rock, give us an indication of the growing strength of the Buddhist faith as well as the increasing influx of foreign motifs. The T'ang Empire, in particular, was an open society and this is reflected in the increasing diversity of art. At Tunghuang the confidence of the age can be seen in the splendid panoramic landscapes that have assumed an almost separate status in the decoration of the caves. The rocky desert landscape depicted behind the canopy of paradise in Cave 112 has strong affinities with *Spring Landscape with Travellers on a Broad River* by Chan Tzu-ch'ien (died *c*. 610). This remarkable painting, first exhibited in Peking in 1954, combines precision of brushstroke, delicate realism and the use of bright colours. It foreshadows the rise of landscape painting in the Sung Empire.

Painting, which later on in China was added to poetry as a chief distraction of the literary class, remained at this time a craft, practised almost exclusively by specialists. The works of that distinguished exception to the rule, Wang Wei, have been lost, though we do know that his usual subject was landscape. Of the paintings executed by Han Kan (born *c*. 715) a certain number survive. From the restored *Shining Light of the Night* a glimpse of the artist's ability to portray animals with curious economy can be obtained. This horse was one of Ming Huang's favourites, a fine specimen from Central Asia. Though of humble origin, Han Kan was highly esteemed in Ch'ang-an: more than fifty of

Mai-chi-shan, Kansu. The three colossi, over fifteen metres high, represent Mi-lo, the coming Buddha, flanked by two *bodhisattvas*. Maitreya, as Mi-lo, underwent a transformation in China and became the centre of a widespread cult in which the devotees prayed to be reborn in Tushita Heaven in order to see the future Buddha face to face. Sacred mountains like this attracted imperial notice in 583 and Emperor Sui Wen-ti commanded that each should have a temple erected at its foot.

SUI AND
T'ANG ART

his paintings found their way into the imperial collection. For this fame he had
to thank Wang Wei, who discovered the talent of young Han Kan when he
worked in an inn. Wang Wei generously sponsored Han Kan, paying for his
education and introducing him into polite society.

Apart from paintings and sculpture, the only art objects that we have to
illustrate the T'ang achievement come from graves. In 1964 the excavation of
Princess Yung T'ai's mausoleum, at Ch'ien-hsien in Shensi, increased this
stock enormously. Princess Yung T'ai was buried at the beginning of the
eighth century, the cause of her death being either enforced suicide for a mis-
taken misdemeanour or the result of childbirth. The large mausoleum, akin to

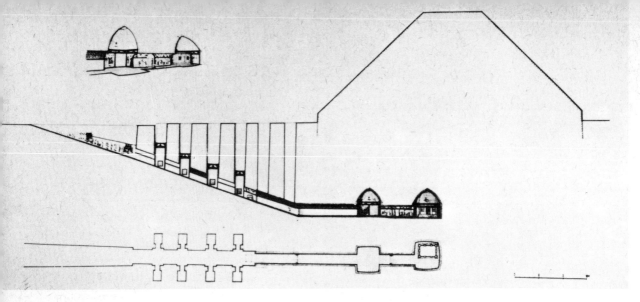

a sunken pyramid, was copiously decorated and contained a wide variety of ceramic figurines and pottery. One group consists of horses, with and without riders, and the influence such pottery sculpture had on Han Kan is obvious. Outstanding are the brightly glazed bowls, the result of technical advances during the T'ang dynasty. To the clear lead glaze potters added mineral colorants to produce browns and yellows, greens and blues.

When Po Chu-i was serving as an official at Chiang-chou, Kiangnan, in 816, he found time to build on a hill behind his house an arbour amid bamboos and white rocks. After work he would lounge here, awaiting the evening sky above the lake. A year later he discovered on the neighbouring Incense Burner Peak a spot which struck him as the perfect setting for a retreat, and he built himself a cottage there. At that time he could not take up permanent residence, but this was his intention once his five years at Chiang-chou were over. 'The situation delighted me,' he wrote to Yuan Chen. 'There is a group of high pine trees in front of the cottage and a fine cluster of bamboos. I have covered the walls with green creepers and made paved paths of white rock. A stream almost encircles it and I have a waterfall at my very eaves. There is a white lotus in my pool and red pomegranate on its banks.' This simple hut with its garden filled Po Chu-i with pleasure, and the thought of it sustained those friends to whom he reported its tranquil beauty. Po Chu-i was one of the most devoted and active amateur gardeners among the T'ang poets. If the country estate of Wang Wei was more central to that poet-painter's life, the continued interest of Po Chu-i in gardens must be all the more impressive when his long career as an official is remembered.

The rise of gardening as an art ran parallel to that of landscape painting. Its roots lie in Taoism, that perennial call to return to Nature, in both an inner and an outer sense, but Buddhism too encouraged the trend. The Society of the White Lotus, which had been founded by Hui Yuan (333–416) and had its headquarters near to Po Chu-i's hut, possessed a large natural park where disciples who came from different provinces received their instruction. Returning to their homes, these Buddhists founded other centres, each with a park of its own. Wealthy converts also made a practice of leaving their gardens

THE CHINESE
GARDEN

to the faith, like the dedication of Wang Wei's country estate after his mother's death. The T'ang statesman, Li Te-yu (787–849), had a pleasure park at P'ing-ch'uan that was the amazement of his contemporaries. It contained wonderful trees and plants, 'wild mountains', tunnels, ponds, winding water-ways and magnificent pavilions. An ardent Taoist, Li Te-yu took drugs and practised all kinds of rites in order to contact the Immortals, whose presence was expected in his paradisal garden.

The Chinese garden was, and still is, an expression of artistic ideas and conceptions that have emerged from an intimate relationship with the natural world. It is a work of art, a unique achievement of Chinese civilization. 'Such gardens,' wrote Oswald Sirén in his fascinating study, 'cannot be described or analyzed as exhaustively as the geometrically arranged gardens of Europe and the more stereotyped gardens of Japan.' For the awareness of natural change, the interaction symbolized in the Yin-Yang theory, has caused Chinese gardeners to seek irregular and unexpected features which appeal more to the imagination than to the reasoning faculty of the beholder. There were certain rules and principles for gardening, but these did not lead to any conformity. The basic elements were the same as for landscape painting, *shan shui*, or mountains and water – these might be. simply gnarled rocks and a pond. In addition, we find flowers and trees as well as decorative architecture, like bridges, pavilions and walls. One fundamental difference between the Chinese view of the garden and ours is that it has always been considered an extension of the dwelling area, something more than a 'picture window'. No real distinction between indoors and out-of-doors can be said to exist in the Chinese house. The 'Well of Heaven', the inner courtyard, was a touchstone for daily life. Even in the city, the *Yuan Yeh* (*Garden Treatise*, 1634), informs us that the impression of a hermitage can be obtained.

> A single 'mountain' may give rise to many effects, a small stone may evoke many feelings. The shadow from the dry leaves of the banana tree is beautifully outlined on the paper of the window. The roots of the pine force their way through the crevices of the hollow stones. . . . If one can find stillness in the midst of the city turmoil, why should one then forego such an easily accessible spot and seek a more distant one?

The *shih* sought to be the countryman in the town; Wang Wei was in the minority when he chose rural seclusion. Gardens in cities and towns were always more numerous than those in the country.

Objects in a Chinese garden have a symbolic as well as an artistic value. They are aids to meditation. Water, so integral to social organization and philosophic thought, is never absent. The lawn finds no place at all, whilst flowers are never formed into patterns. Individual plants seem sufficient, especially when juxtaposed with the cragginess of a rock 'mountain'. We need to reflect on the vast symbolism of Chinese art before we wonder at the economy of many landscape gardens. To name a few: the chrysanthemum, the flower of autumn, stands for retirement and culture – the late fragrance that defies the frost; the water lily, rising stainless from its bed of slime, quietly reposes on the clear pool, a symbol of purity and truth; and the bamboo, unbroken by the fiercest storm, represents suppleness and strength, as well as lasting friendship and hardy age. Neither should the love of garden rocks cause surprise. China

A section drawing of the main axis of the tomb of the T'ang Princess Yung T'ai, in Ch'ien-hsien, Shensi, dating from about 700.

is a land of rivers and mountains. Long after the cultural focus of the country had shifted out of the 'land within the passes' this deeply ingrained fascination for stones and rocks continued unabated. In the eleventh century the Emperor Sung Hui-tsung, a renowned painter himself, dispatched officials to the four corners of the Empire to collect interesting rocks for the imperial gardens at K'ai Feng. Strangeness of shape and texture was most prized because the artificial mountains of the garden had to be wild and rugged. Water-moulded limestone was always in great demand. Such gnarled, convoluted, weather-worn rocks were witnesses of the potency and awe-inspiring aspects of Nature, natural forces with which the Chinese people had long ago learned to live. Asymmetrical and spontaneous, the Chinese garden is a statement of faith in Nature as well as an admission of the lowly place that mankind has in the natural order of things.

The Cho Cheng garden, Soochow, was laid out at the close of the Ming dynasty in the seventeenth century. Over half of this garden is water, a common feature of southern gardens.

ABOVE Pan Mou garden, Peking. This famous garden was arranged by the Ming poet Li Li-weng in the seventeenth century. The drawing, taken from a journal by Lin Ch'ing, shows the official sitting with a friend, both lost in admiration for the beauty about them.

RIGHT The Chu Fang garden of the Ch'ing official Lin Ch'ing, after he had been dismissed from the civil service. An austere charm inhabits this neat little garden in Ch'ing Chiang-pu.

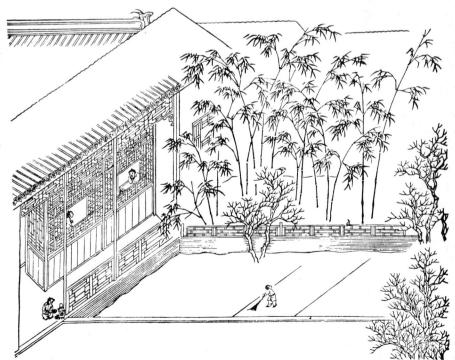

9

The Two Sungs
960–1279

THE FIVE DYNASTIES (907–960) The Five Dynasties and the Ten Kingdoms occupy the fifty-three years of division that separate the T'ang and Sung Empires. The unusual extent of the fragmentation, which even cut across economic areas, may have been caused by advances in military technology. Neglect of hydraulic engineering after the rebellion of An Lu-shan must also have assisted the development of local separatist movements, wherever a military leadership arose to direct them, but the establishment of so many small states in Kiangnan can be explained only in terms of the region's diverse geographical character – a land of mountains and valleys. The economic area had not yet become a homogeneous unit; this was to be accomplished during the Sung Empire.

In the North a series of brief military dictatorships, the Five Dynasties, were unable to hold their own against nomadic incursion. The longest of these dynasties was seventeen years. Taking advantage of such instability, the Kitans, a Mongolian tribe based in South Manchuria, penetrated the north-western frontier. The first ruler of the Later Tsin (936–947) was obliged to cede a large tract of Hopei, including the gates in the Great Wall and what is now Peking. In 947 the Kitans renamed their state Liao, a sinicized name, and adopted Chinese culture. But admiration was not the same thing as absorption, so that the Hopei cession remained outside the Empire for four hundred years, and through it foreign invaders, the Mongols, conquered all China. In the Five Dynasties period, reluctance on the part of the *shih* to serve the northern rulers, who were largely adventurers of barbarian stock, led to a southern exodus. The influx of scholars considerably advanced the civilization of Kiangnan, the states of Nan T'ang and Shu being particularly distinguished. In the South the traditions of the T'ang Empire were preserved. The spread of literary culture was greatly assisted by the contemporary advance in printing. The Confucian Classics were block-printed between 932 and 953; a government department was made responsible for the editing of texts, for the employment of wood-carvers for the blocks and for the printing operation itself. Movable type, invented about 1040, greatly facilitated this revolution. Both Buddhist and Taoist scriptures had been printed in the ninth century; the earliest known example of block printing is a Buddhist charm dating from 770.

In 960 a northern general, Chao Kuang-yin, seized power and, repeating the pattern of Sui reunification, conquered the Ten Kingdoms of the South. When one king begged for independence, the first Sung emperor asked, 'What wrong have your people done to be excluded from the Empire?'

Emperor Sung T'ai-tsu, founder of the Northern Sung dynasty.

A mutiny by troops he was leading northwards against the Kitans forced Chao Kuang-yin to ascend the throne. Chao had been promoted commander-in-chief of the army because of his rectitude and respect for learning; these qualities, it was hoped by the ruling house, the Later Chou (951–60), would make him a trusted protector of the seven-year-old heir apparent, but the plan took no account of the temper of the soldiers. The coup d'état, an uncommon beginning for a successful dynasty in Chinese history, was welcomed in Loyang, where Chao was much esteemed. For the reluctant emperor, Sung T'ai-tsu, proved to be an astute ruler. He spared the ruling house after the manner of the Duke of Chou, gained the allegiance of the *shih* by restoring the civil service to its pre-eminent position, and, not least, rid himself of those military leaders who had placed him on the throne. At a feast Emperor Sung T'ai-tsu ended the vicious circle of suspicion and military revolution that had raised and degraded the Five Dynasties. It was in the first year of his reign; his guests were his chief military officers, those responsible for his elevation. When the company had drunk deeply and were in a cheerful mood, the newly acclaimed emperor said:

> 'I do not sleep peacefully.'
>
> 'Why?' asked the generals.
>
> 'For a very simple reason,' the emperor replied. 'Every person here covets my throne.'
>
> Bowing deeply the army officers protested as one, thus, 'There is nothing to justify your words. Heaven has chosen Your Majesty. Who wishes to oust you?'
>
> 'I do not doubt your loyalty,' the emperor added, 'but if one fine day one of you is suddenly awakened at dawn and compelled to don the yellow robe, as you made me do so, how could he avoid rebellion, no matter his own reluctance?'
>
> The generals replied that not one of them was in possession of sufficient virtue for such a thing to happen, and they entreated the emperor to take whatever measures he felt necessary. At which the emperor said:
>
> 'The life of man is short. Happiness consists of the means to enjoy life, and then bequeath the same to one's descendants. Therefore, resign your commands, retire to the provinces, and there select for yourselves the best estates; on these you will be able to live at ease and die of ripe old age, leaving them to your descendants. To guarantee such domestic accord we shall ally our families with marriages. Isn't this plan better for us all than uncertainties and mishaps?'
>
> The army officers assented, and the next day, every one of them resigned on the grounds of imaginary ill-health. The emperor kept his part of the bargain, ennobling them and generously distributing lands and wealth.

The Ten Kingdoms viewed these events with interest and sympathy. Nan Ping and Shu submitted to the Sung by diplomatic arrangement; Nan Han (971) and Nan T'ang (975) surrendered after short wars, whilst the last independent state, Wu Yueh, held out only till 979. Except for the Liao kingdom, China was reunited under the third great imperial administration, the Two Sungs. The second emperor, Sung T'ai-tsung (976–997) attempted without success to recover the territory occupied by the Kitans. Serious

THE NORTHERN SUNG DYNASTY (960–1126)

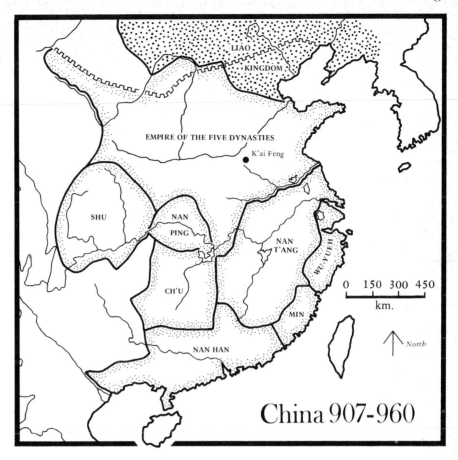

reverses and a long, exhausting war ceased when the third emperor, Sung Chen-tsung (998–1022) agreed to tolerate the Kitan presence and pay a large annual subsidy to Liao (1004). This arrangement was similar to the *ho-ch'in* policy followed during part of the Former Han dynasty. Yet in striking contrast to Han and T'ang, the foreign policy of the Sung was never imperial in design. Containment of the nomad peoples, the maintenance of the *status quo*, not expansion, was the consistent rule. Even though foreign invasion remained a perpetual threat and was the cause of the final overthrow of the Sung Empire, the subjection of military officials to civilian control reflects the pacific tenor of the times. Apart from the Kitans on the northern frontier another group, the Tunguts, a partially sinicized Tibetan tribe, had secured in Hsia a base from which to expand southwards at the expense of the Chinese. Between 1032 and 1044 the Sung generals fought a complicated, defensive war against the Hsia forces.

The century of peace that followed the wars with Liao and Hsia was a splendid epoch for China; not a few people have regarded its achievements as the climax of Chinese civilization. K'ai Feng, the Northern Sung capital, is the historical city that later scholars would have wished to visit most. The early civilization of China can be said to terminate during the Mongol dynasty, to which the Southern Sung fell, officially, in 1279. But it was the years before the capture of K'ai Feng by the Kin (1126), the period of the Northern Sung, that witnessed mature blossoming of the Chinese spirit.

Learning, enshrined in the examination system, formed the basis of the Sung achievement. The imperial administration was modelled on the T'ang. Recruitment to the civil service, now supreme, was perfected. In the capital there were government-sponsored universities and colleges to prepare candidates for the entrance examinations. In the provinces grants of land were made to encourage local scholarship and sustain the widespread movement for popular education. Not only were more students allowed to pass their final examinations and become officials, but also there was a significant widening of the curriculum. During the ascendancy of the reformer Wang An-shih (1021–86), technical and scientific subjects could be offered. Previously the questions set, though concerned with administrative, governmental and economic problems, were expected to be answered within the context of orthodox literature and philosophy. Now engineering and medicine could be discussed from a more scientific point of view. This extension of official knowledge did not long survive the fall of Wang An-shih but its brief introduction reflects the contemporary rise in scientific consciousness amongst the educated classes. Painting was added to the minimum qualifications of would-be officials at Court by Emperor Sung Hui-tsung (1101–26). The extent of Sung preoccupation with higher education can be gauged by the number of candidates sitting for second degrees. Some years there were as many as seventeen thousand.

An efficient and humane civil service ran the Sung Empire. Political conflict within its ranks in the 1060s led to the formation of two main parties, the Traditionalists and the Innovators, but there was no recourse to violent intrigue by either of these opposing factions. Posting or retirement to a distant province became the usual fate of ruined ministers. Before the death of Emperor Sung Shen-tsung in 1085, his Imperial Chancellor, Wang An-shih, the leader of the Innovators, was removed from office in such a civilized manner.

Disaster struck the Sung Empire in the form of the warlike Kin. These untamed nomads were originally vassals of the Kitans, but ten years of war with the Liao kingdom gave them mastery of the frontier and direct contact with the Chinese. Emperor Sung Hui-tsung, the painter and patron of art, misjudged the strength of the Kin army and tried to recover the Hopei concession by force. In 1126 the Kin besieged and captured K'ai Feng; they took prisoner three thousand *shih*, Sung Hui-tsung and his son, in whose favour the disgraced ruler had abdicated. Both these Sung emperors were to die in captivity. For several years the Kin army dominated China. In 1129 Kin cavalry crossed the Yang-tze River and captured Hangchow, where the first Southern Sung emperor, Kao-tsung, had been proclaimed two years earlier. The situation looked grave, but the Empire rallied, particularly the populous southern provinces, and found in Yo Fei a general capable of repulsing the Kin. When fighting had restored Sung control over the Kiangnan, Emperor Sung Kao-tsung decided to come to terms with the Kin (1141). To the dismay of Confucian historians, Yo Fei was secretly executed and China partitioned between two powers, the Sung and Kin Empires. One of the motives for this unprecedented act was fear of the power acquired by military commanders

A bearded huntsman with a cheetah, excavated from the tomb of the T'ang Princess Yung T'ai, who died sometime before 700. These horsemen came from 'the Western Regions', an area that supplied the wealthy Chinese with grooms. The saddle by this time was equipped with stirrups. The figure is of painted pottery.

through fighting the Kin. Yo Fei himself was an honest servant of the throne, but his belief in continued war only served to strengthen the military arm of government. In the event the frontier between Sung and Kin was almost identical to the line drawn across China during the Tartar Partition (317–589). It was the northern boundary of the wet-rice growing valleys of central and southern China, country unsuited to the military tactics of nomad cavalry.

WANG AN-SHIH'S
ECONOMIC
REFORMS

The 'flying horse' from the Wu-wei tomb in Kansu. A Later Han bronze, dating from the second century AD, of the Western breed sought by Emperor Han Wu-ti. The horse is represented at full gallop and the figure balances on a swallow.

OVERLEAF *Going up the river at the Spring Festival* by Chang Tse-tuan, painted about 1125. This detail of K'ai Feng shortly before its fall to the Kin shows a multi-angular soaring cantilever bridge.

The Sung Empire, though smaller in territory than the T'ang, was more populous. In Kiangnan the opening up of new lands for agriculture and improvements in technique led to rapid increases in the number of people dwelling in towns and villages. Before the fall of K'ai Feng the population of the Sung Empire had topped one hundred millions, and the annual revenue of the imperial government was twice as much as the T'ang. Connected with these demographic changes was the growth of a cash economy. The *shang*, the merchants, were becoming a powerful element in society, their affluence directly related to the revolution in money and credit.

Before the period of the Five Dynasties the amount of money in circulation was limited because of three factors: most taxes were assessed in kind, grain being the usual medium of payment; metals used for coinage, such as copper, were generally in short supply; and, there was the problem of maintaining a coinage free from debasement and counterfeiting. The common unit of currency was the 'cash', a circular copper coin with a central square hole that allowed it to be used in strings. After his success in the imperial examination of 800, Po Chu-i had been granted the small salary of 16,000 cash a month; on his appointment as governor of Soochow in 825 his salary was 80,000 cash a month, a very considerable income. Whilst state accountants dealt only with units of one thousand cash, the standard for daily trade was one hundred. The decline in value of this copper coinage towards the end of the T'ang dynasty proved extremely inconvenient. The sheer weight of larger strings hindered commercial transactions – one thousand cash weighed a little under one kilogram. Moreover, it was found that the minting and distribution of new coins cost more than their face value. Other forms of currency, like iron and pottery, seemed equally vulnerable to inflation. But economic pressure for an extension of currency could not be easily diverted. To the household levy and the land tax, a personal tax was added during the Five Dynasties. This new tax was retained after the Sung reunification so the state itself found money was a necessary part of its revenues. A partial solution to the difficulty of handling large amounts of coinage was discovered in paper money, which first appeared in 811, becoming generally accepted from 970. In order to facilitate trade, merchants began to store their copper cash with powerful families, receiving receipts for the amount deposited. These bills could be converted back into cash on request in other cities or towns, wherever other members of the family or their friends lived. This system, known as 'flying money', was extended by the imperial government in the eleventh century, initially by accepting receipts in exchange for its monopoly products, such as salt and tea. Merchants received bills in K'ai Feng which could be converted in the provinces. What this monetary revolution, for that is what it undoubtedly was, represents is the development of a national market. The provinces of the Sung Empire were

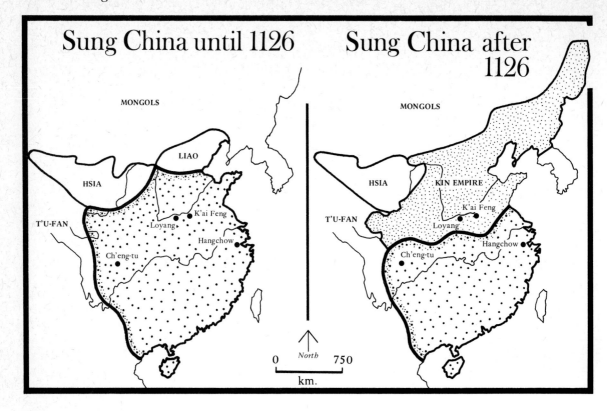

now interdependent, their economic cohesion sustained by improved agriculture and communications.

Above this immense economic transformation towers one man, Wang An-shih, the second great reformer of early Chinese civilization. Unlike Wang Mang, with whom he is often bracketed as a socialist, he had no imperial ambitions, but like him he was an advocate of a more scientific approach to daily problems. Wang An-shih was given the opportunity to reform the Empire by Emperor Sung Shen-tsung (1068–85), a ruler much occupied with strengthening the dynasty. After 1069 Wang An-shih introduced a series of measures, referred to as the 'New Laws', which aroused the blind fury of the traditional *shih*. The policies of the Innovators, the party which he led, were anathema to the Traditionalists, who never tired of warning the emperor that their consequence must be a popular uprising by the *nung*. What seems to have most annoyed the Traditionalists was the originality of Wang An-shih's economic reforms – they were unheard of and new. Suited to the times his methods were primarily financial, the protection of the hard-pressed farmer being his essential aim. Upon the *nung* the Empire rested, Wang An-shih contended, because agriculture furnished both the means of peace and war: food and the manpower for armies came from the peasantry, then harassed by an inefficient imperial administration and the encroachments of the *shang*. Echoes from the School of Law may be found in this argument, though Mencius had placed emphasis on the condition of the tillers of the soil, too. When the barbarian pressure in the north is recalled to mind, this concern for the welfare of the *nung* on the part of the Imperial Chancellor was opportune.

Wang An-shih did not deny the importance of moral leadership. He was frugal. So sparing was he in his own style of life that he has been accused of poor personal hygiene. His clothes were often dirty, and his unkempt head of hair disgusted many acquaintances. On regular occasions his followers forced him to bathe and change into fresh clothes. Personal gain seems not to have interested Wang An-shih, just as the natural portents of flood and famine did not touch any religious or superstitious nerve in his make-up. To him natural catastrophies were the product of natural causes; and the economic ills of the Sung Empire were likewise caused by disequilibrium in the social system. A sceptic in matters of belief, Wang An-shih was a thorough-going realist when it came to reorganization. He perceived the dangers of disintegration in the Empire as the affluence of K'ai Feng and other leading cities contrasted with rural poverty. That his measures, aimed directly at current abuse and deficiency, bestirred the *shih* and not the *nung* to intense opposition indicates that he had largely grasped the economic problems of his times.

At the start of his ministry Wang An-shih rationalized public expenditure. A saving of forty per cent of the national budget resulted. Economies at Court, streamlining of administrative procedures and the reduction of peculation accounted for this improvement in imperial finances. Civil servants were no longer permitted to receive 'gifts' in the way of duty. They were expected to live on their salaries, a policy unlikely to endear the reformer to the vast majority of the official class. He next proposed to abolish the ancient system of transporting tax grain and other produce to the capital. Though K'ai Feng was closer to Kiangnan and the central provinces than had been either Loyang or Ch'ang-an, the business of transportation was expensive and incredibly wasteful. As an alternative system Wang An-shih established government warehouses in urban centres throughout the Empire. Tax grain accumulated in these warehouses could then be sold on the open market and the cash receipts transferred to the capital. This system, called the 'Equalization of Loss', was a further development of the *p'ing chang* or levelling system, first devised during the reign of Emperor Han Wu-ti. Where the two differed was in the role of *entrepreneur* that Wang An-shih gave to officials handling grain-tax. Public granaries were involved in marketing for the benefit of the hungry and the imperial exchequer. Through this measure he hoped to use the cash economy against the new power of the *shang*. In 1072 this system of state intervention in the market was enlarged to include other items of commerce unconnected with taxation. The *shih yi fa* or exchange system was intended to stabilize prices and limit profits on a wide range of products. A commodity depressed because of oversupply could be exchanged at one of the state marketing agencies for another that was in short supply, if the disposer of the commodity preferred not to receive cash payment or a bill of exchange. Hoarding of commodities by the *shang* was thus reduced and the overproduction of luxury goods held in check. Above all, Wang An-shih tried to balance supply and demand.

To raise the condition of the *nung* a large-scale rural aid programme was launched. The 'Young Shoots' law introduced state loans to farmers for the purchase of seeds and tools. The rate of interest was low and farmers were able to pledge as security their growing crops. Again, Wang An-shih sought to exclude the activities of the local moneylender and the merchant, thus en-

TOP A porcelain ewer and bowl for warming wine, decorated with light blue glaze, of the Two Sungs period. It was excavated at Su-sung, Anhui, in 1963.

ABOVE A stoneware pillow of the Two Sungs period excavated at Hsing-t'ai, Hopei, in 1955.

couraging the small farmer to extend the area of land under cultivation. The Traditionalists claimed that the 'Young Shoots' law squeezed the *nung*, but throughout the ministry of Wang An-shih there was no popular uprising to give any support to such a view. Another law designed to ease the burden of the farmer was the 'Remission of Services', which placed the corvée on a fairer basis. Instead of liability for forced labour at the behest of the state the *nung* were made subject to money tax. Whereas the corvée was inflexible, binding men to a certain number of labour days in a given locality, the substitution of a money tax allowed for the hire of coolies when and wherever required. The *shih*, to whom the corvée was the fundamental instrument of imperial control by virtue of its use in the maintenance of waterways on which tax grain could be transported, regarded the 'Remission of Services' law as nothing less than treason. A better land tax, related to the intrinsic value of the soil, goaded these landowning officials further.

The *pao chia* of Wang An-shih had a double objective, internal and external security. Under the *pao chia* every ten families combined as a group with a leader, or headman. Each member was responsible for the crimes of the other members, like the Ch'in punishment of the three *tsu*. Also, every family with two adult males had to provide one soldier, fully trained and armed. These recruits to the standing army during emergencies were to be supported by the other members of the group, thereby reducing the cost to the government of fighting the Kitans. Adoption of this policy was forced on Emperor Sung Shen-tsung and his minister through the collapse of universal conscription. Perhaps the closest parallel would be Ts'ao Ts'ao's agricultural colonists, for Wang An-shih's soldiers were charged with maintaining order in the country-side during peace time as well as strengthening regular armies at the time of war. Families living in the northern and north-western provinces were also required to keep a government horse in fodder during the winter months. Cavalry, a perennial Chinese military weakness, was temporarily brought up to standard. It was unfortunate that the edict lapsed some years before the Kin descended on K'ai Feng.

Wang An-shih was forced to resign and retire to Nanking in 1076. He had lost the emperor's favour, though his policies remained unchanged till 1086. After the death of Emperor Sung Shen-tsung the Traditionalists were able to repeal the 'New Laws'. All seemed undone, but in 1093 Emperor Sung Che-tsung recalled the Innovators to office, where the disciples of Wang An-shih reintroduced the 'New Laws'. It was not a popular rebellion that swept away these advanced economic policies, the earlier fate of Wang Mang, but the on-slaught of Kin horsemen. Whereas the *pao chia* system was disliked and other measures were misunderstood, the *nung* did not resent Wang An-shih's econo-mic reforms. Entrenched resistance came from the official class, who were neither capable nor willing to apply the 'New Laws'. The civil service simply lacked the ability to handle a money economy.

The reunification of China in 960 had been made possible by an economic and technological revolution that we have noted in the arrival of an incipient cash economy. Whilst the expansion of trade via the new development in water transport drew together the various provinces of the Sung Empire, a less

RIGHT AND OVERLEAF Another detail from the Sung scroll *Going up the river at the Spring Festival* by Chang Tse-tuan, shows one of the city gates of K'ai Feng.

THE SOUTHERN SUNG DYNASTY (1126–1279)

cumbersome imperial administration along with well-equipped armies provided no opportunity for renewed political fragmentation. The military officials might be subject to the strict control of the civil service, but the quality of troops and the equipment in use was of the highest standard. The social position of the military, like that of the merchants, was less depressed because of the changing circumstances of the period but there was never any question of serious competition with the *shih*. Commerce in China was massive compared with the parallel development in Europe. Marco Polo, the native of industrious Venice, was to be amazed by the size and intensity of commercial activity in the Yuan Empire (1279–1368). Nothing like it could be found in contemporary Europe. Yet the *shang* were unable to make lasting social and political headway against the official hierarchy. The scholar, the servant of

centralized government, retained his exalted position. Unlike the West, towns and cities acquired no special liberties, never becoming centres of mercantile influence. The *shang* simply became wealthy. Likewise, no dominant military class arose in China, despite the continued need to face the barbarian menace on the northern frontier. For his advocacy of the reconquest of those provinces overrun by the Kin, Yo Fei lost his head.

The fall of K'ai Feng and the loss of the North was not so decisive as first appeared at the time, since Kiangnan contained the key economic area. Improved techniques in rice-growing had spread throughout the Yang-tze Valley. Printed manuals on agricultural method, written in simple language and often illustrated were partly responsible for this advance in farming. In order to strengthen its economic position the Southern Sung dynasty took an

active part in rural education. By 1164 the Sung Empire had recovered: another Kin invasion had been repulsed and these troublesome neighbours were obliged to accept a smaller annual subsidy. Culturally, too, the Southern Sung dynasty rescaled the peaks originally achieved before 1126. Painting and philosophy came into their own, though Chu Hsi (1130–1200), the reinterpreter of Confucius, found his ideas neglected at Court; and Hsia Kuei (1180–1230), the most celebrated Sung landscape painter, was busy working on his marvellous panoramic scrolls.

But on the steppes another nomadic people, the Mongols, were preparing for their world-shattering course of conquest and destruction. In 1206 Genghiz Khan was elected. Chu Hsi, the spokesman for reason, was spared seeing the agony of civilization savaged by the irrational violence of the

Mongol horde. The Kin Empire went down in 1211–12 amid scenes of appalling ferocity. But it was the cold-blooded extermination of the Hsia kingdom, fourteen years later, that proclaimed the inhumanity of the Mongols. So thorough was the devastation that the region became a permanent wasteland, while the language and traditions of the Hsia were lost for ever. In 1235, eight years after the death of Genghiz Khan, the Mongols turned their attention to the Sung Empire. Nearly half a century of war was necessary before the last member of the Southern Sung dynasty perished in a sea battle off what is now Hong Kong in 1279. The terrain of the South handicapped the Mongol cavalry but a crucial factor in slowing down the nomad advance was Chinese military technology. The Two Sungs, though pacifist inclined, did possess the most advanced weapons available in the world.

The San Tan-yin garden, West Lake, Hangchow, dating from the Ming period.

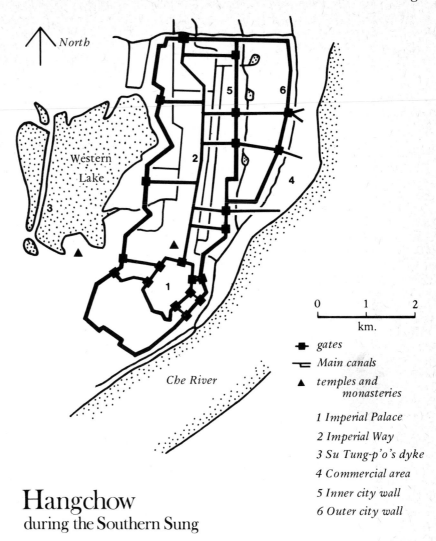

0   1   2

km.

⬛ *gates*

⎯ *Main canals*

▲ *temples and monasteries*

1 Imperial Palace

2 Imperial Way

3 Su Tung-p'o's dyke

4 Commercial area

5 Inner city wall

6 Outer city wall

Hangchow
during the Southern Sung

Gunpowder had been adopted by the imperial armies. Explosive grenades and bombs were launched from catapults at the seige of K'ai Feng; rocket-aided arrows and poisonous smokes were also deployed. The latter, a kind of poisonous gas, caused bleeding from the mouth and nose, and was distinct from the smoky mist derived from a contemporary lime-based projectile. 'Iron fire' bombs, most probably shrapnel, were introduced by the Kin in 1221. Chinese *kung* improved this weapon for their new masters. Flame-throwers were in service from the late eleventh century; they comprised a tank of naphtha upon which was mounted a double-acting pump with two pistons to work continuously. Out of the 'flying fire lance', a Kin invention, the Chinese evolved in 1259 the gun proper, the 'fire-spurting lance'. Instead of emitting a jet of flame the 'fire-spurting lance' shot out pellets from a bamboo tube with a loud report. The iron-plated armoured car had been devised in 1127, as a counter to Kin cavalry charges, whilst the man-powered paddle-wheel warship was used to seal off the rivers and artificial waterways that stood in the way of nomad advance. The nomadic peoples ranged against the Sung, like the Tartars after 317, became irresistible only when they had adopted Chinese military technology. The Mongol fleet that destroyed the last hopes of the Southern Sung dynasty in 1279 had existed but a decade.

Another factor which complicated the Mongol conquest was the presence of barbarian scholar-statesmen like Yelu Ch'u-ts'ai, a Kitan admirer of Chinese culture. A descendant of a noble family from the Liao kingdom, whose desire for sinicization we have already remarked, he did what he could to temper the furious determination of the Mongols, converting an urge to destroy into a desire for a regular empire. The absolute hatred of sown lands typical of Genghiz Khan was transformed into Kubilai Khan's great foundation, the city of Peking (1263). The grandson of Genghiz Khan and the first Yuan, or Mongol emperor, Kubilai Khan, transferred his people and his capital from the steppe to the sown.

LIFE IN TOWN AND COUNTRYSIDE

In 1083 the official census of the Sung Empire recorded 17,211,213 households, or ninety million people. By 1124 there were 20,882,258 households, which gives a population slightly in excess of one hundred million, nearly twice that of the T'ang Empire. Population growth was a startling phenomenon for the Sung Empire. The inhabitants of Hangchow increased from below half a million in 1173 to more than one million in 1270. To feed these people some two hundred tonnes of rice was needed daily. 'New settlers,' an official noted, 'arrive month by month.' Though refugees from the North after the fall of K'ai Feng may account for a part of this novel urban expansion, there was an overall increase in the size of towns and cities throughout the period. Impetus was given by rapid improvements in communications, both in hydraulic engineering and nautics. Methods of circumnavigating natural obstructions on rivers were discovered, canal building progressed and the true junk came into general service. The Yang-tze, an intricate network of rivers, lakes and canals, teemed with shipping; holds were filled with agricultural produce, timber, metals, pottery and every kind of luxury goods. Hangchow, which received more than it produced, was still a specialist centre of manufacture in its own right, notably for jewellery, children's toys, gold brocade and printed books.

Hangchow, a city 'greater than any in the world', in Marco Polo's estimation, had humble beginnings. Between 317 and 589, when the Tartars controlled the North, the imperial capital was Nanking, not Hangchow, then little more than a collection of villages. With reluctance the Southern Sung dynasty admitted that Hangchow would have to become the permanent residence of the Son of Heaven. Apart from the charm and attractiveness of its environs the city had little to commend it for such a dignity. It failed to follow any of the major precepts of classical town planning. Irregular in shape, the walls were pierced by thirteen equally irregular gates; the palace was located in the south, while the centre housed a pig market; multi-storeyed dwellings, indicators of the chronic overcrowding, spoilt the city's aspect and ruled out the urban garden; the lack of internal walls and the uncontrolled activities of

The overhanging eaves and elaborate roof decoration of a pavilion in Hangchow.

commerce substituted an air of human chaos for the order and grandeur of the northern cities. Making the best of the situation at last in 1148, Emperor Sung Kao-tsung decided to extend the city walls to the south-east and construct something approaching an imperial palace.

Scarcity of accommodation was typical, except for the richest inhabitants. Suburbs surrounded the ramparts and the commercial centre was established along the river bank away from the city itself. No space for building existed within the city walls by the end of the thirteenth century, a concentration of population that gave the Chinese themselves reason to pause. The construction of houses of several storeys, unique to Hangchow, gave rise to frequent fires, particularly in the less affluent quarters of the city, where the materials in use were wood and bamboo. In 1132 a single conflagration destroyed as many as thirteen thousand houses. Earlier in K'ai Feng, a city with fewer open spaces than either the Han or T'ang capitals, the menace of fire had led to the institution of a fire-fighting service. Every ward possessed a watch-tower manned by soldiers who were properly trained and equipped. The system was introduced in Hangchow after the fire of 1137, which gutted ten thousand houses. Plenty of water was, of course, ready at hand in such an emergency because of the lattice of canals on which the city was built. These canals were connected with the Western Lake, whose waters collected from the surrounding hills by an encircling dyke met the city's needs for irrigation and supply; and to the east they joined the Che River, thus providing access to the city for smaller craft. Marco Polo also commented that they carried 'with them all the filth into the river, and ultimately to the sea'. Once a year, like Venice, there was a general clearing out of the canals, but a daily refuse collection service did exist. Whereas the rich had cesspools that could be emptied periodically, ordinary citizens used buckets which were collected by the nightsoil men each morning. They then sold this human waste to local market gardeners for conversion into fertilizer. The streets themselves were cleansed by the authorities. Indeed, a high standard of public and private cleanliness was maintained in Hangchow. Both toothbrushes and toilet paper, for instance, were widely used. The Chinese were aware of the medical reasons behind this policy; the relation between epidemics and hot, dirty, overcrowded towns was early perceived.

Public safety was naturally a prime concern of the *shih*. To save drunken revellers from drowning themselves in water rather than wine the local authorities had solid balustrades set up along the edge of the canals. Too many of them had fallen in at night; perhaps it was even something of a fashion after the celebrated death of Li Po. Limitations, however, were not placed on the night life of the city, a feature of Hangchow that Marco Polo discovered to have survived the Mongol curfew. For the wealthy there were amusements galore. Tea houses, restaurants, pleasure grounds, theatres, concert halls or nightclubs welcomed those with taste and money. Each social class had its own favourite resorts, but during the great festivals, like New Year, the Festival of Flowers, the Festival of the Dead and the Festival of the Moon, all the citizens took part in the celebrations. Nevertheless, beneath this outward gaiety there was an inner strife and bitterness. Numerous in Hangchow and other cities

A pavilion on the edge of West Lake, Hangchow.

were poverty-stricken *nung* from the surrounding countryside, magnetized by the possibilities of freedom and employment. These urban poor were homeless and made their way, if at all, by a mixture of cunning and intense specialization. Unless they managed to secure a post as servant in a powerful family or became the employee of a merchant, the jobs open to them were few. Some became street vendors or porters; others entered the entertainment industry as mimics, comedians, jugglers, animal trainers, singers, dancers or prostitutes; those who fell out of regular employment altogether ended as vagrants and thieves. Unrest amongst these lower orders prompted officials and wealthy members of society to increase their donations to charity in an attempt to head off trouble.

Although the rural exodus of small farmers was a symptom of the concentration of wealth in the towns and the impoverishment of the countryside throughout the Sung Empire, it is likely that the stresses and strains in Hangchow were greater than elsewhere. The authorities never seem to have exercised complete control over its inhabitants; it was too well established before the Court arrived. From the Yuan Empire onwards there was to be a return to the classical Chinese city. Three small pieces of evidence would suggest the discomfort experienced by the Southern Sung dynasty in Hangchow. First, edicts forbidding officials entering into partnership with merchants were issued on a number of occasions. Secondly, the southern custom of cremation was felt to undermine one of the basic tenets of state religion, namely ancestor worship. In Kiangnan, the focus of this new practice, there could have been a Buddhist influence at work. Yet Imperial disapproval was unable to reduce its popularity among the mass of the urban dwellers. Lastly, the waiving of criminal action against male prostitutes, another lapse from Confucian ethic, may represent an enforced adjustment to southern *mores*.

The economic policies of Wang An-shih were aimed at a regeneration of the rural community. The continued drift of landless *nung* to the towns during the Southern Sung dynasty are indicative of shortcomings in the 'New Laws'. Protection against the large-scale landowner was not obtained; wealthy families were able to purchase land with the tenants on it, a revival of the quasi-feudalism evident in Later Han. Free *nung* who sold their land because of poverty were sometimes compelled to stay on as tied-tenants of the new owner. This was liable to happen when the interests of the landowners and the local administration were found to coincide. Large farms started to become common, though the *nung* remained the foundation of the rural work-force. A money economy, related to the new urban markets, was the driving force behind these changes. Agricultural production soared but the profits were not reaped by the hard-working *nung*. This increase in output rested on improved techniques. New knowledge about fertilizers and crops helped farmers to get more from their land; manure, silt and lime were used to prepare the soil in Kiangnan. Seeds, better adapted to growing conditions in the southern provinces, allowed two crops in the same field. Improvements in water control, either as a byproduct of canal building or actual land reclamation, added to the fertility of many areas; whilst seed-drills in the North and heavy ploughs and harrows in the South brought a higher degree of mechanization to the farm. In sum, a sophisticated agriculture evolved to sustain the extra population of the Sung Empire.

10

The Sung Achievement

Intense activity marked every aspect of Sung culture. The heritage of the T'ang was taken over and in the intellectual ferment of the period of the Two Sungs reached a zenith of achievement. Emperor Sung T'ai-tsu inaugurated this era of philosophical, scientific and artistic advance when he revitalized education in order to obtain for his imperial administration a regular intake of scholars. In consequence of this policy there was the revival of Confucian scholarship, once again the official philosophy of government. But there were deeper forces at work too. Neo-Confucianism, as the Sung reinterpretation of Confucian tradition is called, was a response to the changing conditions of the time. Buddhism, less potent a force after the tenth century, still exposed the paucity of cosmological explanations in traditional Confucianism. Neo-Confucian philosophy more than made amends for this shortcoming by the judicious incorporation of elements from Taoist speculation and contemporary scientific knowledge. As Joseph Needham has remarked, it was 'an empirical rationalism, a kind of scientific humanism'. The Neo-Confucian thinkers felt compelled to take into full account the new scientific knowledge.

Chou Tun-i (1017–73), a scholar who preferred philosophical study to an official career, wrote *On the Supreme Pole*. In this analysis of the ancient cosmological diagram, which includes the Pole, Yin-Yang, the Five Elements and other related concepts, he postulated the fundamental idea of Neo-Confucianism, namely that the universe was a single organism. He reached this position through a marriage of the *Tao Teh Ching* and the *I Ching*. 'Motion and rest alternate, each being the root of the other,' Chou Tun-i explains. The Supreme Pole, the *t'ai chi*, or axis, in movement produces the Yang, at rest the Yin. Upon the interaction of the Yin-Yang all else depends; it transforms and generates 'the myriad things'. But *t'ai chi* is not something outside or beyond the world; within 'the myriad things' its presence can always be found. In effect, it constituted them, as an aggregation of 'matter-energy'. *Li*, a character which in its most ancient meaning stood for pattern, was the principle of organization underlying the *t'ai chi*. Rather than a force, a consciousness, or an ideal, the form behind matter in Greek philosophy, *li* was conceived as the pattern in Nature that gave ordered direction to the movements of the axis. Imminent in every part of the universe, the power derived from the *t'ai chi* followed the pre-established harmony of *li*. The universe, therefore, was a unity, self-sufficient and without any single controller. This grand conception led Chu Hsi (1130–1200) to deny the immortality of the soul and existence of the deity. 'There is,' he said, 'no man in heaven judging sin.'

The names of Chu Hsi and Confucius are always linked together because it

An anonymous fan painting in ink and water colour on silk entitled *The Haunt of the Sage*, dating from the thirteenth century, the Two Sungs period.

was above all this Sung philosopher who recast the sage of Lu's teaching in a form that has been accepted as orthodox ever since. In his voluminous writings Chu Hsi achieved a synthesis of the Taoist and Confucian elements in Neo-Confucian thought, an event nearly coincidental with the synthesis of Christian-Aristotelian thinking in the *Summae* of St Thomas Aquinas (born 1225). Apart from this contemporaneity, there is nothing that encourages a comparison between these two thinkers, the European cleric and the Chinese civil servant. The gulf between them can be best illustrated by that cynical Chinese proverb, 'The educated believe nothing, the uneducated believe everything.' For Chu Hsi re-interpreted the Confucian Classics in a modern idiom, downgrading the supernatural as the operations of natural phenomena. The few references to the spirits, malevolent and benign, were explained away with little difficulty. Scepticism had been a feature of Confucianism from the beginning. The wind, rain, thunder and lightning became natural forces, though the same characters were used to denote them. The learned, however, knew what was what. But in no way could Neo-Confucianism be regarded as amoral. On the contrary, its distinctive feature was its ethical teaching. Throughout his writings the overriding concern of Chu Hsi was morality; how should a man best lead his life? The answer to this question, the philosopher maintained, was attunement to *li*. Because the pattern in Nature encompassed the entire world, it behoved mankind to live in accordance with this pre-established harmony. Only when individuals pursued such a course of action was there a possibility of human perfection. Hence, Chu Hsi reasserted the view that the nature of man was good, explaining evil conduct as the result of neglect or the absence of proper education. One of his favourite comparisons was between man in society and a pearl in a bowl of dirty water. Though the pearl appears grey and spoilt, it has lost nothing essential. Taken from the bowl it shines forth in all its original brilliance. Should man seek his true nature, or *hsing*, and live according to its dictates, then his original goodness will become clear likewise. Natural virtue, Chu Hsi agrees with Mencius, becomes clouded and dull through the false values of social life. The way of moral cultivation is to follow the Mean, the human manifestation of that natural balance upon which the universe rests.

Like Confucius, Chu Hsi was intent upon ethical and political problems. The condition of the Sung Empire was a cause of grave anxiety to him. Acquiescence in Hangchow to the permanent loss of the northern provinces seemed a dereliction of duty, something that a loyal *shih* needed to speak out against. Chu Hsi criticized openly those in power, much to the annoyance of ministers and the Son of Heaven. The first duty of the Southern Sung emperor, he repeatedly announced, was revenge on the Kin for death in captivity of Emperor Sung Hui-tsung and his son (1135). Despite such frankness as well as a large measure of backing from the *shih*, the pacifist policy adopted after Yo Fei's execution was never reversed. The philosophical stature of Chu Hsi received nodding recognition at Court, but relations between him and leading officials were often strained, even antagonistic. He was kept out of high office and usually posted to distant provinces. To register protest against things he disliked about the government Chu Hsi would decline appointments. But it was a negative gesture and he failed to find ways of applying his philosophy. On succeeding generations rather than his own was the real impact of his

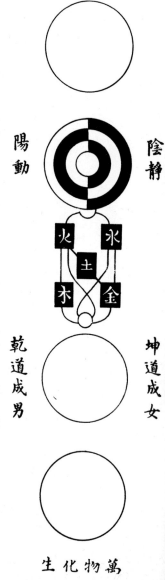

The Supreme Pole, the *t'ai chi*, of Chou Tun-i.

thinking felt. Though state ceremonial and rites continued down to the end of the nineteenth century, this public worship was increasingly seen by the *shih* to relate more to the political framework than to religion. It underpinned the claim of the emperor to rule on behalf of Heaven, as a quintessential part of the social order. From the Sung Empire onwards, Confucian scholars tended to be agnostic and humanistic. After all Buddhism and Taoism were there to provide for those who might seek other-worldliness.

This rational emphasis was to impress profoundly thinkers outside China. The European scholars of the Enlightenment, when they first became aware of Chinese philosophy at the end of the seventeenth century, were very interested in Neo-Confucianism. They responded to a morality that managed without supernatural sanction. What stirred Gottfried Wilhelm Leibniz (1646–1716) was the organic basis of Chu Hsi's thought. Leibniz wanted an explanation of the universe that was realist, but not mechanical. He rejected the current Western view that the world was a vast machine, and proposed the alternative concept of it as a living organism, every part of which was also an organism, or 'monad'. These 'monads' fitted into a pre-established harmony, not unlike the *li*. The organic view of the world, as first put forward by Leibniz, was to be crucial in the nineteenth century; witness Hegel, Darwin, Marx, Pasteur and Spencer. It has been suggested that Neo-Confucianism provided crucial confirmation. 'Thus we may applaud the modern Chinese interpreters,' Leibniz wrote in his *Letter on Chinese Philosophy*, 'when they reduce the government of Heaven to natural causes, and when they differ from the ignorant populace, which is always on the look out for supernatural (or rather supra-corporeal) miracles, and Spirits like *deus ex machina*. And we shall be able to enlighten them further on these matters by informing them of new discoveries of Europe, which have furnished almost mathematical reasons for many of the great marvels of Nature. . . .' The Enlightenment, then, warmed to the Chinese predilection for a universe founded on an underlying harmony and unity rather than on struggle and chaos. Chu Hsi was able to wonder at the mysterious perfection of Nature without needing to abstract a creator or a personal god; he was awed but never unintelligent. He had devised a philosophy suited to an age of scientific discovery and technological advance. 'Nevertheless,' Joseph Needham reminds us, 'all these achievements did not bring Chinese science to the level of Galileo, Harvey and Newton.'

SCIENCE AND TECHNOLOGY

During the Two Sungs China reached the edge of modern science and underwent a minor industrial revolution. No country could compare in the application of natural knowledge to practical human needs. The world's first mechanized industry was born at the same time that the printing of books facilitated the exchange of scientific knowledge derived from observation and experiment. But it remains a fact that the early civilization of China, far ahead of other cultural areas in scientific and technical understanding between the first century BC and the fourteenth century, did not generate modern scientific method. Nor was the commercial development in the Sung Empire followed by anything which faintly resembled the rise of capitalism in the West. China was to continue on its own distinct course for centuries, a society dominated by the scholar-bureaucrat. Only in the late nineteenth century were the *shih* convinced that the country needed to import modern technology, the origins of which had been acquired by the West from China.

Western debts to Chinese science are now admitted. The major information flow occurred after the end of the Southern Sung dynasty, when the Mongol conquest of all between the Don and the Mekong rivers encouraged overland travel and trade. Yet the fundamental ideas of Chinese science were largely neglected in favour of specific inventions or processes. An instance of this short-sightedness is Marco Polo. His *Travels* hardly touch upon scientific topics even though for three years he had been governor of Yangchow, a centre specializing in the production of armaments and military supplies. By the thirteenth century Europeans were using the magnetic compass, the stern-post rudder and the windmill, and in the fourteenth century mechanical clocks, water-powered textile machinery, blast furnaces, gunpowder, seg-mental-arch bridges, and block printing are recorded. Although the exact source of these inventions was unknown to the inhabitants of Europe at this time, their significance as agents of social and economic change was not unnoticed. In the early 1600s Francis Bacon, Lord Chancellor to James I, was aware that the metamorphosis of Europe stemmed from the application of these inventions. He wrote:

> It is well to observe the force and virtue and consequences of discoveries. These are to be seen nowhere more conspicuously than in those three which were unknown to the ancients, and of which the origin, though recent, is obscure; namely, printing, gunpowder, and the magnet. For these three have changed the whole face and state of things throughout the world, the first in literature, the second in warfare, the third in navigation; whence have followed innumerable changes; insomuch that no empire, no sect, no star, seems to have exerted greater power and influence in human affairs than these mechanical discoveries.

The clue to this acute observation was Bacon's own scientific activities. He was pointing out a crucial watershed in European history: what we call modern times were beginning. Knowledge became readily available in printed form whereas previously only the very rich layman could afford the long, tedious and expensive process of hand-copied manuscripts. The Renaissance and the Reformation followed. Gunpowder inaugurated large-scale warfare, eclipsing both knight and castle. The Thirty Years' War, which raged shortly after Bacon's death, was the nearest experience of total warfare in Europe before 1914. The magnetic compass had sent Columbus to America in 1492 and helped Magellan circumnavigate the globe in 1520.

Before looking at science and technology in the Sung Empire, 'the major focal point' for both, a word or two on the reasons so far adduced for the later slackening of pace in Chinese technical progress ought to be written. A number of hypotheses have been put forward to explain the initial progress of Chinese science and its eventual overtaking by the scientific revolution of the late Renaissance in Europe. The work of Joseph Needham, at present nearing completion, is shedding new light on this difficult subject, but few historians have charted the relations of science and society in Europe, not to mention China. The impact on the West of discoveries and inventions emanating from early Chinese civilization lends weight to the argument that the answer must lie in the different social and economic structures as well as the intellectual systems upon which they rested. Despite the commercial activity of the great Chinese cities – Marco Polo was stunned by the sheer size of the economy – the merchants were never permitted to accrue to themselves any influence in state affairs. Neither were cities free as in the mercantile centres of Europe, where a 'charter' granted privileges to the burghers not enjoyed in the surrounding countryside, nor were the merchant guilds of any social standing. The *shang*, victims of sumptuary laws and state interference, sought admission for their sons to the official class. To be a civil servant was the ambition of all. Because of his unchallenged position of authority and the intimate relation of mankind with Nature in Chinese thought, the *shih* were interested in the benefits of technology. Hydraulic engineering was a case in point. But the tradition of public works and nationalization kept the control of science in the hands of the government, and it led to a number of early state-sponsored inventions, like paper. A driving force behind the Sung achievement was imperial interest, which Wang An-shih institutionalized by the introduction of technical and scientific papers in the civil service examinations. Only astronomy remained 'classified', but the scholar-bureaucrat was likely to hinder any other scientific development that might be seen to threaten the social structure. Inhibition may have taken its toll of later invention and experiment.

Very careful experimentation was, of course, carried out. An instance of systematic study was the revival of dissection in Northern Sung. Yet the conception of Laws of Nature did not arise in the Chinese mind. The experimental method, coupled with mathematics, was never tried as a means of discovering the rules that governed the workings of a mechanical universe. Law, since the Legalists in the reign of Ch'in Shih Huang-ti, was in bad odour and little attempt at abstract formulation was made. Without a universal creator too, there was no need to justify his ways to men by the discovery of his imprint on creation; that is, Nature's laws. *Li*, re-interpreted in Neo-Confucianism, explained natural harmony, whose integrative levels are not so abstruse to us today. 'Here again the Chinese shot an arrow close to the spot where Bohr and Rutherford were later to stand, without ever attaining to the position of Newton.' In the Newtonian phase, apparently a prerequisite of modern science, however, China found itself left behind in knowledge, an entirely new experience and one that cost dearly in the conflicts of the nineteenth century.

One of the beneficiaries of the Sung reunification was undoubtedly Chinese science, which was second to none in the world prior to the scientific revolution of the late European Renaissance. In every branch major developments were recorded, and the number of efficient applications has made the Sung Empire the age of technical innovation. Wang Chen, whose *Nung Shu* (*Treatise on Agriculture*) was published in 1313, describes two fascinating arrangements for the large-scale use of the water-wheel. One of them was an advanced metallurgical bellows, worked through the conversion of longitudinal motion by crank, connecting-rod and piston-rod. Motive power was derived from a horizontal water-wheel with a flywheel above. Extraction of iron from iron ore was also assisted by the use of coal and possibly coke. 'In Cathay,' Marco Polo records, 'there is found a sort of black stone which they dig out of the mountains, where it runs in veins. When lighted, it burns like

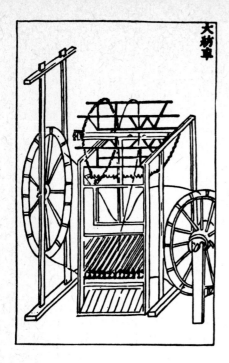

Water-powered textile machinery, the vertical wheel on the right providing the motive power. An illustration from Wang Chen's *Nung Shu* (*Treatise on Agriculture*), published in 1313.

charcoal, and retains the fire much better than wood.' The other invention was water-powered textile machinery. Thirty-two spindles, Wang Chen tells us, could spin thread at the same time. In different versions it was used for silk-reeling and hemp-spinning. The leather driving-belt of this textile machinery had an interesting parallel in the chain-drive of Su Sung's astronomical clock. Between 1088 and 1092 the pioneer work of the Buddhist monk I-Hsing (eighth century) on hydraulic clockwork was brought to perfection in the imperial observatory at K'ai Feng. Su Sung (1020–1101) and other engineers applied the principle of regular and controlled water flow to an armillary sphere, a model of the heavens used in astronomy. It allowed the sphere to move in accordance with the apparent movements of the planets and the stars. As a break-through in the accurate measurement of time Su Sung's astronomical clock cannot be gainsaid: it stands between the primitive water-clock and the spring-driven clock because its time-keeping ability could be adjusted by weights. Though not seen by its inventors as primarily a clock, it did strike a gong to indicate the passing hours by a system of bamboo 'revolving and snapping springs'.

Efforts directed towards understanding the heavens were matched by those intended to add to the store of knowledge concerning the immediate environment. Meteorology, a science that seemed to encompass the two, was taken up by the imperial government. A network of rain-gauge and snow-gauge stations was probably established in the western provinces, their purpose being the collection of information on river levels and the likelihood of flooding. Sung mathematicians spent a great deal of time considering the proper shape of rain-gauges. Map-making, another precise application of mathematics, had started with the seismologist, Chang Heng (78–139). In the T'ang period an expedition manned a line from the Great Wall to Annam and established the meridian arc, perhaps the first evidence of a spherical earth. Nine observation stations collected data on the heavens, which was then interpreted by leading

Su Sung's astronomical
clock at K'ai Feng, built
between 1088 and 1092.

scientists, including I-Hsing. Chinese cartography was given its classic form
in the *Kuang Yu T'u* (*Great Atlas*) of Chu Ssu-pen (1273–1337). The Yuan
Empire inherited the geographical tradition of the Sung; Kubilai Khan dispatched several expeditions to ascertain the source of the Yellow River. Chu
Ssu-pen, too, had the advantage of Arab knowledge then reaching China for
the first time; but the oldest printed map known is of China in 1155.

Behind the rise of science in the Han Empire there had been a remarkable
body of mathematical theory. Decimal place-value and the concept of zero
were understood, whilst the *kung* possessed sliding calipers decimally graduated. This tradition, continued by the T'ang scientists, culminated in the Sung
and Yuan Empires when mathematics was encouraged by the fusion of Taoist
and Confucian doctrines in Neo-Confucianism. Taoism had developed a
strong numerology, possibly under Buddhist pressure. At this time China was
ahead of the world in the solution of equations, because more than one unknown could be handled; whilst algebra has always seemed profoundly suited
to the Chinese mind. Primers of arithmetic for daily needs were also printed
during the Southern Sung dynasty. Trade and industry relied on the abacus, an
effective calculating instrument still in use today. But the upsurge in commercial activity must be seen as part of the improvement in national communications. Besides an extension of the road network in Kiangnan and
Kwangtung, there occurred significant advances in nautical and hydraulic
engineering. Though a continental rather than a maritime nation, we have seen

how the Chinese fully exploited their numerous rivers for transportation from the beginning of centrally organized political life. After the establishment of the Empire in 221 BC, it became a tenet of imperial policy that waterways held the provinces together. They carried tax-grain as well as the other bulk items of government concern, like the products of the Iron and Salt Bureaux. The comparative neglect of canals, typical of the periods of late T'ang and Five Dynasties, ended with the Sung reunification.

Sluice-gates were common in the Later Han, and further attempts to control water flow eventually led to the invention of the lock some time before the T'ang dynasty. During the Two Sungs large locks with a roof like a shed were constructed. These gave protection to the cargo and sailors from the elements or robbers, while the change in the level of water was effected. Reinforcement and repair of canals and river banks became more sophisticated with piling and gabions, huge cylinders of kaoliang stalks fastened with bamboo rope. Greater control over the turbulent Yellow River was gained because galions could be lowered into breaches by coolies manhandling them with cables. Preventive action in the form of dredging was taken by Sung hydraulic engineers. Wang An-shih set up the Yellow River Dredging Commission in 1073, a year that witnessed devastating floods in Hopei. Government dredgers, using a toothed rake or bucket, cleared the accumulation of silt along the river-bed. Careful checks were maintained on waterways by means of graduated poles and floating signs, data from which was fed by observers to the administrators responsible for water-conservancy. Across these numerous waterways were thrown an impressive array of bridges. Though Marco Polo never ceased to marvel at the stone bridges in Hangchow, the oldest extant segmental arch bridge, the An-chi bridge at Chao-hsien, Hopei, was built in 610 by Li Ch'un, civil engineer to Emperor Sui Yang-ti. The single arch of the An-chi bridge has a span of thirty-seven metres but rises barely seven metres from foot to crown. Its beauty and architectural merit have been justly celebrated ever since its erection. The flatness of the crown was not emulated in Europe until the sixteenth century. In Kiangnan and Szechuan the rugged, mountainous interior presented the Sung engineers with an even greater variety of problems. Either wooden cantilever bridges or cable suspension bridges were placed across gorges and torrents. The latter were originally composed of plaited bamboo strips, whose tensile strength had already led to their use for marine cordage, but in the T'ang dynasty iron chains were introduced. The suspension bridge was slung between two or more towers containing winding gear to adjust the tension of the cables. Such mountain bridges increased in number and size during the Two Sungs; they became centres of strategic and commercial importance.

In nautical technology the Sung Chinese were supreme. The *Ling Wai Tai Ta (Information on What is Beyond the Passes)*, written by Chou Ch'u-fei in 1178, describes the sea-going junk thus:

> The ships which sail the southern sea and south of it are like houses. When their sails are spread they are like great clouds in the sky. Their rudders are several tens of feet long. A single ship carries several hundred men, and has in the stores a year's supply of grain. Pigs are fed and wine fermented on board. . . . A great ship with heavy cargo has nothing to fear of high seas, but rather in shallow water it will come to grief.

The Pao-tai bridge at Soochow, built in 806 and much admired
by foreign visitors like Marco Polo.

The great ship was built with nails and iron pins; it had a double hull, water-tight bulkheads and buoyancy chambers; waterproofing was achieved with a mixture of t'ung-oil and lime; there were multiple masts, life-boats and tenders; oars were stored in case of calm weather; gunpowder offered a means of defence; several heavy anchors were carried as well as floats to stabilize the ship in stormy seas; the massive rudder ensured that the steering was no problem; and the magnetic compass freed the captain from shore-line sailing. What struck Marco Polo a hundred years later was the appointment of living space. Cabins were commodious and well-aired. When he left Chuang-chou on his homeward journey, an imperial envoy accompanying a Mongol princess to her betrothed, Arghun, the Mongol ruler of Persia, the Yuan fleet in which he sailed consisted of fourteen four-masted vessels, each manned by six hundred men and provisioned for two years. Confirmation of the spaciousness of the sea-going junk is given by Ibn Battutah, the great Arab traveller. In 1347 he noticed that Chinese merchants were accustomed to take with them their wives and concubines on sea voyages. Often a man might remain privately in his cabin, like his own house, so that others on board would not be aware of his presence until disembarkation.

The distant shores that Chinese junks were to reach in the Ming period included the countries of South-East Asia (1405-7), Ceylon (1409-11), India

LEFT The stern of an early Ming grain freighter on the Grand Canal. These ships were never less than 12 metres long and employed sails, poles and oars. Up to 140 tonnes of grain could be transported at a time. This illustration dates from the Ch'ing period.

ABOVE Early iron technology. The forging of a ship's grapnel anchor; an illustration from the Ming period.

and Persia (1413–15), the eastern coast of Africa south of Zanzibar (1417–19) and Arabia (1421–2). These voyages listed above, were undertaken by the Imperial Fleet under the command of the eunuch admiral, Cheng Ho. The first expedition carried twenty-eight thousand men in sixty-two four-decked ships, whose dimensions were one hundred and thirty-four metres long and fifty-five metres in the beam. Such junks were larger versions of traditional craft, whose earlier voyages for commercial purposes had gained the nautical expertise required in deep-ocean shipbuilding. The Mongol conquerors took advantage of Chinese seamanship to launch attacks on Japan (1281) and Java (1294), but Ming expeditions were not aggressive in design. Local rulers were expected to acknowledge the Ming emperor and to offer tribute. In return, however, they received substantial gifts as well as emblems of office, like the umbrella, possibly a Chinese invention. Commercial and diplomatic success was Cheng Ho's objective, in contrast with later Western mercantile activity in the Indian Ocean. Unlike the Chinese, Portuguese sailors wanted goods from the East but had nothing to offer in exchange, and their 'conquistador' mentality led to slaving and warfare with the 'heretics' they encountered. Little control was exercised from Lisbon because these ventures were based on private enterprise – desperately in search of El Dorado. Even Alfonso de Albuquerque, the second Portuguese viceroy in the East, who captured Goa (1510) and Malacca (1512), was arrogant enough to tell the Sultan of Calicut that he had come 'for Christians and spices'. What Albuquerque failed to understand – indeed, what few in the West today quite appreciate – was that the Indian Ocean and the China Sea had been previously Chinese lakes. The scrapping of the navy after the voyages of Cheng Ho led to a power vacuum in the area that the Portuguese unwittingly filled. Even their rudders and magnetic compasses, the very means of exploration and conquest, had been obtained indirectly from China.

Innovation in military technology and printing having been discussed elsewhere, we come to the last great aspect of Sung science, namely medicine. The medical profession had received formal recognition during the T'ang dynasty; between 619 and 629 the Imperial Medical College in Ch'ang-an was enlarged and an associate institution set up in each provincial capital. The Sung Imperial Medical College in Hangchow had two hundred and fifty students. In 1111 the twelve most eminent practitioners compiled the *Sheng Chi Tsung Lu* (*The Imperial Medical Encyclopedia*). This work was part of a general movement towards the codification of medical disorders – symptoms, diagnosis and treatment. It sought to standardize medical practice, early theory being reassessed in the light of new evidence. Anatomy, largely neglected after the death of Hua T'o in 265, was supplemented by dissection, the bodies of rebels providing the specimens for analysis. Clinical observation acquired, it may be said, a remarkable accuracy, with the result that new diseases were properly identified and described. In pharmacy there were astounding developments, such as the manufacture of steroid sex hormones by Shen Kua (1031–95). This polymath official, a friend of the poet Su Tung-p'o, was connected with the Imperial Drugs Office, established in 1076 as a government watchdog over the pharmaceutics industry. Only satisfactory drugs were recommended to medical circles for prescription, whilst these preparations from state factories were sold to the public slightly below market prices.

Open-minded and fascinated by the world about him, Shen Kua has left us much detailed information about Sung science. His *Meng Ch'i Pi T'an* (*Dream Pool Essays*) provides the first account of the magnetic compass, a description of movable type and discussions on astronomy and mathematics, besides noticing fossils as extinct creatures and recording matters of more contemporary geographical interest. The book is instructive; its survey of Sung culture and institutions takes just over half of the space available to deal with scientific and technical subjects.

Knowledge of anaesthetics was an off-shoot of the work done on drugs. Its diffusion along with pharmaceutical developments resulted from the extensive printing of medical textbooks. The Two Sungs encouraged this process even to the extent of a state subsidy for the more popular works. In the fifty years prior to the fall of K'ai Feng it has been estimated that no less than one thousand medical officials were responsible for the health of the Empire.

The Painting Academy, founded during the Five Dynasties period as a department of the Imperial University, was made an independent institution by Emperor Sung Hui-tsung, who reigned from 1101 until 1126. This ruler elevated the social status of the visual artist by introducing painting as one of the examinations for entry to the civil service. The examination question, closely modelled upon that in the Literary Examination, consisted of a line or phrase taken from the Classics or a well-known poem, which had to be illustrated in an original way. Ingenuity of composition was rewarded rather than any ability in reproducing a likeness, an exact copy of natural objects. Such a literary approach to painting was not without its dangers and might have led to mere cleverness had not that Chinese preference for reticence led the artist away from self-indulgent complexity. Another safeguard during the Two Sungs was that neither the Court nor the official class could dominate creative effort when major artists were working at a distance from society. There were, for instance, leading painters living as monks or, like the T'ang poet Li Po, simply wandering the provinces.

Apart from enhancing the imperial gardens at K'ai Feng and encouraging the *shih* to take up painting, Emperor Sung Hui-tsung produced a number of fine bird-and-flower paintings. In these compositions, popular during the Northern Sung dynasty, the emperor excelled and led something like a movement. But it was in another form that Chinese art found its perfect mode of expression. That is the painting of landscape, which had begun to replace figure and animal painting as the pre-eminent form towards the end of the Five Dynasties; it was fostered as much by Ch'an Buddhism as the mystical elements in Taoism. China itself abounded with splendid natural scenery, long enjoyed by the Chinese people; but it was the T'ang poets who fully articulated the pleasures of the hermit, remote from the dust of cities, so that a romantic appreciation of the landscape became a general sentiment amongst the literary classes. Between the painters of the Northern Sung and the Southern Sung there was a difference of attitude. The few surviving landscapes of Li Cheng (late tenth century), Fan K'uan (*c.* 990–1030) and Kuo Hsi (1020–90) reflect the austere countryside of North China. Wintry scenes inspired them, Fan K'uan's *Abbey in the Snowy Mountain* being deservedly the

THE SUNG
PAINTERS

most famous. Yet the brushwork of Kuo Hsi when combined with one of his daring compositions produces an inimitable expression of natural beauty. One is astonished by the harsh splendour of *A Scene in Clouds and Mists*.

A softer, warmer landscape appears in the paintings of the Southern Sung dynasty. Mei Fei (1051–1107), the younger contemporary of Kuo Hsi, was the precursor of the later school. He had an official career, spending a number of years in Kiangnan, and he exhibited a fastidiousness that verged on madness. A phobia for dirt caused him to wash his hands and change his clothes with alarming frequency. But he was a close friend of Su Tung-p'o, with whom he wrote marvellous calligraphy, and his *Mountains, Clouds and Pinetrees* has a serenity that beggars description. Its style, the antithesis of Fan K'uan's, depends on liberal use of water. In this painting, too, we can readily observe the Chinese treatment of perspective, odd to Western eyes which have been trained to see things from a single point. In China there never was a Brunelleschi to insist upon scientific perspective; therefore, the Chinese painter was free to imagine himself to be looking down from the top of a small hill in order that he might gain a 'total' vision of every part. Another surprise about Chinese art may be the restricted palette, the sparse use of colour. But the saying, 'Black is ten colours', indicates the importance of the brush, whose cursive line gives rhythm and vitality to the composition. Skill with the brush, regarded as an art in calligraphy since the Later Han, comprised the 'bones' of Chinese painting. For simplicity the works of Ma Yuan (1190–1224) spring to mind; often he would manage with ink on silk.

The disaster of 1126 has cost us all but a few paintings of the Northern Sung masters, but fortunately Kuo Hsi left a record of his views on landscape. His *Advice on Landscape Painting* explains how it is human nature to desire flight from the rush and tear of society in order to see 'immortals hidden in the clouds'. But filial duty and social responsibilities prevent most people from seeking peace in retirement amid forests, streams and hills. To salve the troubled mind through the sights and sounds of Nature, the artist recreates in his landscape painting what nourishes the secluded hermit. Thus, Kuo Hsi believes, 'mountains and water' can be brought to the living room of any house, providing the observer adopts the correct frame of mind. The popularity of paintings in Chinese homes in Hangchow was referred to in *The Travels*, but Marco Polo's aesthetic interest does not seem to have been awakened by what he saw. He must have missed the landscapes of Hsia Kuei (1180–1230), the one painter it is impossible to miss in a discussion of Sung art. Hsia Kuei, whose style has affinities with that of Ma Yuan, was the most celebrated artist in an unrivalled era. In his scrolls, usually long panoramas measuring many feet, the romantic spirit of Chinese art is fulfilled. His fiery brushwork has remained the admiration of later generations, though there have been critics of his romantic impetuosity. The famous *Distant View of Rivers and Hills* subsumes the Chinese attitude to Nature – the only sensible one for the descendants of P'an-ku's fleas.

LITERATURE   *Ku wen*, classical prose, was continued by Ou-yang Hsiu (1007–72), whom Su Tung-p'o compared to Han Yu. Through his historical writings and essays the Classical Prose Movement was firmly established as standard for the *shih*.

Mountains, Clouds and Pinetrees by Mei Fei.

'Nowadays,' Ou-yang Hsiu noted with satisfaction, 'everyone studies the writing style of Han Yu. It is indeed a great phenomenon.' Ou-yang Hsiu came from the same area of Kiangnan as Wang An-shih and had befriended the younger scholar until his reforms made him a political opponent. The other outstanding prose-writer of the day, Ssu-ma Kuang (1018–86), was also a bitter critic of the 'New Laws', and his monumental work, *Tzu-chih T'ung-chien* (*History As A Mirror*), whose historical span reminds the Western reader of Gibbon, traces the history of China from 403 BC to AD 959, a period of 1,362 years. *History As A Mirror*, written between 1067 and 1084, eventually became the source for orthodox historiography, and the most read history of China in the simplified version of Yuan Shu (1131–1205).

It was during the T'ang Empire that Chinese poetry first scaled the peaks. Empress Wu had introduced poetical composition into the *k'o-chu*, or examination system, thereby concentrating the minds of the *shih* on poetry. In a similar way the Sung emphasis on educational attainment allowed an uprush of creative energies: not only were there more poets writing in the Two Sungs than the T'ang but they were even more prolific. Some nine thousand poems by Lu Yu (1125–1209) survive, and even Wang An-shih has to his credit four hundred poems above the thousand left by Li Po. Su Shih (1036–1101), usually known as Su Tung-p'o, was a poet, calligrapher and painter. There was no definite boundary between poetry and pictorial art – one complemented the other. Su Tung-p'o's official career foundered badly; he was harassed under the ministry of Wang An-shih, not enjoying senior posts till after the death of Emperor Sung Shen-tsung in 1085. As governor of Hangchow, he initiated there and in Canton the installation of water-mains, large bamboo trunks both caulked and lacquered. Holes were provided at intervals for freeing blockages, and ventilator tapes for the removal of trapped air. In 1097 further differences with leading officials caused his banishment to Hainan, the island off the southern coast of China. Recalled to K'ai Feng in 1101, he contracted dysentery on the journey and died at the age of sixty-five.

Another aspect of Sung literature was the taste for collections of anecdotes, a fashion dating from T'ang times, to which printing and the spread of literacy gave encouragement. The two roots of the Chinese short story, often fantastic and humorous, were anecdotes found in the writings of classical philosophers and cautionary tales used to explain the Buddhist scriptures. The fable is common to every civilization, but by the Chinese brush it was endowed with something more innate than a literary sense. Fable and proverb seem to isolate the basic elements of life, giving at the same time a feeling of the unending continuity of human affairs. The persistent intrusion of humour, the irrepressible smile that has greeted so many tales of apparently hopeless circumstances and futile endeavour, depends on affection and awe of the eccentricity in human character. It both humbles and exalts the individual at once. The *shih* had begun to collect and edit such oral literature towards the end of the Classical Age. *Hsiao-lin* (*The Forest of Laughter*), compiled by Han Tan-chun, an official of Wei in the third century BC, was one of the earliest collections. Examples of this genre are to be found at the end of this section.

It was the exclusion of the *shih* from the imperial civil service after the Mongol invasion that stimulated the development of two new forms of literature, namely the play and the novel. Preoccupation with the Classics was

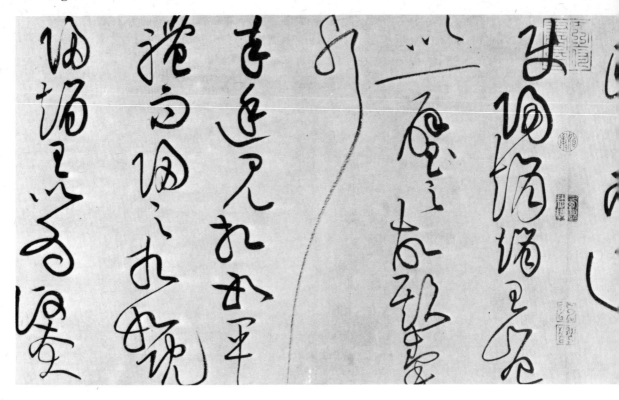

A marvellous example of wild cursive script dating from the Northern Sung period. This detail of the calligraphy of Huang T'ing-chien (1045–1105) is in ink on paper.

relaxed while the examinations were discontinued. Scholars found themselves free to venture beyond the confines of history, philosophy and poetry and they took up the popular play and novel. A kind of creative split occurred in Chinese culture, which lasted till 1911. Court patronage in the Ming dynasty (1368–1644) and the Manchu (1644–1911) was inclined to be traditional, antiquarian and backward-looking, the officials wistfully recalling the lost splendours of K'ai Feng and Ch'ang-an, while the more vital and exciting artists worked in the provinces.

The great novels were to be *The Romance of the Three Kingdoms* by Lo Kuan-chung (late Yuan dynasty); *All Men Are Brothers*, a story woven out of popular Sung tales concerning the exploits of a certain Sung Chiang and his bandits, and possibly edited by Lo Kuan-chung; the anonymous *Chin Ping Mei* (*Golden Lotus*), first printed at Soochow in 1610 and immediately acclaimed as the masterpiece of the novel of manners; and, the fantasy, *Pilgrimage to the West*, by Wu Cheng-en (1505–80). The last book illustrates the colloquial power of both new forms because it is a novel which draws on the folk stories and plays that had collected around the pilgrimage to India of Tripitaka, the historical Hsuan-tsang. Possibly it is the most widely read book in Chinese literature. The knockabout humour may surprise Western readers, though the wisdom of laughter was appreciated by Chuang-tzu long before the Ch'in Empire and the sceptical tradition of Confucian thought discovered in ridicule a potent weapon against religious fanaticism. Moreover, a sense of humour has always been something very close to the Chinese heart. In literature it ranged from the Rabelaisian to the Shavian. To conclude our treatment of literature

here are several examples of humorous tales from the Ming period, when the most famous collections after the manner of Han Tan-chun were made.

Love of Wine
A bibber, dreaming that he was warming some excellent wine, woke up. He said, regretfully, 'I should have drunk it cold'.

Husbands' Lib
When all the henpecked husbands assembled to discuss what should be their proper rights, some people tried to scare these men by saying that their wives had got wind of the meeting and were gathering to come presently and beat them up. Immediately they dispersed, except for a single husband. He alone remained seated, apparently unafraid. However, on closer examination it was realized that he had died of fright.

Shooting the Tiger
One man was carried away by a tiger. His son tried to shoot the tiger with a bow and arrow. From the tiger's mouth the father shouted, 'Aim at the legs. Don't spoil the hide!'

The Monk Is Here
A monk committed an offence and was arrested by an official. On the way to the law court they had to spend a night at an inn. During the evening the wily monk persuaded his captor to drink himself under the table. Then he shaved off the official's hair and made a getaway. In the morning the official woke from his drunken stupor and looked throughout the inn for the monk, but he was nowhere to be seen. Pausing to think he happened to touch his head and found it bald.

'The monk is here,' he exclaimed, 'but where am I?'

In Praise of Farting
A most distinguished scholar died and found himself standing before the King of the Underworld. When the monarch accidentally farted, the *shih* sang a eulogy of the fart in endless verses. At one point he declaimed:

> Let regal steam free passage find
> From golden buttocks raised behind,
> As when such sounds of music soft
> Of organ pipes and strings doth waft;
> Such fragrance is not held a stain
> Though quivering scent the nostrils strain;
> While rapt in thrall thy servant low
> Exults, o'erwhelmed by massy blow.

So pleased was the King of the Underworld by the poetry that he extended the scholar's life for ten years. The *shih* returned to the world of the living and at length the time came for him to leave again. When on his second arrival the King of the Underworld asked who the scholar was, one of the little devils answered, 'He's the Crap Poet!'

A mongol archer on horseback by an anonymous artist of the fifteenth
century; ink and colour on paper with imperial seals in the top corner.

11

The Mongol Conquest
1279–1365

The Mongols ruled over China for about a century. Though the beginning of the Yuan or Mongol Empire is considered to be 1279 by Chinese historians, there has been a Mongol dynasty established in North China since the accession of Kubilai Khan, and from 1263 Peking, not Karakorum, was the centre of Mongol world power. For Chinese civilization the period was one of partial eclipse, a temporary snuffing out of the cultural activities associated with the imperial administration; in contrast with the brilliance of K'ai Feng and Hangchow, it was, inevitably, an opaque era.

The Mongol Terror was unleashed on the world by Genghiz Khan, who laid down the rule that any resistance shown to Mongol arms should be punished by total extermination; it proved an effective deterrent. He was notoriously devoid of pity. On occasions his fury extended to even animals and plants. When in 1222 his favourite grandson, Mutugen, fell at the siege of Kakrak, a fortress city in Bamiyan, the once famous Buddhist centre in the Hindu Kush, Genghiz vowed to kill every living soul in that rich and populous valley. Accordingly, total destruction was visited upon the unfortunate region. Such ruthlessness was almost a natural instinct to the Mongols who delighted in ferocious actions. 'The greatest joy,' Genghiz once said, 'is to conquer one's enemies, to pursue them, to seize their belongings, to see their families in tears, to ride their horses, and to possess their daughters and wives.'

Every Mongol tribesman was a soldier. Between campaigns both men and horses were kept fit and in constant training by means of seasonal hunting expeditions, personally supervised by the Khan himself. Physical endurance was most prized. Concerning the original vigour of the Mongols – 'at the present day they are much corrupted' – Marco Polo wrote,

> Each man has, on an average, eighteen horses and mares, and when that which they ride is fatigued, they change it for another. They are provided with small tents made of felt, under which they shelter themselves against rain. Should circumstances render it necessary, in the execution of a duty that requires despatch, they can march for ten days together without dressing victuals, during which time they subsist upon the blood drawn from their horses, each man opening a vein and drinking from his own cattle.

Slaves performed the few domestic duties the restless Mongols considered necessary. The continuous military activity started by Genghiz forced them to rely more and more on servile labour, even in the crucial task of cattle-breeding. When the occasion warranted, both women and children entered the fray and acted as military auxiliaries. Personal hygiene was never a Mongol virtue. They were unkempt, custom forbidding them to wash themselves or to have an article of clothing washed in running water. These people of the Mongol tribes, whose entire population may not have reached two millions, were welded by Genghiz Khan into the most efficient war machine the world had ever seen. At most there were three hundred thousand Mongol males of fighting age, but this horde had several inestimable advantages over rival armies. The Mongol warriors were unswervingly loyal and obedient to their leaders: the *yasa*, or military code, prescribed death for nearly all breaches of discipline. In these fierce tribesmen too, Genghiz possessed a highly trained and mobile cavalry. 'Their horses,' *The Travels* records, 'are so well broken-in to quick changes of movement, that upon the signal given, they instantly turn in every direction; and by these rapid manoeuvres many victories have been obtained.' Not least the Mongol horde proved capable of adopting military technology from other countries, especially the Kin and Sung Empires. They supplemented their forces with conscripts from conquered states and put to good use the new weapons these soldiers brought with them. Polish chroniclers relate how at the battle of Wahlstadt in 1241 the Mongols employed a smoke-producing device to cause disarray among the combined forces of the Poles and the Teutonic Knights.

What the Mongol onslaught represents is the greatest clash in world history between the nomadic culture of the steppe and the civilization of intensive agriculture. There is a revealing incident reported in *The Secret History of the Mongols*, commissioned by Genghiz's successor Ogodei (khan, 1229–41). During one of his campaigns in Central Asia, Genghiz Khan questioned two learned men from Khiva, in Turkestan, about the puzzling phenomenon of the city. To the Mongol leader, the city was something alien, a threat to the world of the nomads, whose power during the thirteenth century for the first and last time in their history came very close to a world imperium. But to Genghiz, comprehension was never acceptance; cities remained natural targets for plunder and destruction.

When the Mongols overran those provinces of China under the control of the Kin Empire and the Hsia kingdom, the nomad fear and hatred of a settled pattern of life was indulged to the utmost. The brunt of this fury was borne by Hopei, Kansu and 'the land within the passes': the last, the ancient seat of Chinese civilization, ceased to have any cultural importance from this time onwards. The decimated *nung* were no longer able to maintain the extensive hydraulic works, and many northern frontier towns had to be abandoned. Yet one voice was raised against Mongol devastation and, luckily for China and the world, his words convinced Genghiz.

Here is an account of the discussion which led up to this momentous alteration of policy:

When Genghiz Khan invaded the countries of the West, he had neither baggage train nor regular supplies. When he entered China, his Mongol advisers said, 'This country is useless. Exterminate all the Chinese. Turn the land back to pasture. Then, we can graze our cattle.' The Mongol leader was about to implement these proposals, when Yelu Ch'u-ts'ai intervened.

The face of a tomb figure, probably an official. The earthenware body is covered with a white slip and painted with coloured pigments. It dates from the T'ang dynasty.

OVERLEAF A bird-and-flower painting by Emperor Sung Hui-tsung, who died in Kin captivity after the fall of K'ai Feng (1126). This emperor was renowned for both his painting and calligraphy.

'Now that you have conquered everywhere under Heaven and all the riches within the Four Seas,' he told Genghiz Khan, 'you can have everything you want. You should tax land and commerce and should make profits on wine, salt and iron, and the produce of mountains and marshes. In this way the revenue for a single year will equal half a million ounces of silver, eighty thousand rolls of silk and four hundred thousand *piculs* of grain. . . .' Genghiz Khan agreed that it should happen.

Yelu Ch'u-ts'ai, a Khitan noble descended from the royal house of Liao, had been summoned by Genghiz to Mongolia in 1218. The khan expected that such a nobleman would welcome service in the Mongol cause because of the enmity between Khitan and Kin. But Yelu Ch'u-ts'ai spoke respectfully of the Kin, to whom both his father and grandfather had rendered loyal service. Pleased by such rectitude and honesty, Genghiz found a place for him in his retinue. The Khitan nobleman became his secretary-astrologer and through his administrative talents he finally rose to become Head of the Secretariat under Ogodei Khan.

The attitude adopted by Yelu Ch'u-ts'ai on his arrival in Karakorum and expressed in his later advice about state affairs bears the unmistakable stamp of a Confucian training. Profoundly influenced by Chinese civilization, Yelu Ch'u-ts'ai made it his personal duty to mitigate the harsh rule of the Great Khan and to provide an administration for the unwieldy nomad state. Whilst Yelu Ch'u-ts'ai was not slow to play on Mongol cupidity in an emergency like the extermination debate, he hoped that wisdom and learning would triumph at last. In his diary he tells us that he hoped Genghiz Khan would accept the teachings of the Three Sages – Lao-tzu, Confucius and the Buddha. This was the reason he supported Ch'an-ch'un, whom he 'also intended to be the advocate of Confucianism and Buddhism'. Ch'an-ch'un, a leading Taoist, had attracted the notice of the Mongol Court because of a rumour that he was in possession of the elixir of life. At this period in China it was generally believed that the teachings of the Buddha, Lao-tzu and Confucius had a common origin. To follow the Three Ways was 'to stand firmly in the world like the three legs of a tripod'. In spite of Ch'an-ch'un turning out to be a disappointment because of his use of the acquaintanceship with Genghiz to further the interests of his own sect, Yelu Ch'u-ts'ai did achieve successes at Court. On the election of Ogodei Khan he introduced a number of Chinese procedures designed to stabilize the dynasty, but more important for the administration of the provinces, he opened the secretariat to Chinese scholars by having examinations restarted in 1237. This measure alone freed a thousand *shih* from Mongol slavery. But agitation from the anti-Chinese faction soon brought about the end of the practice, and the influence of Yelu Ch'u-ts'ai on government policy ceased in 1239 when tax-farming was permitted by Moslem businessmen.

Yelu Ch'u-ts'ai died of a broken heart four years later. The Yuan dynasty, which he believed had the Heavenly Mandate, went on to become a non-Chinese régime, supported by officials of foreign origin. Had the wish expressed in his diary been fulfilled, the Mongols might have saved themselves from the great Chinese rebellion that was to drive them out of the country in 1368.

A gilded silver plate of the T'ang dynasty. The two birds, possibly phoenix, with feathers in their beaks, symbolize matrimonial harmony and good fortune.

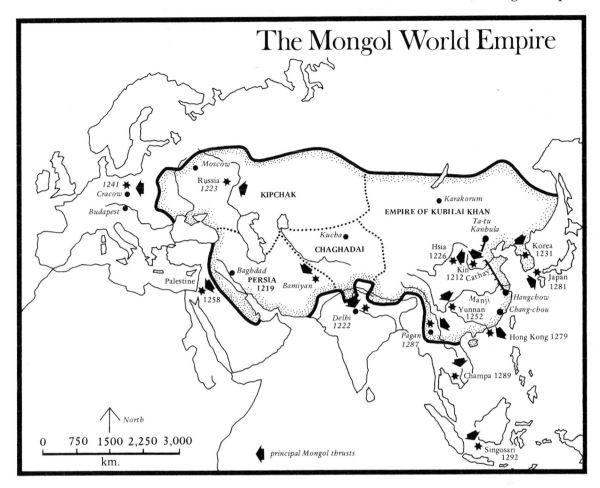

The Mongol World Empire

1241 Cracow ✶

Budapest

Moscow

Russia 1223

KIPKCHAK

Karakorum

EMPIRE OF KUBILAI KHAN
Ta-tu Kanbula

Kucha

CHAGHADAI

Baghdad
PERSIA 1219
Bamiyan

Palestine

1258

Hsia 1226

Kin 1212 Cathay

Korea 1231

Japan 1281

Manji Yunnan 1252

Hangchow
Chang-chou

Delhi 1222

Pagan 1287

Hong Kong 1279

Champa 1289

↑ *North*

0   750 1500 2,250 3,000
km.

◀ *principal Mongol thrusts*

Singosari 1292

THE MONGOL
WORLD EMPIRE

The authority of Kubilai Khan (1260–94) extended in theory over a unified World Empire, stretching from Budapest to Peking and from Baghdad to Canton. In practice the Mongol territories spanning Europe and Asia, encompassed so many diverse peoples and places that Genghiz Khan had been compelled to divide it into four *ulus*, or dominions, whose lesser khans gradually asserted their own authority. The four khanates were China, Chaghadai (Central Asia), Persia and Kipchak (West Asia and Russia). Kubilai Khaghan, 'the khan of khans', remained nominal head of state until the conversion of the Western Mongols to Islam in 1295 completed the process of disintegration, because the Muslim khans were unwilling to recognize the Buddhist Kubilai or his successors. The westward sweep of the Mongol hordes had hesitated at the borders of Christian Europe on two occasions. Domestic politics stopped the Mongols exploiting the 1223 raid on Russia for permanent advantage. Then, in the campaigns of 1239–42, Mongol arms were halted by the news of the death of Ogodei. The Mongol commander-in-chief, Batu, was anxious to return to Karakorum for the election of the new khan. Batu's forces retired after sacking Sandomir, Cracow, Budapest and Zagreb, turning back from the walls of Vienna. Should the Mongols have pressed home their attack on Europe, at this moment in time, it is hard to imagine how

Genghiz Khan, the instigator of the Mongol Terror.

A lama prayer-wheel in Peking; a legacy of the Yuan interest in Tibetan Buddhism.

any effective resistance could have been made. Only in the Holy Land were the Mongols unable to have things all their own way. In 1258 the Egyptian sultans managed to halt their encroachment there.

Despite the growth of internal divisions within the Mongol World Empire, the reign of Kubilai Khan became a legend in the West. Overland travel was comparatively safe and foreigners with skills or special abilities were welcomed in Cathay. The reports of the wonders they saw there fed our ancestors' avid imaginations; a fantastic tapestry was thus woven around this monarch. Marco Polo, whose chronicle we shall examine in the next section, was one of these travellers. Another was Friar William of Rubruck, a Franciscan missionary in Mongolia between 1253 and 1255; he was taken aback by the religious tolerance evident at Karakorum. What he failed to realize was the motive behind this Mongol outlook, namely that holymen were thought to be capable of obtaining good fortune and longevity for those mentioned in their prayers. Kubilai later embraced Buddhism under the influence of his Tibetan adviser, Phagspa, but he continued this policy of toleration. His recognition of Christianity in 1289 was no more than what had been customary practice in China for the previous millennium, with the difference that the basis of this action was superstition. Campaigns undertaken by the Yuan dynasty met with mixed success. Yunnan and Burma were easily annexed, but defeats were sustained in South-east Asia and Japan. Against Champa, modern South Vietnam and Cambodia, the Mongol expeditionary force made no headway at all: it found the guerrilla tactics employed by the Champs utterly debilitating. Fever and jungle warfare hastened a Mongol withdrawal into a frantic retreat, which has been compared with the experience of Western powers in the area since 1945. The invasion of Japan was a disaster. A violent storm wrecked the invasion fleet of 1281 and those warriors who managed to wade ashore were cut down by the flashing swords of the Japanese *samurai*. A similar though less complete reverse overtook the sea-borne expedition against Java in 1292. King Kertanagara of Singosari, then predominant on the island, had disdained to offer homage to Peking, and the Mongol failure against Champa in 1289 encouraged his independence. Though King Kertanagara lost his own life in a revolt prior to the Mongol attack, his kingdom survived through a mixture of guerrilla warfare and double-dealing.

The Yuan Empire was already showing signs of decay before the death of Kubilai Khan. The destructiveness of the initial Mongol advances had impoverished whole provinces: one official census of those liable to taxation gives the figure of 58,837,711, a marked drop. Though the government paid attention to 'water benefits', notably in the improvement of the Grand Canal between the Yellow River and Peking and irrigation schemes in Yunnan under the direction of the Muslim governor, Said Ajall Shams al-Din, the administration was fundamentally unconcerned with the welfare of its Chinese subjects, and most officials were corrupt and unreliable. The *shih* and the *nung* discovered themselves united in opposition to the Yuan dynasty. In 1315 the belated restarting of the examination system for entry to the civil service failed to rally support from the long-excluded *shih*. Succession troubles disturbed the peace, and a series of mediocre emperors, displaying the characteristic Mongol weaknesses for drink and the harem, were found incapable of handling the rising tide of discontent. Active in popular opposition was a secret society known as the 'White Lotus', whose doctrines were an amalgam of Taoist and Buddhist cosmology. It was centred on the Huai River valley, the scene of repeated famines in the 1350s. This movement was suppressed by the authorities but others arose in the Yang-tze Valley and Hopei. From 1348 open rebellion was continuous with various groups jostling for position. Chu Yuan-chang, the founder of the Ming dynasty, eventually destroyed all of his Chinese rivals and drove the Mongols out of the country in 1368. His leadership was of the highest quality – a man of humble origins, he managed to bring into concert the *shih* and the *nung*, upon whose cooperation Chinese society always depended. He demolished the Yuan Empire, exposing the hollowness behind the façade of legend. The last Yuan ruler fled to Mongolia, whither a Ming army under general Hsu Ta marched in 1372, sacking Karakorum and pursuing the remnants of the Mongol horde into the fastness of Siberia. A hundred years after the death of the last of the Sung another Chinese ruler sat on the dragon throne.

MARCO POLO AND THE WESTERN IDEA OF CATHAY

After his return to Italy, to whose cuisine he probably added spaghetti, Marco Polo was taken prisoner in the war between Venice and Genoa. In a Genoese prison he dictated to a writer of romantic fiction named Rusticiano what he had observed in China and many other countries he had visited. Just under half of the space in *The Travels* is devoted to the Mongols and the Yuan Empire. Though Marco Polo does not penetrate very deeply into conditions in China, the impact of his narrative on medieval Europe was tremendous for the reason that he gave a simple, eye-witness account of a more advanced civilization, something which was credited with great difficulty in the contemporary European mind. There were other visitors to East Asia during the Mongol supremacy, but *The Travels*, by an intriguing combination of traveller's tale and storyteller's craft, became the Baedeker for Cathay and Manzi. It opened a window onto another world, whose magnificence and splendour dazzled those who peered out from the confines of Western Europe. Even today, the popularity of Marco Polo's book has not wholly diminished. He remains the stock-in-trade of the history teacher, and in the memory of many people he is permanently linked with China, just as Kubilai Khan is sometimes thought of as a Chinese emperor. *The Travels* are valuable to the historian of China, as they furnish details of the Mongol occupation, but they contain only an aspect of the early civilization of China. To round off our study of this ancient tradition we shall examine a few of the things that Marco Polo remembered about his seventeen years as a Yuan civil servant when he lay in the Genoese cell. By setting each one of them in its proper historical context, there will be an opportunity to reflect on the greatness of the civilization which the Mongol invasion so rudely interrupted.

Marco Polo's account of Peking is a good starting-point because it was the first city within the borders of China that he visited. 'The great city of Kanbula' as Peking was known to the Mongols, contained the winter residence of Kubilai Khan; '. . . here, on the southern side of the new city, is the site of his vast palace. . . .' Enclosed by two outer walls, one eight miles square and the other six miles square, the inner wall of the palace enclosure was:

A pottery figure of an actor, dating from the Yuan dynasty; excavated at Chia-tso, Honan, in 1963.

> . . . of great thickness, and its height is full twenty-five feet. The battlements or crenated parapets are all white. . . . Within these walls, which constitute the boundary of four miles, stands the palace of the grand khan, the most extensive that has ever been known. It reaches from the northern to the southern wall, leaving only a court where persons of rank and the military guards pass and repass. It has no upper floor, but the roof is very lofty. . . . The inside of the roof is contrived in such a manner that nothing besides gilding and painting represents itself to the eye. . . . The palace contains a number of separate chambers, all highly beautiful and so admirably disposed that it seems impossible to suggest any improvement to the system of their arrangement. . . . Not far from the palace, on the northern side and about a bow-shot distance from the surrounding wall, is an artificial mount of earth, the height of which is a full hundred paces, and the circuit at the base about a mile. It is clothed with the most beautiful evergreen trees; for whenever his majesty receives information of a handsome tree growing in any place, he causes it to be dug up, with all its roots and the earth about them, and however large and heavy it may be, he has it transported by means of elephants to this mount, and adds it to the verdant collection. From this perpetual verdure it has acquired the appellation of the Green Mount. On its summit is erected an ornamental pavilion. . . .

Nearby were two artificial lakes, used for 'watering the cattle' and raising fish. Across a stream stood 'a new-built city', Ta-tu, in which all the Chinese were obliged to live, because astrologers had warned that they were 'destined to

Mongol armies attack a Chinese fortress; a sixteenth-century Indian miniature from the court of Akbar the Great.

become rebellious to his authority'. The new city was 'of a form perfectly square, and twenty-four miles in extent, each of its sides being neither more nor less than six miles. . . . The whole plan of the city was regularly laid out by line, and the streets in general are consequently so straight, that when a person ascends the walls over one of the gates, and looks right forward, he can see the gate opposite to him on the other side of the city. . . .' The dwellings were 'handsome, with corresponding courts and gardens', and 'the whole interior of the city is disposed in squares, so as to resemble a chess-board, and planned out with a degree of precision and beauty impossible to describe'.

Kanbula, 'the city of the sovereign', followed the classical Chinese pattern for the city, a rectangular layout on a north–south axis. That the Mongols adopted what had been normal practice in China from Chou times is illustrated by the Ming attitude to Peking. In a reaction against the unplanned, sprawling cities of Kiangnan, such as Hangchow and Chang-chou, the Chinese dynasty that followed the Mongols transferred the capital northwards to Peking and had little more to do than extend the existing plan of Kubilai's foundation. The size of city planning involved in Ta-tu baffled Marco Polo: there was no Western metropolis which approached its dimensions. About the presence of the bell-tower in the centre of the city, Marco Polo, the citizen of the Venetian Republic, was in no doubt that it resulted from 'the declaration of astrologers'. Uninformed of the history of Chinese town-planning, he did not appreciate that strict government control of urban populations dated from the reign of Ch'in Shih Huang-ti. Resentment of Mongol rule certainly existed amongst the 'Cathaians', but Marco Polo tends to attribute it to specific examples of maladministration, like the 'acts of injustice or the flagrant wickedness' of individual officials. He records the plot directed against the Saracen Achmac, and the punishment inflicted upon this corrupt minister and his sons by Kubilai. Besides the concentric series of enclosures around the Yuan palace, common from the Sui and T'ang periods, there is so much in Marco Polo's outline which recalls Chinese official architecture, like the Green Mount, an obvious adaptation of the Chinese garden. Whereas Emperor Sung Hui-tsung had ransacked the Empire for gnarled rocks, or little 'mountains', Kubilai Khan had a live forest of 'handsome' trees moved to cover his artificial eminence. Again the two lakes, connected by a rivulet, must have had both aesthetic and practical functions.

Although *The Travels* deal at length with such Mongol pleasures as hunting and feasting, there is a record of various towns and cities through which Marco Polo passed on his tours of duty. It is in these brief descriptions that many of the features of early Chinese civilization are mentioned. At Kanbula he noted the issue of paper money by the mint, which 'may truly be said to possess the secret of the alchemists'. But he seems unaware of the adverse influence this almost unrestricted practice was having on the national economy. One of the reasons for the alacrity with which the Yuan dynasty issued notes may have been the drain of wealth to Tibet. The Tibetan form of Buddhism became the official religion through the activities of the lama Phagspa, who died in 1280. By 1291 there were 42,318 temples, and in 1322 when copper for coins was becoming very scarce, a three-hundred-ton statue of the Buddha was cast for a temple near Kanbula. Even the *p'ing chang* still existed in some measure, but state intervention in the grain market alone could not redress the economic

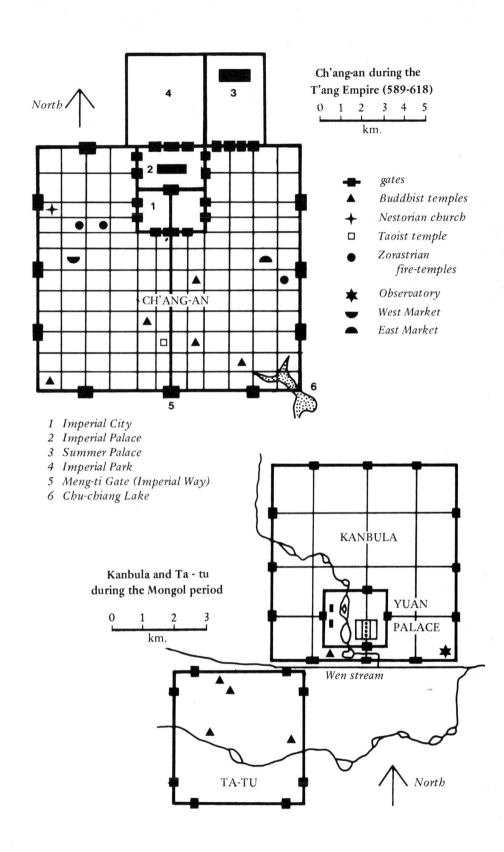

North

Ch'ang-an during the T'ang Empire (589-618)

0 1 2 3 4 5
km.

CH'ANG-AN

gates

▲ Buddhist temples

✦ Nestorian church

☐ Taoist temple

● Zorastrian
  fire-temples

★ Observatory

◗ West Market

◖ East Market

1 Imperial City
2 Imperial Palace
3 Summer Palace
4 Imperial Park
5 Meng-ti Gate (Imperial Way)
6 Chu-chiang Lake

**Kanbula and Ta - tu
during the Mongol period**

0 1 2 3
km.

KANBULA

YUAN
PALACE

Wen stream

TA-TU

North

229

imbalance caused by the acquisitiveness of the lamas. Charity, not an original custom of the Mongols, was learned from the teachings of Buddhism, though characteristically Kubilai overdid it.

The populousness of China was not missed by Marco Polo, nor was the cultural function of a walled-city-in-the-countryside. He says, 'A degree of civilization prevails amongst all the people of this country, in consequence of their frequent intercourse with the towns, which are numerous and but little distance from each other.' They acted as centres for commerce and manufacture, and often housed sizeable foreign communities. At Ka-chan-fu, possibly Ch'ang-an, he encountered Nestorian Christians, Turks from Asia Minor and Saracens. This city was then active in silk production. The mixture of peoples must have given Marco Polo reason to reflect on the xenophobia of some European cities, though China had not barred settlement to outsiders from earliest times. Taking the mountainous road to Szechuan from Ch'ang-an on one occasion, he was impressed by Li Ping's irrigation scheme in the countryside around Cheng-tu, where 'the city is watered by many considerable streams, which descending from the distant mountains, surround and pass through it in a variety of directions'. The antiquity of these public works is not recorded in *The Travels*: they had been in service for a millennium and a half when Marco Polo arrived. In the same way he seems to regard the Grand Canal as a contemporary feat of engineering. Looking at the section near Yangchow, he says it was 'a wide and deep canal which the grand khan has caused to be dug, in order that vessels may pass from one great river to the other, and from the province of Manji by water, as far as Kanbula, without making any part of the voyage by sea'.

Here was something special, a 'magnificent work . . . deserving of admiration', the grand trunk canal of the Chinese waterways system. But Marco Polo never knew that in far distant times the first steps had been taken by Yu the Great Engineer. Myriad vessels plied their trade and on all transactions in the port of Zaiton, or Chuang-chou, there was a ten per cent tax on cargoes, whence 'the grand khan derives a vast revenue'. The pepper trade alone 'is so considerable, that what is carried to Alexandria, to supply the western parts of the world, is trifling in comparison, perhaps not more than the hundredth part'. This tax on the *shang* and the 'ample revenue' obtained by the government from the manufacture of salt did not lead the Venetian to inquire into the recent history of commercial enterprise. Neither Wang An-shih nor Yelu Ch'u-ts'ai were known to him.

Let us be grateful to Marco Polo for his readable chronicle, and admit the dangers that intrepid travellers like him faced on journeys to the East in those days, but not for one moment should we be content with the picture of the early civilization of China that he offers. In order to enter into the spirit of that ancient tradition, so modern and advanced when the Mongols invaded, it is necessary to have, as it were, an inside view, and to look through the eyes of its own philosophers, scientists, artists and historians. It has been our aim in the foregoing pages to provide such a perspective without falling into the trap of over-partiality. If we have helped to identify certain features of early Chinese culture missed by the Venetian traveller, and still often lamentably unknown to many Western readers, then perhaps another window has been opened on a world of human endeavour and achievement which vanished long ago.

Epilogue

The early civilization of China, it can be said, ended during the Yuan Empire. The Mongol invasion was a definite rupture in the pattern of Chinese history. The full extent of the destructiveness and disruption was not evident to Marco Polo during the reign of Kubilai Khan because he lacked knowledge of the level to which civilization in China had attained prior to the capture of K'ai Feng and, later, Hangchow. On his tomb in 1398 the first Ming emperor, Hung-wu, had carved this piece of advice, 'Rule like the T'ang and the Sung'. His successors were to restore Chinese unity and tradition; they did so, but in the process of repair what we have termed the early phase of Chinese civilization disappeared. The Ming restoration, thorough if somewhat antiquarian, could not bypass the changes which had occurred in thirteenth and fourteenth centuries. Society was in the throes of a vast transformation during the Two Sungs, with the emergence of a cash economy, and the continued expansion of population under the Ming to an unprecedented one hundred and fifty millions put increasing strain on institutions as well as the means of production. By the middle of the fourteenth century eighty-five per cent of the people lived south of the Huai River, relegating the northern provinces to economic obscurity in spite of the situation of the imperial capital at Peking. In the Ming Empire, the 'bright' age, Chinese civilization revived and continued along its own distinct path. There were new achievements in many fields, but for the first time since the Classical Age the levels of science and technology in China lagged behind those of other countries. Decline and self-elected isolation from the world marked the close of the Ming dynasty, the century before the Manchus conquered all of China (1682). Although these semi-nomadic people were rapidly assimilated as the Ch'ing dynasty, national resurgence had to await the coming of the twentieth century.

In this brief outline of the remainder of Chinese history we do not intend to denigrate in any measure the second phase of cultural development, which ran from the beginning of the Ming dynasty in 1368, through the final dissolution of the imperial system in 1911–12, to the massive political, social and economic reconstruction of the present day Peoples' Republic of China. This more recent period is another part of the history of Chinese civilization, less splendid perhaps, but no less fascinating.

All that needs to be said now concerns the magnificence of the early civilization of China, to which contemporary interest is turning in earnest. We welcome this long overdue attention from the West and confidently anticipate that ancient Chinese culture will be a constant delight to those who penetrate its mysteries.

A blue porcelain octagonal vase, with a lid, decorated with a striking dragon design dating from the Yuan dynasty. It was excavated at Pao-ting, Hopei, in 1964.

Chronology
from earliest times to the Ming dynasty

PREHISTORIC PERIOD   Old Stone Age *c.* 500,000–7000 BC

New Stone Age *c.* 7000–1500 BC

(Hsia dynasty *c.* 2000–1500 BC?)

BEGINNING OF HISTORICAL   Shang dynasty 1500–1027 BC

     PERIOD   Chou dynasty 1027–256 BC

Ch'un Ch'i period 722–481 BC

Warring States period 481–221 BC

IMPERIAL UNIFICATION   Ch'in dynasty 221–207 BC

Former Han dynasty 202 BC–AD 9

Hsin dynasty (Wang Mang's usurpation) AD 9–23

Later Han dynasty 25–220

AGE OF DISUNITY   Three Kingdoms 221–265

Shu-Han kingdom 221–264

Wei kingdom 220–265

Wu kingdom 220–280

Six Dynasties 265–587[1]

Western Tsin dynasty 265–316

Eastern Tsin dynasty 317–420

Liu Sung dynasty 420–479

Southern Ch'i dynasty 479–502

Liang dynasty 502–557

Ch'en dynasty 557–587

Tartar Partition 317–589

Toba Wei dynasty (Northern, 486–535; Eastern 534–543; Western 535–554) 386–554

Northern Ch'i dynasty 550–577

Northern Chou dynasty 557–581

REUNIFICATION	Sui dynasty 581–618	
	T'ang dynasty 618–906	
PARTITION	Five Dynasties[2] and the Ten Kingdoms 907–960	
		Later Liang dynasty 907–936
		Later T'ang dynasty 923–936
		Later Ch'in dynasty 936–948
		Later Han dynasty 946–950
		Later Chou dynasty 951–960
REUNIFICATION	The Two Sungs 960–1279	Liao kingdom 907–1125
		Northern Sung dynasty 960–1126
		Hsia kingdom 990–1226
		Kin Empire 1125–1212
		Southern Sung dynasty 1127–1279
MONGOL INVASION	Yuan dynasty 1279–1368	
CHINESE RECOVERY	Ming dynasty 1368–1644	

1. This period of division is also known as the Northern and Southern Dynasties, the distinction being drawn between the Tartar and Hsien Pei rulers of the North and the Chinese rulers of the South.
2. These houses were non-Chinese and mainly Turkic.

Notes and References

Names of authors listed below are always followed by a number in brackets corresponding to the full reference in the bibliography, e.g. 'Needham (3)'. When a translation made by a previous author is used without change in the text, the reference is given thus: 'tr. Waley'. As far as practical, details of the exact source of the Chinese original is indicated in front of such a citation. When a translation has been made by the authors, the ascription is: 'tr. auct.'. The references and notes are identified by folio and paragraph numbers.

INTRODUCTION

11.1 BRIDGES: Marsden (1), pp. 290–300.

CHAPTER 1: *Prehistoric and Feudal China. From earliest times to 771 BC*

15.1 PATTERN OF DIFFERENCES: Needham (1), p. 55. A detailed discussion of this question can be found in Chi Ch'ao-Ting (1).

15.2 STABLE ENTITIES: Elvin (1), p. 17.

15.3 FLOODS: Cheng Te-K'un (1), p. 66. The Yellow River valley is not an ideal area of settlement. 'In the course of the last 2,000 years, history witnessed 1,828 reports of flood and famine in the Huangho basin.'

16.3 SINKING OF COASTAL REGION: Goodrich (1), p. 42.

18.1 FERTILIZATION: Chi Ch'ao-Ting (1), p. 24.

18.2 PEKING MAN: Andersson (1), p. 142. This view can be found repeated in contemporary surveys of prehistory, like Watson (1), p. 2, though Pierre Teilhard de Chardin, the late French palaeontologist, was inclined to regard *Sinanthropus* (Peking Man) and *Pithecanthropus* (Java Man) as pre-hominids. This distinction was made rather from the standpoint of the anatomical progression of forms, because these early types do enable us 'to glimpse a whole wave of mankind' for the very important reason that they achieved a significant advance in mental ability. Indeed, he wrote, 'they were already, both of them, in the full sense of the word, intelligent beings', de Chardin (1), p. 195.

18.2 'ABOUNDED ... LIONS': Cheng Te-K'un (1), p. 18.

18.3 LAN T'IEN MAN: The brain capacity of Peking Man ranges from 850 to 1,220 cc., while Lan-t'ien Man only reaches 780 cc. In comparison modern man averages 1,350 cc.

18.4 PAN-P'O: Cheng Te-K'un (3). A concise explanation of the significance of Pan-p'o, first reported in 1962, is contained in this volume. The author notes, 'Among Pan-po-ts'un human skeletal remains there are 3 complete and 32 partially preserved skulls, 12 mandibles, 2 of which are in association with their skulls, 7 femora, 8 tibiae, 2 humeri and 1 radius. They represent at least 61 individuals, 51 adult males and 10 adult females. The stature of the former is estimated as around 169.45 centimetres and his cranial capacity ranges from 1,330 to 1,450 cc', pp. 20–1.

20.2 MIAO-TI-KOU: The Miao-ti-kou potter produced mainly fine red ware. Pots were all hand-made; the potter's wheel first appears in Lung-shan culture. At Miao-ti-kou three levels have been recognized and they represent three cultures: Miao-ti-kou I: Yang-shao culture; Miao-ti-kou II: Lung-shan culture; Miao-ti-kou III: Eastern Chou culture. *Ibid.*, p. 22.

20.2 ACCELERATED DEVELOPMENT: Watson, W. (1). p. 1: 'The cultural luminaries: the western Asiatic states of immemorial antiquity in the west, and in the east the civilization of bronze-age China, the state of the Shang and Chou kings on the middle course of the Yellow River. These were younger than the early civilizations in the west, but they outmatched their western compeers in speed and vigour of growth, and in some important technical inventions.'

22.4 'ALL ... REVEALED': Li (1), p. 34.

24.1 'SO ... PEOPLE': Legge and Waltham (1), p. 4.

24.2 'THE INUNDATING ... STREAMS': *Ibid.*, p. 31.

24.2 'THE FACT ... POLITICS': Chi Ch'ao-Ting (1), pp. 1–2.

24.3 SHANG DYNASTY: Needham (1), p. 88. See this volume for a discussion of the Shang and the Hsia and early chronology.

24.4 SHU CHING: Fitzgerald (2), p. 49.

25.1 'OH! ... PEOPLE': Legge and Waltham (1), pp. 69–70. Heaven manifested clear signs of disapproval. 'Two suns fought in the sky. The earth shook. Mountains were moved from their strong foundations. Rivers dried up. Chieh was routed....' p. 63.

26.2 BRONZE AGE: Watson, W. (1), pp. 38–9. 'So far no trace has been found in China of a rudimentary bronze industry which might represent a stage equivalent to the chalcolithic of the Near East, or the early bronze age of temperate Europe ... an inescapable conclusion from the facts thus far established is that the comparatively sudden rise of metallurgy in central China must follow a cultural borrowing. This influence from elsewhere in Asia may have been no more than the basic idea of bronze smelting and casting. It does not follow that any considerable packet of cultural influence – still less a migration of people – reached

China simultaneously with the technical information. The archaeological record shows that this did not happen.'

26.2 POTTERY KILNS: *Ibid.*, pp. 67–8. 'Kilns of both neolithic and Shang date have been preserved almost intact on a number of sites through their being built partly underground. In design they are similar. . . . In the history of ceramics in general the principle of the clear separation of furnace, heat-flue and firing chamber is one mastered at an advanced stage of development. In China it was the rule from Yang-shao times on.'

26.3 SHANG DECISIONS: Cheng Te-K'un (2), p. 204.

27.2 HUMAN BURIALS: *Ibid.*, pp. 73–4. In some cases the position of the bodies shows no sign of a struggle – the result, perhaps, of suicide by followers or relatives of the dead king – but the decapitated victims may well have been convicts, slaves, or captured enemies.

27.3 HAN PRINCE: Creel (1), p. 118.

28.1 MONARCH'S UNWORTHINESS: Legge and Waltham (1), p. 73. After defeating Chieh, T'ang announced his acceptance of responsibility as ruler. 'When guilt is found in you,' he said to the people, 'who occupy the myriad regions, let it rest on me, the One Man. When guilt is found in me, the One Man, it shall not attach to you who occupy the myriad regions.'

28.1 SEISMOGRAPH: Needham (8), p. 17, 'Poverties and Triumphs of the Chinese Scientific Tradition'.

28.2 DIVINATION: Needham (2), p. 347.

28.3 ORACULAR INSCRIPTIONS: Wieger (1), pp. 369–74.

28.4 GOD OF SOIL: Fitzgerald (2), p. 36. See his treatment of the ancient gods of the Chinese, ch. 2.

28.4 'WHEREAS . . . CHILD': *Ibid.*, p. 45. He continues, 'The clear evidence of these customs, preserved in the *Odes*, later caused much embarrassment to the Confucian scholars and gave rise to many ingenious interpretations and explanations.' Not unlike the Christian treatment of *The Song of Solomon*.

29.1 CEREMONY OF EXPOSURE: See Maspéro (1) and De Groot (1).

29.2 YIN-YANG: Needham (2), pp. 273–8.

30.1 LITERACY: Chu T'ung-tsu (1), p. 104.

30.2 COMMON SCRIPT: Karlgren (1), p. 37. And the language of the *shih* themselves provided a continuum of both space and time; because 'the literary language had been an artificial thing for a thousand years and more, for all its stylistic variations it had been essentially the same throughout the ages. Once a Chinese has succeeded in mastering it, it is the same to him, from the linguistic point of view, whether the poem he is reading was written at the time of Christ, a thousand years later, or yesterday; it is just as comprehensible and enjoyable in either case. In other countries, when the written language has followed the evolution of the spoken, a practically new literary language has been evolved in the course of a few centuries. An ordinary Englishman of today can hardly go further back than three or four hundred years in his own literature; the earliest periods he can appreciate only after special philological study. To the Chinese the literature of millenia is open; and his unrivalled love for and knowledge of the ancient culture of his country is largely due to the peculiar nature of his literary language.'

31.2 FALL OF SHANG: Cheng Te-K'un (4), p. xxiv.

31.2 'THE KING . . . DWELLINGS': Legge and Waltham (1), p. 178.

31.3 'BROKEN . . . US': Waley (1), p. 236.

33.1 SLAVERY: Accurate historical data is scarce for the Chou period, but the Han Empire, contemporary with that of Rome, offers an interesting contrast. The *tsu*, corvée labourers, provided an inexhaustible supply of cheap labour. 'Every male commoner between the ages of twenty and fifty-six was liable to one month's labour service a year; technical workers performed these obligations in the imperial workshops or factories, which were never primarily staffed by slaves.' Needham (8), 'Poverties and Triumphs of the Chinese Scientific Tradition', p. 25. Chu T'ung-Tsu (1), p. 144, notes that the government used corvée labourers and convicts for construction purposes, whilst the massive grain transport service was entirely in the hands of corvée labourers. Such slaves as existed were condemned criminals or their relations, captives, rebels, the destitute, and presents from barbarian allies, *ibid.*, p. 135.

33.2 'UNPITYING . . . RECEIVED': Legge and Waltham (1), p. 183.

33.3 RAIDERS: Lattimore (1), p. 319. He points out that many of the 'barbarians' against whom the feudal lords were constantly fighting were most likely the more backward Chinese tribes. The various walls built before the Great Wall itself were intended to separate the steppe from the sown. They sought to protect the peasant-farmers, the agricultural foundation of feudal society.

CHAPTER 2: *The Classical Age 770–221* BC

35.2 'A MAN . . . MAN': *Chan-Kuo Ts'e*; *Ssu-pu Ts'ung-k'an*, 2.13a, *Kuo-ts'e K'an-yen*, 6.12; tr. Crump (1), p. 51.

36.2 'THE LOVELY . . . EARTH': *Kuo Yu (Ch'i Yu)*, ch. 6, p. 141; tr. Needham (7), p. 2. In the paper from which the translation is taken the author posits China as an iron culture from the fourth century BC. Archaeology, so far, has not been able to turn up a find so early as the lifetime of Prince Huan (710–643 BC). See also Watson (1), pp. 80–1.

37.2 'TO . . . HEAVEN?: *Chan-Kuo Ts'e*; *Ssu-pu Ts'ung-k'an*, 4.63a, *Kuo-ts'e K'an-yen*, 27.8; tr. Crump (1), p. 217.

38.1 'THAT . . . CANAL': *Shih Chi*, ch. 29, p. 3, tr. auct. The canal was 124 kilometres long (300 *li*); the area irrigated was 266,800 hectares (40,000 *ch'ing*); there were 100 *mou* in a *ch'ing*; one *chung* was equal to about forty litres.

38.2 FIRST KEY ECONOMIC AREA: Chi Ch'ao-Ting (1) p. 77.

42.2 IN THE . . . LORD': Birch (1), pp. 54–5.

42.3 LAND TAX: Elvin (1), p. 23.

43.2 NATIONALIZATION: A governmental Fermented Beverages Authority was set up in the Former Han dynasty, somewhat later than Iron and Salt Bureaux.

44.1 SHANG/MERCHANTS: Wilhelm, H. (1), p. 50. The *shang*, he suggests, were impoverished nobility belonging to the Shang period. Instead of sinking to the level of the *nung* they found outlets in commerce and other lucrative activities connected with government.

44.2 CHING TIEN: *Meng Tzu*, III, iii, pp. 13–20, tr. auct. See Chi Ch'ao-Ting (1), pp. 50–3; and Legge (3), pp. 243–5. In Needham (6), pp. 256–60, there is an interesting discussion of the origins of irrigation. *Ching* has two distinct meanings: on one hand it is connected with water; and on the other it refers to a nine-plot division of land.

46.1 KILL TYRANTS: Needham (8), pp. 168–9, 'Science and Society in Ancient China'. 'If the mass of the people as a whole were in possession of a powerful offensive weapon, and the ruling class were not in possession of superior defensive means, one can see that the balance of power in society was different from what it was in, for example, the time of the early Roman Empire, where disciplined legions were rather well armoured, with bronze and iron. A slave population was possible because it was not in possession of the arms and armour of the legionaries, nor did it have access to power bows. The principal Roman weapons were always the spear and the short sword. We know what trouble the slaves could give on the few occasions in which they did gain access to substantial stores of weapons, as in the revolt of Spartacus.'

47.1 'AMONG . . . UPRIGHTNESS': *Analects*, 13:18; tr. auct.

48.4 GREAT WALL: Lattimore (1), p. 25. 'The Great Wall only approximates to an absolute frontier. It is the product of social emphasis continuously applied along a line of cleavage between environments. The difference of environment is not equally sharp along every sector of the Great Wall, and this corresponds historically to the fact that there are many loops and variations and alternative lines of 'the' Great Wall. Indeed, Ch'in Shih Huang-ti, who 'built' the wall in the third century BC, did so by linking together different sectors that had already been built by several border states before his time.'

48.4 MARTIAN ASTRONOMERS: Needham (6), p. 47.

51.1 'WOULD CONTROL . . . CH'IN': *Chan-Kuo Ts'e; Ssu-pu Ts'ung-k'an*, 3.70b, *Kuo-ts'e K'an-yen*, 19.19; tr. Crump (1), pp. 135–6.

51.3 DIPLOMATIC MISSIONS: Elvin (1), p. 25.

52.1 GRAND CANAL: Needham (6), p. 374.

CHAPTER 3: *Classical Philosophy and Art*

56.1 LU: Creel (1), p. 17. Between 722 and 481 BC, Lu was invaded only twenty-one times, which though often enough, is little for the period. Yet it engaged in warfare itself when the opportunity for gain arose.

56.1 MO-TZU: See Mei (1) and (2).

58.2 HSUN-TZU: Hsun-tzu's philosophy was completely rationalistic. He denied the existence of a spiritual realm, regarding heaven as purely naturalistic. The ruler, a man whose intelligence and knowledge has outstripped his fellow men, governs, according to *li*, and his firmness is needed socially because of the inherent badness found in human nature. Rites and ceremonies were considered necessary for society, not heaven; their functions were educative and aesthetic. See Dubs (2).

58.2 'THE PRINCE . . . NEGLIGENCE': *Shang Chun Shu*, ch. 7; synopsis by Needham (2), p. 207.

59.3 'EXISTENCE . . . OPENS': Bynner (1), ch. 1. We have used this American poet's version of the first chapter of the *Tao Teh Ching* for the sake of impact. The lapidary style of the ancient Chinese is hard to translate, but we consider that Witter Bynner has succeeded in giving an impression of its

polished character without too much sacrifice of meaning. A more literal translation of the same chapter might run, 'The ordinary way easily talked about is far from the real and extraordinary and indescribable and infinite Way. The ordinary name easily named is far from the real and extraordinary and unnamable and infinite Name. The Nameless is the beginning of heaven and earth; the namable is the mother of all things. Therefore, it is known that whereas the detached observer can see into the unnamable mysteries, the attached observer can only see its namable surface manifestations. Yet these two things are the same in origin, though different in name. Their sameness is called a mystery. Indeed, it is the gateway of all mysteries.'

60.1 'AS . . . MEN': *Ibid.*, ch. 43.

60.3 LAO-TZU'S ISOLATION: Perhaps the Taoist mistrust of words goes some way to account for the obscurity surrounding the life of Lao-tzu. He is one of the most shadowy figures in Chinese history and there has been much argument about his probable date. The traditional birthdate of 604 BC, which would make him an elder contemporary of Confucius, has been disregarded in favour of the fourth century BC. However, it is recognized that the germinal ideas of Taoist thought did exist two centuries earlier than this revised date.

60.3 'CONFUCIAN . . . NATURE': Needham (2), pp. 33–4. Talking of the two diverse origins of Taoism, he explains that 'science and magic are in their earliest stages indistinguishable. The Taoist philosophers, with the emphasis on Nature, were bound in due course to pass from the purely observational to the experimental.'

61.1 'THE PRINCE . . . HERE': *Chuang-tzu*, ch. 17; tr. auct.

61.2 'THE ANCIENTS . . . ACCORDINGLY': *Ibid.*, ch. 16; tr. auct.

61.3 'THE WISE . . . WORDS': *Tao Teh Ching*, ch. 2; tr. auct.

61.3 'POTLATCH': See Granet (2).

61.3 THE TALE OF YU: Giles, L. (1), p. 107. A complete translation of this story is provided.

61.3 LIEH-TZU'S ISOLATION: Like Lao-tzu, details of the life and writings of Lieh-tzu are uncertain. Taoist tradition ascribes Lieh-tzu to the period 600–400 BC, when he travelled by riding the wind. Whilst some scholars have identified a certain Lieh Yu-k'ou in Cheng not long before 398 BC, the general view would put the composition of the *Lieh-tzu* as late as AD 300. Nevertheless, there are sections of the book dating from the Warring States period. In many ways his writings form the easiest introduction to Taoism for the Western reader. See Graham (1).

62.1 'PRINCE HUI'S . . . LIFE': *Chuang-tzu*, ch. 3; tr. auct.

62.2 'TUNG . . . COMPLETELY': *Ibid.*, ch. 22; tr. auct. see Legge (4), vol. 2, p. 66; Giles, H. A. (1). p. 215; and Needham (2), p. 47.

64.1 'I AM . . . IT': *Analects*, 7; tr. auct.

65.1 'DEATH . . . LI': *Ibid.*, 12.5; tr. auct.

65.2 DIVINATION: Smith (1), p. 46.

65.2 'HIGH . . . RELATIONS': Fung Yu-lan (1), p. 3.

65.2 'ALMOST . . . ANCHORAGE': Gerth and Mills (1), p. 293. Yet there was a strong sense of the spiritual in the philosopher. As Needham (9), p. 63, has put it, 'Confucianism was a religion, too, if you define that as something which involves the sense of the holy, for a quality of the numinous is very present in Confucian temples (the *wen miao*); but not if you think of religion only as theology of a transcendent creator-deity.'

67.1 'HUMAN-HEARTEDNESS . . . PATH': *Meng Tzu*, 6a, 12; tr. auct.

71.1 'FOR . . . GRANDSONS': Watson, W. (2), p. 81, no. 93.

72.1 MUSIC: Wilhelm, R. (1), p. 74. Confucius, himself a contemporary of Marquis Chao of Ts'ai, was so susceptible to music that he forgot to taste meat for three months while he practised. He regarded the practice of music 'as all-important for the cultivation of the aesthetic side of human nature', p. 141.

72.1 'PRIMITIVE . . . PERCUSSION': Needham (4), p. 200.

72.3 'THE SHANG . . . NORTH-EAST': Watson, W. (1), p. 59.

CHAPTER 4: *Imperial Unification: the Ch'in and Former Han Empires 221 BC–AD 9*

77.1 'BURNING OF THE BOOKS': See Bodde (1).

79.1 AVENGING ARMY: Bishop (1) has underlined the geographical and cultural antagonism that originally existed between North and South China: the people of Ch'in, wheat-eating charioteers, possibly influenced by Persia and Central Asia, confronting the people of Ch'u, rice-eating river dwellers, whose cultural relations were with South-East Asia and India.

79.1 POWERFUL FAMILIES: *Han Shu*, 90: 16a–17a; Chu T'ung-tsu (1), p. 437, III, 37.

81.1 'SO . . . STRONGLY': *T'ung Chien Kang Mu*, ch. 3, p. 46b; tr. auct.; see Weiger (2), vol. 1, p. 299. Pan Ku, the Later Han historian, also refers to the slowness of Emperor Han Kao-tsu in cultivating literary studies; see Dubs (1), vol. 1, p. 18 and p. 146.

81.3 THE HISTORIES: Macgowan (1), p. 94. This volume encompasses the official history of China from the original myths down to the end of the Ming dynasty. The Ch'ing Empire (1644–1911) is represented by a narrative woven from various sources. The official historians composed documents about contemporary events and then deposited them in an iron-bound chest, which remained locked up until that dynasty had ceased to rule. It was later opened by imperial command and the documents were edited into the history of the previous dynasty.

81.3 CIVIL SERVICE EXAMINATIONS: The origin of school and civil service examinations is not generally known, despite unequivocal historical evidence of the adoption of the Chinese system by Western countries. From the Former Han period a system of recommendation and examination was used, though it was the T'ang dynasty which gave precedence to the successful examinee (622). The Sung Empire (960–1126) witnessed the triumph of the civil arm of government. In July 1835, Robert Inglis, a British resident in China, wrote, 'The British East India Company . . . have adopted the principle as far as election to the civil service. . . . The full development in India of this Chinese invention is destined one day, perhaps, like those of gunpowder and printing, to work another great change in the states-system even of Europe.' Quoted in a full account of this important cultural transfer by Teng Ssu-yu, in MacNair (1), p. 448.

83.1 LIU PEI AND MI CHU: Chu T'ung-tsu (1), p. 116.

83.2 'WAS CAREFUL . . . CONFUCIUS': *Ibid.*, p. 343, II, 23.

86.1 'NOW . . . MEAN': Chao T'so presented his famous memorial on the condition of the *nung* in 178 BC. Ssu-ma Ch'ien agreed that the *shang* had grown in strength and wealth. He records that nobles sought loans from money-lenders.

86.2 'FORMERLY . . . FACTIONS': Needham (5), pp. 21–2. The *Yen T'ieh Lun (Discourses on Salt and Iron)* dates from 81 BC. It is supposed to be the record of a debate between leading *shih* on the question of state involvement with industry. The speaker in the extract quoted is the Imperial Grand Secretary. See Gale (1).

87.2 CHIA-I: Yu Ying-shih (1), p. 37.

87.2 HSIUNG NU ABANDONED: *Ibid.*, p. 40.

87.3 BACTRIA: After the death of Alexander in 323 BC, the eastern provinces of his empire were ruled by the Seleucid dynasty from Antioch in Syria. But around 250 BC they broke off as an independent Greek kingdom. Under Demetrius I Bactrians, Greeks and Indians merged as a single people in the Buddhist kingdom of Bactria. Coins with bilingual inscriptions survive; they used Greek and Indian languages, combining visual motifs from both cultural areas. Demetrius's general, Menander, invaded the north of India about 190 BC and was made a separate king. A famous Indian book, the ancient *Milinda Panha*, records Menander's own conversion to Buddhism. Other Greek kings established themselves in north-western India, but they were swept away by the great invasion of the Kushan tribes during the first century BC. Bactria and Ferghana, to the north, had many magnificent cities and towns at the time of Chang Ch'ien's arrival. Large scale irrigation schemes permitted intensive agriculture, while international trade brought in commodities and wealth. Chang Ch'ien reached Bactria shortly after the Kushan conquest; the Han envoy was amazed by the urban development in Ta Hsia and Ta Yuan, though he does not seem to have appreciated that the former kingdom had been on the fringe of the Hellenistic world. It is interesting to speculate on the historical consequences for the world of a significant cultural interchange between Han China and the Graeco-Roman West. The cultural heritage of mankind might have been much richer for it. In the event, the Chinese became aware of other worlds, but the only foreign influence came from India, as Buddhism. The transplanting of this faith confirmed the oriental frame of Chinese society and continued China along its separate course, so remote from the historical experience of Western Europe. Specific things brought back by Chang Ch'ien included the grape-vine, the walnut, the jointed bamboo, and the hemp plant. See Wilheim, R. (1), p. 182. It should be recalled that the present-day desolation and obscurity of what was once Bactria is due to the fury of the Mongols. Early in the thirteenth century Genghiz Khan devastated the entire region. See Tarn (1) and Rawlinson (1).

88.1 POLICY TOWARDS WESTERN REGIONS: Yu Ying-shih (1), p. 137.

88.3 'IN . . . CH'IN': Elvin (1), pp. 29–30.

90.1 'KUAN-CHUNG . . . EMPIRE': *Shih Chi*, ch. 129, p. 7; tr. auct.; see Watson, B. (3), p. 332 for a translation of the chapter in which Ssu-ma Ch'ien discusses commerce and industry. The chapter is simply entitled 'The Biographies of the Money-makers'.

90.2 'UNLIKE... ASTRONIMICAL': Watson, B. (2), p. 4.

90.2 'SEEMS... WORKS': Beasley and Pulleyblank (1), p. 35. See Hulsewé, A.F.P., 'Notes on the Historiography of the Han Period'.

90.2 SSU-MA CH'IEN'S PUNISHMENT: Ssu-ma Ch'ien refused to make a heavy payment to the Imperial Treasury in order to commute the punishment. He accepted the indignity of castration – the worst possible fate in a society that prized the continuity of the family – rather than impoverish his near relations.

90.3 RECORDS OF THE HISTORIAN: Beasley and Pulleyblank (1), p. 3. The three main traditions of historical writing in the world are identified as the European tradition, which looks back to its Greek and Roman origins, the Islamic tradition, and the Chinese tradition, 'unique in the volume of its output and the length and continuity of its record.' p. 1.

90.3 'ONE OF... RULE': Watson, B. (2), p. 5.

CHAPTER 5: *The Later Han Empire AD 25–220*

92.2 'EARTH FAT': Chu T'ung-tsu (1), p. 94.

94.1 DRASTIC ECONOMIC ACTION: In 7 BC the Emperor Han Ai-ti imposed a limit on landholdings. This restriction did not stay in force for very long, since the Emperor himself ignored it in order to present an enormous gift of land to a favourite. The Later Han dynasty was placed in a less independent position because in the restoration of the imperial house the first rulers had to rely on support from the big landowners. In AD 39 Emperor Han Kuang-wu found it impossible to conduct a survey of the cultivated land in the Empire for the purpose of reassessing the land tax. The edict of the Hsin Emperor required that a family with less than eight male members, but with more than a hundred *mou* of farmland each, should divide up the surplus and give it to neighbouring families in need.

94.2 FAMINES: Elvin (1), p. 32. Wang Mang's reign seems to have coincided with a period of severe droughts, but famine relief was inadequate and mismanaged even in Kuan-chung, the seat of the imperial capital. In addition, the 'water benefits' schemes in the province were in a state of disrepair and neglect, including the network of irrigation channels connected to the old Chengkuo Canal. For a detailed discussion of the reasons for Wang Mang's fall, see Dubs (1), vol. 3, pp. 112–24.

94.2 'RED EYEBROWS': Secret societies were usually of Taoist inspiration and flourished in North China. Emperor Han Kuang-wu experienced some difficulty in suppressing the movement of the 'Red Eyebrows'. Such popular agitation was a symptom of imperial decline – a sign that the dynasty was approaching eclipse – and though useful to contenders for the throne, the forces unleashed could take on anarchic characteristics that terrified the Confucian *shih*. At the end of the Later Han dynasty another movement arose named the 'Yellow Turbans'.

95.1 'WORE... PIGS': Chu T'ung-tsu (1), p. 110.

95.1 EXTENDED FAMILY: Small families were common in Ch'in and Han times. The average family then included only

five persons. It will be recalled that the break-up of large family units was a social policy of the Ch'in rulers, whilst Emperor Han Wu-ti used 'harsh officials' to destroy powerful families.

95.1 'THE HOUSES... HALLS': Elvin (1), p. 33. This description by Chung-ch'ang Tung at the beginning of the third century AD is quoted by the author who argues persuasively that this period represents a crisis for the survival of Chinese civilization.

95.3 PICUL: Equals 60 kilograms; it refers to grain.

96.1 PARTHIA: The Parthians were concerned to keep Rome and China separated for the commercial reason that Parthia played an intermediary role in the silk trade. Parthia was able to tax the caravans that passed down the Silk Road and enrich itself without adding anything of value. When Kan Ying, the ambassador Pan Ch'ao sent to establish direct relations with Ta Ts'in, or the Roman Empire, reached the Black Sea, he was given to understand that the rest of his journey was hazardous and long. Thus, the Parthians persuaded him to turn back, lest he perish in the attempt. The trade between Rome and China was extensive; the Emperor Tiberius (14–37) was forced to prohibit the wearing of silk because Roman gold had to be exported to pay for it. See Yu Ying-shih (1), pp. 156–8.

96.2 'A TYPICAL... KINGDOMS': Chi Ch'ao-Ting (1), p. 96.

97.1 CENSUS: Loewe (1), p. 62. The sixty millions of the Han Empire compares with the seventy to ninety millions of the Roman Empire at the time of Augustus (27 BC–AD 14). But the Chinese figure may be an underestimate of the total population because it is doubtful whether an accurate survey was conducted to the south of the Yang-tze River.

97.1 ADMINISTRATIVE CENTRES: Ch'in Shih Huang-ti had centralized power at his capital, Hsienyang, the site of which was on the opposite bank of the Wei River from Ch'ang-an. It could be said that 'the First Emperor' used the city to hold the *first* Empire together. Hsienyang and the provincial capitals founded in the *hsien*, or prefectures, formed a network of administrative centres from which imperial control could be exerted over the people. Although during the Han Empire these settlements developed cultural and commercial functions, they were all dominated by the imperial officials stationed in them.

99.3 'THE CHINESE... LORD': Needham (6), p. 71. The passage continues thus, 'originally, before the first millenium, the proto-feudal chieftains appropriated the centres of assembly where people exchanged commodities and came together for the seasonal festivals. There was no distinction through Chinese history between the feudal castle and the town; the town *was* the castle, and was built so that it could serve as protection and refuge, as well as the administrative centre, of the surrounding countryside. Towns and cities in China were not the creation of burghers, and never achieved any degree of autonomy with regard to the State. They existed for the state of the country and not vice versa; they were planned as rational fortified patterns imposed from above upon carefully chosen portions of the earth's surface.' For this reason the Chinese Communist Party has looked to the countryside for revolutionary support. 'It was the struggles of the peasants,' Chairman Mao wrote in 1939, 'the peasant uprisings and peasant wars that constituted the real motive force of historical development in Chinese feudal society.'

99.4 TREES: *Ibid.*, p. 74. 'In Peking, figures for residential areas reached 55,000 per square mile, and for working areas 85,000. But the city maintained a garden character owing to the abundance of trees, which paradoxically were more numerous within the walls than outside, and to this day Peking seen from some vantage-points resembles a forest, with only the most important buildings visible above the tree tops.'

100.1 COLOURFUL ARCHITECTURE: *Ibid.*, p. 65.

100.3 LESSONS FOR WOMEN: Pan Chao was the sister of the historian Pan Ku and the general Pan Ch'ao, who reconquered Central Asia. Emperor Han Ho-ti (89–105) ordered Pan Chao to complete her brother's unfinished *Han Shu* (*History of the Han*). Although she was given no official title, her son was ennobled as a marquis and appointed an official, apparently as a reward for her work on the *Han Shu*. The famous *Nu-chieh* (*Lessons for Women*) may have resulted from her stay at Court, where she was treated as a teacher by the Empress and some of the imperial concubines.

100.3 'THE WAY . . . LI . . .': Swann (2), p. 84.

100.4 SLAVES: Ch'u T'ung-tsu (1), p. 142.

103.1 HO SUICIDE: *Ibid.*, p. 184.

103.1 'IN . . . ANIMAL-POWER': Needham (5), p. 28.

104.1 'AGRICULTURE . . . DROUGHT': Chi Ch'ao-Ting (1), p. 83. This edict has been translated from the *Han Shu*, 29:7.

104.2 TERRACED FIELDS: *Ibid.*, p. 9.

104.3 MOU: One *mou* equals about 0.06 hectares.

104.3 CHAO KUO'S SYSTEM: Loewe (1), p. 168.

105.2 JEN FAMILY: *Han Shu*, 91:96–10a; tr. Chu T'ung-tsu (1), p. 260, 1, 10.

106.1 'IF WE . . . IT': Needham (3), p. 193.

106.2 'ON . . . ANTARES': Needham (10), p. 3: 'Astronomy in Classical China'.

109.2 CHANG HENG: Chang Heng also made the most accurate calculation of **π** at that time, besides casting 'a network (of coordinates) about the heaven and the earth, and reckoned on the basis of it'.

109.2 'THE BOOKS . . . VAPOUR. . . .': Needham (3), p. 219. Chinese astronomy had little in common with the Greek tradition. The Chinese felt no desire for a concrete geometrical model; they had nothing like 'the rigid Aristotelian-Ptolemaic conception of concentric spheres, which fettered European thought for more than a thousand years'. Matteo Ricci (arrived at Peking in 1598) was impressed by the Hsuan Yeh ideas. They had 'a distinctly Taoist flavour'. But Buddhism 'also contributed . . . with its conceptions of infinite space and time and a plurality of worlds'. Finally, 'Chu Hsi gave to these views his great philsophical authority – the Heavens, he said, are bodiless and empty', p. 221.

109.3 SCIENCE AND TECHNOLOGY: *Science and Civilisation in China*, as our frequent references to individual volumes in it imply, forms the basis of this current reassessment. Dr Needham's original intention was the improvement of intercultural communication between East and West, particularly in respect of the history of science, but the volumes he has completed so far have become a major contribution to world history in their own right. In them the interested reader will find a great deal to amaze him.

110.2 'THE PILING . . . CONTENT': Needham (10), p. 109. 'Iron and Steel Production in Ancient and Medieval China'.

110.2 PAPER-MAKING: Ts'ai Lung's invention created a profound impression on his contemporaries. His perfection of a pre-existing process – he substituted vegetable fibres for the fibres of animal origin, such as silk refuse, used previously – provided an inexpensive and inexhaustible supply of paper, an indispensable precondition of a literate civilization like China. Laufer (1) notes, 'The ancient Sumerians, Babylonians, Egyptians, and Greeks may have reached a flourishing civilization long before the Chinese, but all their achievements, however great, do not equal in importance the invention of paper which we owe to the Chinese and the art of printing that was born of it. . . . Without paper there would be no adequate record of the past, no history, no science, no progress. The manufacture of paper denotes a landmark in the intellectual development of mankind; it sets off civilization from the stage of savagery,' p. 16.

The battle of Talas River in AD 751 ended the Chinese monopoly over the manufacture of paper. Chinese captives of the Arabs introduced the technique in Samarkand, whence it spread throughout the world of Islam. It reached Christian Europe in 1150 when a paper-mill was founded in Fabriano, Italy.

Preference for manuscripts amongst the Confucian *shih* delayed the development of printing, though Buddhist monks availed themselves of its advantage in disseminating information during the T'ang dynasty. The *Diamond Sutra* seems to have been printed as an act of filial piety 'by Wang Chee, for free general distribution, that the memory of my parents be reverently perpetuated'. Feng Tao (881–954), an official under four of the Five Dynasties, is credited with the invention of block-printing. Although movable type followed soon afterwards, block-printing remained prominent for the reason that it preserved accurately the beauty of form of the characters and the handwriting of the individual scholar.

110.3 'TO SHARE . . . TRANSPORT': Needham (6), p. 373.

110.3 TAN: 6,000,000 *tan* equals 420,000 tonnes.

110.3 CH'ANG-AN CANAL: Chi Ch'ao-Ting (1), p. 81.

112.1 'FOR NEARLY . . . TIME': Needham (6), p. 375.

112.3 'IT AFFECTED . . . CIVILIZATION': Needham (8), pp. 86–7, 'Science and China's Influence on the World'.

117.1 'THE GREATEST . . . PHYSICS': Needham (4), p. 229.

117.1 'BUT . . . SOUTH': *Ibid.*, pp. 261–2. The 'south-controlling spoon' needs to be distinguished from the 'south-pointing carriage', invented in 260. The carriage was a mechanical device, with compensating gears.

117.1 'THE FIRST . . . OBSERVATION': *Ibid.*, p. 239.

117.2 MEDICAL STUDIES: Needham (10), p. 384, 'China and the Origin of Qualifying Examinations in Medicine'.

117.3 DIAGNOSIS: *Ibid.*, p. 269, 'Medicine and Chinese Culture'.

CHAPTER 6: *The Age of Disunity: the so-called Six Dynasties 200–587*

119.1 SHU-HAN: Chinese historians have considered the

rulers of Shu-Han to be the legitimate rulers, the continuation of the Han house, because they were relatives of the Later Han. Therefore, the first of the Six Dynasties was Western Tsin, which was not founded till 265.

119.2 MIDDLE KINGDOM: Chi Ch'ao-Ting (1), p. 9. Of the economic history of China Chi writes, '*The first period of unity and peace* covers the Ch'in and Han dynasties . . . the Ching, Wei, Fen, and lower Huang Ho (Yellow River) valleys as the Key Economic Area. *The first period of division and struggle* (a most important transitional period) covers' . . . this period (221–589) 'with Szechuan and the lower Yang-tze valley, gradually developed by irrigation and flood-control, emerging as important areas of agricultural production to challenge the dominance of the Key Economic Area of the earlier period. *The second period of unity and peace* covers the Sui and T'ang dynasties, with the Yang-tze valley assuming the position of a Key Economic Area and the simultaneous rapid development of Grand Canal transportation connecting the capital with the new Key Economic Area.'

120.3 'IT IS . . . WAR': Elvin (1), p. 41.

122.1 'POSSESSED . . . ENGINEERING': Needham (1), p. 119.

122.1 'CHINA . . . CULTURE': Goody (1), p. 36. From 'The Consequences of Literacy' by Goody, J. and Watt, I.

122.2 'THE OLD . . . ROOTED': Wilhelm, R. (1), p. 205.

123.1 'WE . . . BASIS': Elvin (1), pp. 48–9.

126.2 TAOISM POPULAR: Between 326 and 342 a series of revelations were granted to a woman Taoist living in the South. This tradition of revelation was collected by T'ao Hung-ching, the famous Taoist physician of the Liang dynasty, in his book, *True Reports*, written in 489. In the North the Toba Wei were particularly sympathetic to Taoism. The head of the Taoist church was accorded the official title of *T'ien Shih*, Heavenly Teacher, in 423. The Northern Ch'i dynasty actually called a joint congress of Buddhists and Taoists in 555; the initial idea of the gathering, namely the unification of the embattled faiths, was forgotten in the heat of the argument and the Taoists suffered an ignominious defeat.

127.1 'WHO . . . CLIFF': Bynner (1), ch. 39.

127.4 'NO . . . ANOTHER': Babbit (1), p. 27, XII, 165.

127.4 YOGA: Zimmer (1), p. 8.

128.2 'THEREFORE . . . MAHAYANA': Zimmer (2), p. 68.

128.3 BRAHMANIC HINDUISM: The Muslim invasion of India brought about the final extinction of Buddhism. In 1199 Ikhtiyar Khiliji's soldiers destroyed Odantapura monastery, Bihar, the last centre of Buddhist learning, dispersing those monks who managed to escape to Burma, Tibet and Ceylon.

129.2 AVALOKITESVARA: (Chinese: Kwan-yin; Japanese: Kwannon) was originally the Lord of Compassion, but by the time of the Sung Empire the bodhisattva had been transformed into a woman, the Goddess of Mercy.

129.2 BENIGN TRANSFIGURATION: Zimmer (1), p. 540.

129.2 SANGHA: Dutt (1), p. 22.

130.1 MONASTIC SYSTEM: Brown (1), pp. 96–103.

130.2 SANG-MEN: Zürcher (1), vol. 1, p. 26. Prince Liu Ying, Duke of Ch'u since 39, had sent a gift to Emperor Han Ming-ti in 65, during a general amnesty for political opponents. The Emperor returned the rolls of silk, disclaiming any

suspicion against the Prince, and suggesting that the gift be used to entertain the *upasakas (i-p'u-sai)* and *sramanas (sang-men)*. At this time Prince Liu Ying was living in Shantung, a province noted for its interest in out of the ordinary philosophies, ever since Prince Huan encouraged scholarship in the seventh century BC.

130.2 TRANSLATION: Zürcher (1), vol. 2, p. 21, note 1. The first Chinese who is known to have mastered Sanskrit is Chu Fo-nien.

130.2 'A FORM . . . CULTURE': Zürcher (1), vol. 1, p. 32.

130.2 'EARLY . . . PHENOMENON': *Ibid.*, p. 59.

134.3 DECORATED BOX: Sullivan (1), p. 88.

135.2 TUN-HUANG: De Silva (1), p. 202.

CHAPTER 7: *Reunification: the Sui and T'ang Empires 581–906*

137.1 'HE . . . ACCOMPLISHMENTS': Chi Ch'ao-Ting (1), p. 122.

137.2 PEASANT-SOLDIERS: Elvin (1), p. 55.

144.4 'WISHED . . . REGIONS': Fitzgerald (3), p. 114.

147.2 AN LU-SHAN'S VETERANS: Pulleyblank (1), p. 26. The author views the rebellion as one of the chief turning points in Chinese history. 'Never again,' he writes, 'did a native dynasty reach the summit of glory from which An Lu-shan rudely pushed Emperor Hsuan-tsung and his brilliant court in 755–6,' p. 1.

148.1 UNREGISTERED FAMILIES: *Ibid.*, p. 31.

149.4 'THE WAY . . . EMPIRE': *T'ang Hui Yao*; Wieger (2), vol. 2, p. 1351, tr. auct. The edict was issued in 638.

150.2 NEO-CONFUCIANISM: Needham (2), p. 413.

150.2 PARENTAL LOVE . . . : Ch'en (1), p. 20–3; a synopsis of a filial *Jataka* tale. Upon Ch'en's fascinating study the section entitled 'The Buddhist Challenge' is founded.

151.1 'THE DEEPLY . . . IT': Radharkrishnan (1), p. 133.

151.1 THE BUDDHA AND HIS MOTHER: Ch'en (1), p. 34.

151.1 IMPERIAL ANCESTOR WORSHIP: *Ibid.*, p. 52.

152.1 'DOWN . . . CASE': Beal (1), vol. 1, p. xxxviii.

152.4 'IN . . . GENERATIONS': *Chi Sha-men pu-ying pai-su ten-shih*, 3; tr. Ch'en (1), p. 78. See also Wieger (2), vol. 2, p. 1343.

152.4 'IN . . . GENERATIONS': *Ibid.*, p. 79.

155.1 HOMAGE LIMITED: *Ibid.*, p. 81.

155.2 REGISTRATION OF CLERGY: *Ibid.*, p. 85.

155.3 HAN-SHAN: See Snyder (1), pp. 31–41. This is a free and exciting translation of Han Shan.

CHAPTER 8: *The T'ang Renaissance*

156.1 LITERARY EXAMINATIONS: Perhaps the Empress Wu deserves the title of 'True Patron of Chinese Poetry'. It was through her influence that poetry became a requisite in examinations for higher qualifications and promotion.

156.1 COLLATOR OF TEXTS: The imperial archives contained all kinds of material: literature, philosophy, historical writings, calligraphy, paintings and so on. In the T'ang Empire the imperial catalogue had more than 80,000 entries; the names of 3,000 T'ang poets were recorded.

158.2 LACQUER GARDEN: *Wang Yuch'eng Chi Chienchu* (collected by Chao Tien-ch'eng; 1736), ch. 13; tr. Robinson (1), p. 31.

158.4 IN ... AUTUMN: *Ibid.*, ch. 7; tr. Robinson (1), p. 75.
159.1 LI PO'S BACKGROUND: Lai Ming (1), p. 149.
162.1 WAKING ... DAY: *Ssu-pu Pei Yao* edition of Li Po's Works, XXIII, 8; tr. Waley (5), p. 48.
162.2 FIGHTING ... RAMPARTS: Waley (5), p. 34.
163.2 'SAGE OF POETRY': Yoshikawa (1), p. 43.
163.3 AUTUMN MEDITATION: Tr. Graham, A.C., in Birch (1), p. 252.
164.2 THOUGHTS ... JOURNEY: Tr. Birch; *ibid.*, p. 255.
164.3 THE CHANCELLOR'S ... DRIVE: Tr. Waley (4), p. 103.
166.1 'ONE ... PLACES': Tr. Waley (3), p. 160.
166.1 ON HIS BALDNESS: Tr. Waley in Birch (1), p. 293.
167.1 'THE TRENDS ... PEOPLE': Lai Ming (1), p. 169.
167.2 'A SOLDIER ... COUNTED': Ch'en (1), p. 270. This extract is taken from an account of the same ceremony held in 873.
167.2 'I ... COMPLAIN ... !': Tr. auct., see Weiger (2), vol. 2, pp. 1471–2; and for a discussion of the incident see Dubs (3).
168.1 MAI-CHI-SHAN: Sullivan (2), p. 48.
170.2 'THERE ... BANKS': Tr. Waley (3), p. 120.
170.3 BUDDHIST GARDENS: Sirén (4), p. 71. Essential reading for all lovers of Nature.
171.1 LI TE-YU: *Ibid.*, p. 76.
171.2 'SUCH ... JAPAN': *Ibid.*, p. 3.
171.2 'A SINGLE ... ONE?': *Pan Mu Yuan* (compiled by Li Li-weng, Ming period); tr. Sirén (4), p. 5.

CHAPTER 9: *The Two Sungs 960–1279*

175.1 KIANGNAN: Chi Ch'ao-Ting (1).
176.1 'I DO ... WEALTH': *Hsu T'ung Chien Kang Mu*, ch. 1, p. 24b; tr. auct.; see also Wieger (2), vol. 2, p. 1559.
178.2 SECOND DEGREES: Out of these only a few hundred would pass. This represented, however, a definite increase in the number of successful candidates because during the T'ang Empire less than fifty were permitted to pass the highest examination at the same time. Wang An-shih's concern was quality. He wanted the most capable minds recruited into the civil service and, though by no means a philistine, he remained sceptical of officials whose interests were primarily literary. He added medicine, botany, geography and hydraulic engineering.
181.3 PAPER MONEY: The shortage of copper was a recurrent problem in the T'ang and Sung Empires. Emperor T'ai-tsu of the later Chou, the dynasty overthrown by Chao Kuang-yin, issued the 'Edict Sweeping Away the Buddhas' in 956. This measure was an attempt to increase the circulation of copper coinage by melting down statues and other religious objects. Though six million strings of new coins were issued in 1073, the supply of money always lagged behind demand. Bills of exchange, the antecedents of paper money, were commonplace from the late T'ang. Overprinting of paper notes eventually caused chronic inflation in the twelfth century. From 1265 the imperial government put out notes backed by gold and silver; they were valid throughout the Empire. For a detailed treatment of Sung finance refer to Elvin (1), ch. 11.
186.1 EXTEND AREA OF CULTIVATION: Reclamation of waste land was not a controversial policy. Wang An-shih's methods were challenged, rarely his objectives. It has been estimated that through the 'Young Schools' law and direct government schemes some five million acres of new land were brought into cultivation.
193.2 SCARCE ACCOMMODATION: Gernet (1), p. 30. This book concentrates on Hangchow and it is recommended to any reader who may wish to learn more about urban life in the Southern Sung period.
195.2 MALE PROSTITUTES: Gernet (1), pp. 98–9. Male prostitution would seem a phenomenon peculiar to the big cities during the Two Sungs.

CHAPTER 10: *The Sung Achievement*

196.1 'AN EMPIRICAL ... HUMANISM': Needham (1), pp. 137–8.
196.2 TAO TEH CHING AND THE I CHING: Needham (2), p. 464.
196.2 'MOTION ... OTHER': *Ibid.*, p. 460.
199.2 'THUS ... NATURE ....': *Ibid.*, p. 502.
199.2 'NEVERTHELESS ... NEWTON': *Ibid.*, p. 496.
200.2 'IT ... DISCOVERIES': *Novum Organum*, bk. 1, aphorism 129.
200.4 'MAJOR FOCAL POINT': Needham (1), p. 134.
201.1 MERCHANT GUILDS: Braudel (1), p. 410. The author contrasts the Chinese and the European city in the Middle Ages: the former firmly under the control of the official class and undifferentiated from the countryside; the latter, privileged and at the very centre of social and economic change.
201.2 'HERE ... NEWTON': Needham (2), p. 467.
201.3 'IN CATHAY ... WOOD': Marsden (1), p. 215.
202.1 ASTRONOMICAL CLOCK: Needham (2), p. 363. The outlook of the T'ang monk, I-Hsing, mathematician and astronomer, contrasts sharply with that of James Ussher, Archbishop of Armagh. As a practical horologist, I-Hsing considered that the world had been in existence for millions of years, whilst the Anglican divine calculated in the early century from evidence in the Old Testament that the date of Creation was 22 October, 4004 BC at six o'clock in the evening. Although the oriental way of regarding existence is exemplified in its eternal time-scale, whether Indian or Chinese, the point to notice here is the scientific approach of the Buddhist monk. The modern scientific awareness of prehistory and the vast geological age of the planet itself is not two hundred years old yet.
202.2 METEOROLOGY: Needham (3), p. 471.
204.2 LOCKS: Needham (6), p. 351.
204.2 GOVERNMENT DREDGES: *Ibid.*, p. 336.
204.3 'THE SHIPS ... GRIEF': *Ling Wai Tai Ta*, ch. 6, p. 7b; tr. Needham (6), p. 464.
206.2 CHINESE EXPLORATION: Duyvendak (1).
208.4 BUDDHISM AND PAINTING: Ch'an Tsang, the 'Inner-light School' of Buddhism produced a host of monk-painters. The chief exponents were Shih K'o (tenth century), Mu-ch'i (early thirteenth century) and Liang K'ai (thirteenth century): the last two artists lived in monasteries on the shores of the Western Lake in Hangchow.
209.3 ADVICE ON LANDSCAPE PAINTING: For a translation of this work see Lin Yutang (1), p. 71.
211.1 'NOWADAYS ... PHENOMENON': Lai Ming (1), p. 177.
211.2 WATER-MAINS: Needham (5), p. 129. In these urban

waterworks Su Tung-P'o had the help of a Taoist, Teng Shou-an. But as a Szechuanese he knew of the brine-pipes in his own province.

212.1 NOVELS: Lu Hsun (1), pp. 234–5. Writing of *Golden Lotus*, Lu Hsun, the father of twentieth century Chinese literature comments: 'The author shows the most profound understanding of the life of his time, his descriptions are clear yet subtle, penetrating yet highly suggestive, and for the sake of contrast he sometimes portrays two quite different aspects of life. His writing holds such a variety of human interest that no novel of that period could surpass it. . . . It is not true that *Chin Ping Mei* deals only with the profligates and loose women of urban society, for Hsimen (the central character) comes of a wealthy family and his friends include nobles, influential men and scholars. Hence this presentation of such a family is in effect a condemnation of the whole ruling class, not simply a story disparaging low society,' pp. 134–5. The other name by which *Pilgrimages to the West* is known to Western readers is *Monkey*. The translation by Arthur Waley is recommended.

213.1 HUMOUROUS TALES: These tales are taken from *Hsiao-tsan (Explanations of Laughter)* by Chao Nan-sing and *Hsiao-fu (The House of Laughter)*, by Feng Meng-lung. We have translated them from *Ming Ch'ing Hsiao Hua Szu Chung (Four Kinds of Humourous Tales from the Ming and Ch'ing dynasties)*, 1956. As they appear in the text, their originals can be found on pages 93, 62, 104, 8 and 6 respectively. By way of comment we note the Chinese interest in dreams. Besides *Love of Wine*, there is an underlying meaning to *The Monk Is Here* that connects with it. Chuang-tzu dreamed he was a butterfly. On waking the Taoist philosopher could not be certain whether he was a man dreaming he was a butterfly, or a butterfly dreaming he was a man. Compare the utterance of the Greek sceptic Pyrrho (third century BC) on his death-bed. When asked by one of his followers if he were still alive, he replied that he was not sure. This is, of course, imperturb-ability. Our pseudo-Miltonics in *In Praise of Farting* provide, we hope, some inkling of the poetical flourishes of the admirably opportunist *shih*, ready to use his education in a dire emergency.

CHAPTER 11: *The Mongol Conquest 1279–1365*

215.3 'EACH . . . CATTLE': Marsden (1), p. 129.

216.1 'THEIR . . . OBTAINED': *Ibid.*, p. 130.

216.1 BATTLE OF WAHLSTADT: De Rachewiltz (1), p. 76. After the battle the Mongols cut one ear off every enemy corpse and filled nine large bags with them.

216.2 MONGOL ATTITUDE TO CITIES: Waley (6) and (7).

221.4 'WHEN . . . HAPPEN': *Yuan Shih*, ch. 146, p. 4a; and *T'ung Chien Kang Mu*, ch. 19, p. 27b; tr. auct. See Weiger (2), vol. 2, pp. 1656–7. The issue, of course, in the mind of Genghiz Khan was the value of North China as a war supply base. Yelu Ch'u-ts'ai steadily opposed the Mongol tendency to massacre. Often he quoted the dictum of Lu Chia, 'Though you conquered the Empire on horseback, by administration alone you will keep it.'

221.3 CH'AN-CH'UN AND YELU CH'U-TS'AI: *Hai-yu-chi*: in Wright and Twitchett (1), p. 196: 'Ye-lu Ch'u-ts'ai' by I. De Rachewiltz.

225.1 SINGOSARI: Fitzgerald (4), pp. 84–5.

225.2 SAID AJALL SHAMS AL DIN: Needham (6), pp. 306–20 and pp. 297–8 respectively.

226.3 '. . . OF . . . PAVILION': Marsden (1), bk. II, ch. VI.

226.4 'DESTINED . . . DESCRIBE': *Ibid.*, bk. II, ch. VII.

228.2 TA-TU: Ho Ping-Ti (1). He draws attention to the large dimensions of Chinese cities. Comparative figures in square miles are: Roman and medieval London, 0.52; Loyang (300), 3.9; Byzantium (447), 4.63; Rome (300), 5.28; Baghdad (800), 11.6 (walled part, 1.75 only); Ch'ang-an (750), 30.0; Peking (1410) 24.0. Also, see Sirén (2) and (3).

228.2 ACHMAC: Marsden (1), bk. II, ch. VIII.

228.3 'MAY . . . ALCHEMISTS': *Ibid.*, bk. II, ch. XVIII.

228.3 P'ING CHANG: *Ibid.*, bk. II, ch. XXI.

231.1 CHARITY: *Ibid.*, bk. II, ch. XXIV.

231.2 'A DEGREE . . . OTHER': *Ibid.*, bk. II, ch. XXVIII.

231.2 KA-CHAN-FU: *Ibid.*, bk. II, ch. XXXIV.

231.2 'THE CITY . . . DIRECTIONS': *Ibid.*, bk. II, ch. XXXVI.

231.2 'A WIDE . . . SEA': *Ibid.*, bk. II, ch. LXIV.

231.2 ZAITON AND ALEXANDRIA COMPARED: *Ibid.*, bk, II, ch. LXXVII.

231.3 COMMERCIAL ENTERPRISE *Ibid.*, bk. II, ch. LVI.

Bibliography

All references made in the notes to the text are given in full here. Other authors are included too, but this is by no means an extensive list of works in Western languages. We have, in fact, adopted part of the system for bibliography used in the monumental series *Science and Civilisation in China*, which readers needing further information are advised to consult.

Each entry comprises the name of the author, the title of the book or article, and relevant bibliographical details with dates. Entries are presented alphabetically.

Andersson,J.G. (1), *Children of the Yellow Earth*, London, 1934.

Babbitt,I. (1) (trans.), *The Dhammapada*, New York, 1936, 1965.

Beal,S. (1) (trans.), *Buddhist Records of the Western World, translated from the Chinese of Hiuen Tsiang*, 2 vols, London, 1881, 1884.

Beasley,W.G. and Pulleyblank,E.G. (1) (eds), *Historians of China and Japan*, London, 1961.

Birch,C. (1) (ed.), *Anthology of Chinese Literature*, New York, 1965; Harmondsworth, 1967.

Bishop,C.W. (1), 'The Geographical Factor in the Rise of Chinese Civilisation', *Geographical Review*, XII, 1922, p. 19.

Bodde,D. (1), *China's First Unifier, a study of the Ch'in Dynasty as seen in the Life of Li Ssu (280 to 208 BC)*, Leiden, 1938; Sinica Leidensia, 3.

Bodde,D. (2), *Statesman, Patriot, and General in Ancient China: Three 'Shih Chi' Biographies of the Ch'in Dynasty (255–206 BC)*, New Haven, 1940. Translation and discussion.

Braudel,F. (1), *Capitalism and Material Life, 1400–1800*, trans. M.Kochan, London, 1973.

Brown,P. (1), *The World of Late Antiquity; from Marcus Aurelius to Muhammad*, London, 1971.

Bruce,J.P. (1) (trans.), *The Philosophy of Human Nature by Chu Hsi (chs 47–9 of the Chu Tzu Ch'uan Shu)*, London, 1922.

Bruce,J.P. (2), *Chu Hsi and his Masters: an Introduction to Chu Hsi and the Sung School of Chinese Philosophy*, London, 1923.

Budge,E.A.W. (1), *The Monks of Kublai Khan, Emperor of China*, London, 1928.

Bynner, Witter (1) (trans.), *The Way of Life according to Lao Tzu*, New York, 1962.

Bynner, Witter (2) (trans. with the assistance of Kiang Kang-Hu), *The Jade Mountain; A Chinese Anthology, being Three Hundred Poems of the T'ang Dynasty, 618–906*, New York, 1929, and 1972.

Cameron,A.S. (1), *Chinese Painting Techniques*, Tokyo, 1968.

Carus,P. (1) (trans.), *The Canon of Reason and Virtue, being Lao-tze's Tao Teh King, Chinese and English*, Chicago, 1913, 2nd edn 1927.

de Chardin, Teilhard (1), *The Phenomenon of Man*, London, 1959.

Chavannes,E. (1) (trans.), *Les Mémoires Historiques de Se-Ma Ts'ien*, 5 vols, Paris, 1895–1905.

Ch'en,K.K.S. (1), *The Chinese Transformation of Buddhism*, Princeton, 1973.

Ch'en,K.K.S. (2), *Buddhism in China*, Princeton, 1964.

Cheng Te-K'un (1), *Archaeology in China, 1: Prehistoric China*, Cambridge, 1959.

Cheng Te-K'un (2), *Archaeology in China, 2: Shang China*, Cambridge, 1960.

Cheng Te-K'un (3), *Archaeology in China, supplement to 1: New Light on Prehistoric China*, Cambridge, 1966.

Cheng Te-K'un (4), *Archaeology in China, 3: Chou China*, Cambridge, 1963.

Chi Ch'ao-Ting (1), *Key Economic Areas in Chinese History, as revealed in the Development of Public Works for Water-Control*, London, 1936; New York, 1970.

Chiang Yee (1), *The Chinese Eye*, London, 1935.

Chiang Yee (2), *Chinese Calligraphy*, London, 1950.

Chu T'ung Tsu (1), *Han Social Structure*, ed. J.L.Dull, Seattle, 1972.

Cooper,A. (1) (trans.), *Li Po and Tu Fu*, Harmondsworth, 1973. Selected poems with Chinese calligraphy by Shui Chien-Tung.

Creel,H.G. (1), *Confucius and the Chinese Way*, New York, 1960; originally published as *Confucius; the*

Man and the Myth, New York, 1949; London, 1951.

Creel,H.G. (2), *Chinese Thought from Confucius to Mao Tse-Tung*, Chicago, 1953.

Crump,J.I. (1) (trans.), *Chan-Kuo Ts'e*, Oxford, 1970.

Dawson,R. (1) (ed.), *The Legacy of China*, Oxford, 1964.

Dubs,H.H. (1) (trans. with the assistance of P'an Lo-chi and Jen T'ai), *History of the Former Han Dynasty, by Pan Ku, a Critical Translation with Annotations*, 3 vols, Baltimore, 1938, 1944 and 1955.

Dubs,H.H. (2), *Hsun Tzu; the Moulder of Ancient Confucianism*, London, 1927.

Dubs,H.H. (3), 'Han Yu and the Buddha's Relic; an episode in medieval Chinese religion', *Review of Religion*, 5, 1946.

Dutt,S. (1), *Buddhist Monks and Monasteries of India; Their History and Contribution to Indian Culture*, London, 1962.

Duyvendak,J.J.L. (1), *The Book of the Lord Shang; A Classic of the Chinese School of Law*, London, 1928.

Duyvendak,J.J.L. (2), *China's Discovery of Africa*, London, 1949.

Elvin,M. (1), *The Pattern of the Chinese Past*, London, 1973.

Fitzgerald,C.P. (1), *Son of Heaven; A Biography of Li Shih-Min, founder of the T'ang Dynasty*, Cambridge, 1933.

Fitzgerald,C.P. (2), *China; A Short Cultural History*, London, 1935, 3rd edn 1961.

Fitzgerald,C.P. (3), *The Empress Wu*, Melbourne, 1955; London, 1956 and 1968.

Fitzgerald,C.P. (4), *The Southern Expansion of the Chinese People; Southern Fields and Southern Ocean*, London, 1972.

Fitzgerald,.C.P. (5), *A Concise History of East Asia*, Hong Kong, 1966.

Fung Yu-Lan (1), *The Spirit of Chinese Philosophy*, trans. E. R. Hughes, London, 1947.

Gale,E.M. (1) (trans.), *Discourses on Salt and Iron (Yen T'ieh), a Debate on State Control of Commerce and Industry in Ancient China*, chs 1–19, Leiden, 1931; Sinica Leidensia, 2; chs 1–28, Taipei, 1967.

Gernet,J. (1), *Daily Life in China on the Eve of the Mongol Invasion, 1250–1276*, trans. H.M. Wright, London, 1962.

Gerth,H.H. and Mills,C.Wright (eds and trans.), *From Max Weber: Essays in Sociology*, New York, 1946.

Giles,H.A. (1) (trans.), *Chuang Tzu; Taoist Philosopher and Mystic*, London, 1889, 2nd edn 1926, reprinted 1961.

Giles,L. (1), *Taoist Teachings translated from the Book of Lieh-tzu*, London, 1912, 2nd edn 1947.

Goodrich,N.Carrington (1), *China*, Berkeley, 1946.

Goody,J.(1) (ed.), *Literacy in Traditional Societies*, Cambridge, 1968.

Graham,A.C. (1) (trans.), *The Book of Lieh-tzu*, London, 1960.

Granet,M. (1), *La Religion des Chinois*, Paris, 1922.

Granet,M.(2), *Danses et Légendes de la Chine Ancienne*, 2 vols, Paris, 1926, 2nd edn 1929.

De Groot,J.J.L. (1), *The Religions of China*, 6 vols, Leiden, 1892. Comprehensive study of indigenous belief, especially useful on *wu* magicians.

Grousset,R. (1), *Conqueror of the World*, trans. D. Sinor and M.MacKellar, Edinburgh and London, 1967.

Herrmann,A. (1), *An Historical Atlas of China*, Edinburgh, 1966; based on *Historical and Commercial Atlas of China*, Harvard-Yenching Institute, Monograph Series, 1, 1935.

Ho Ping-Ti (1), 'Loyang (495 to 534); A study of Physical and Socio-Economic Planning of a Metropolitan Area', *Harvard Journal of Asiatic Studies*, XXVI, 52, 1966.

d'Hormon,A. (1) (ed. and trans.), *Lectures Chinoises*, Peking, 1945.

Hung,W. (1), *Tu Fu, China's Greatest Poet*, Cambridge, Mass., 1952.

Karlgren,B. (1), *Sound and Symbol in Chinese*, Oxford, 1923, reprinted 1946. English translation of *Ordet Och Pennan i Mittens Rike*, Stockholm, 1918.

Lai Ming (1), *A History of Chinese Literature*, London, 1964.

Lattimore,O. (1), *Inner Asian Frontiers of China*, Oxford and New York, 1940; American Geographical Society Research Monograph Series, 21.

Lattimore,O. (2), 'Chingis Khan and the Mongol Conquests', *Scientific American*, CCIX, August 1963, pp. 55–68.

Lau,D.C. (1) (trans.), *Mencius*, Harmondsworth, 1970.

Lau,D.C. (2) (trans.), *Lao Tzu; Tao Te Ching*, Harmondsworth, 1963.

Laufer,B. (1), *Paper and Printing in Ancient China*, New York, 1931; Caxton Club Publication no. 24, 1973.

Legge,J. (1), *Shu Ching, Book of History, a modernized edition of the translations of James Legge by Clae Waltham*, London, 1972.

Legge,J. (2) (trans.), *The Chinese Classics, etc.*, 1: *Confucian Analects, The Great Learning, and the Doctrine of Mean*, Hongkong, 1861; London, 1861; reissued Hongkong, 1960.

Legge,J. (3) (trans.), *The Chinese Classics, etc.*, 2: *The Works of Mencius*, Hongkong, 1861; London, 1861;

reissued Hongkong, 1960.

Legge,J. (4) (trans.), *The Texts of Taoism*, 2 vols, Oxford, 1891; reprinted 1927.

Legge and Waltham: *see* Legge (1).

Li Dun,J. (1), *The Ageless Chinese*, New York, 1965.

Lin Yutang (1), *The Chinese Theory of Art*, London, 1967.

Lin Yutang (2), *The Gay Genius; the Life and Times of Su Tung-p'o*, London, 1948.

Loewe,M. (1), *Everyday Life in Early Imperial China, during the Han Period, 202 BC–AD 220*, London, 1968.

Lu Hsun (1), *A Brief History of Chinese Fiction*, Peking, 1964.

Macgowan,J. (1) (trans.), *The Imperial History of China*, London, 1897 and 1973.

Macnair,H.F. (1) (ed.), *China*, Berkeley, 1946.

Marsden,W. (1) (trans.), *The Travels of Marco Polo*, London, 1908.

Maspéro,H. (1), *La Chine Antique*, Paris, 1927.

Medley,M. (1), *A Handbook of Chinese Art, for Collectors and Students*, London, 1964.

Mei,Y.P. (1), *The Ethical and Political Works of Mo Tzu*, London, 1929.

Mei,Y.P. (2), *Mo Tzu, the Neglected Rival of Confucius*, London, 1934.

Needham,J. (1), *Science and Civilisation in China*, 1: *Introductory Orientations*, Cambridge, 1954.

Needham,J. (2), *Science and Civilisation in China*, 2: *History of Scientific Thought*, Cambridge, 1956.

Needham,J. (3), *Science and Civilisation in China*, 3: *Mathematics and the Sciences of the Heavens and the Earth*, Cambridge, 1959.

Needham,J. (4), *Science and Civilisation in China*, 4: *Physics and Physical Technology*, I: *Physics*, Cambridge, 1962.

Needham,J. (5), *Science and Civilisation in China*, 4: *Physics and Physical Technology*, II: *Mechanical Engineering*, Cambridge, 1965.

Needham,J. (6), *Science and Civilisation in China*, 4: *Physics and Physical Technology*, III: *Civil Engineering and Nautics*, Cambridge, 1971.

Needham,J. (7), *The Development of Iron and Steel Technology in China*, London, 1958. Second Biennial Dickinson Memorial Lecture, 1956, Cambridge, 1964.

Needham,J. (8), *The Grand Titration: Science and Society in East and West*, London, 1969.

Needham,J. (9), *Within the Four Seas: The Dialogue of East and West*, London, 1969.

Needham,J. (10), *Clerks and Craftsmen in China and the West; lectures and addresses on the history of science and technology*, Cambridge, 1969.

Phillips,E.D. (1), *The Mongols*, London, 1969.

Pulleyblank,E.G. (1), *The Background of the Rebellion of An Lu-shan*, London, 1954. London Oriental Series, 4.

de Rachewiltz,I. (1), *Papal Envoys to the Great Khans*, London, 1971.

Radhakrishnan,S. (1), *India and China*, Bombay, 1944.

Rawlinson,H.G. (1), *Bactria, from the Earli⁀ Times to the Extinction of Bactrio-Greek Rule in the Punjab*, Bombay, 1909.

Robinson,G.W. (1) (trans.), *The Poems of Wang Wei*, Harmondsworth, 1973.

Shryock,J.K. (1), *The Origin and Development of the State Cult of Confucianism*, New York, 1932, reprinted 1966.

Sickman,L., and Soper,A. (1), *The Art and Architecture of China*, Harmondsworth, 1956.

de Silva, Anil (1), *Chinese Landscape Painting in the Caves of Tun-Huang*, London, 1964.

Sirén,O. (1), *History of Early Chinese Painting*, 2 vols, London, 1933.

Sirén,O. (2), *The Walls and Gates of Peking*, London, 1924.

Sirén,O. (3), *The Imperial Palaces of Peking*, 3 vols, Paris and Brussels, 1927.

Sirén,O. (4), *Gardens of China*, New York, 1949.

Smith,D.Howard (1), *Confucius*, London, 1973.

Snyder,G. (1), *Collected Poems*, London, 1966.

Stein, Sir Aurel (1), *Ruins of Desert Cathay*, 2 vols, London, 1912; recently reprinted.

Sullivan,M. (1), *An Introduction to Chinese Art*, London, 1961.

Sullivan,M. (2), *The Cave Temples of Maichishan*, London, 1969.

Swann,N.L. (1), *Food and Money in Ancient China*, Princeton, 1950.

Swann,N.L. (2), *Pan Chao: Foremost Woman Scholar of China*, New York, 1932.

Tarn,W.W. (1), *The Greeks in Bactria and India*, Cambridge, 1951.

Teggart,F.J. (1), *Rome and China; A Study of Correlations in Historical Events*, Berkeley, 1939.

Tregear,T.R. (1), *A Geography of China*, London, 1965.

Waley,A. (1) (trans.), *The Book of Songs*, London, 1937.

Waley,A. (2), *The Way and its Power; a study of the Tao Teh Ching and its Place in Chinese Thought*, London, 1934.

Waley,A. (3), *The Life and Times of Po Chu-I*, London, 1949, several reprints. Translation and discussion.

Waley,A. (4) (trans.), *One Hundred and Seventy Chinese Poems*, London, 1918, several reprints.

Waley,A. (5), *The Poetry and Career of Li Po*, London,

1950. Translation and discussion.

Waley, A. (6) (trans.), *The Secret History of the Mongols and Other Pieces*, London, 1963.

Waley, A. (7) (trans.), *The Travels of an Alchemist; the Journey of the Taoist Ch'ang-Ch'un from China to the Hindu-Kush at the summons of Genghiz Khan, recorded by his disciple Li Chih-Ch'ang*, London, 1931. Broadway Travellers series.

Waley, A. (8) (trans.), *Monkey, by Wu Ch'eng-en*, London, 1942.

Waley, A. (9) (trans.), *The Analects of Confucius*, London, 1938.

Waley, A. (10), *An Introduction to the Study of Chinese Painting*, London, 1923.

Watson, B. (1) (trans.), *Records of the Grand Historian of China* (from the *Shih Chi* of Ssu-ma Ch'ien), 2 vols, New York, 1961.

Watson, B. (2), *Ssu-ma Ch'ien, Grand Historian of China*, New York, 1958.

Watson, B. (3) (trans.), *Records of the Historian* (selected chapters from *Shih Chi*), New York, 1969.

Watson, W. (1), *Cultural Frontiers in Ancient East Asia*, Edinburgh, 1971.

Watson, W. (2), *The Genius of China*, London, 1973. Catalogue of the Chinese Exhibition.

Watts, A. W. (1), *The Spirit of Zen; A way of life, work and art in the Far East*, London, 1936, several reprints.

Watts, A. W. (2), *The Way of Zen*, New York, 1957; Harmondsworth, 1962. Includes a discussion of Taoism.

Watts, A. W. (3), *Psychotherapy, East and West*, New York, 1961; London, 1971.

Wieger, L. (1), *Chinese Characters. Their Origin, Etymology, History, Classification and Signification. A Thorough Study from Chinese Documents*, trans. L. Davrout. Original edition 1915; reprinted New York 1965.

Wieger, L. (2), *Textes Historiques. Histoire politique de la Chine, depuis l'origine, jusqu'en 1929*, 2 vols, Hsienhsien, 1929. Chinese and French.

Wilhelm, H. (1), *Chinas Geschichte: Zehn einführende Vorträge*, Peking, 1942.

Wilhelm, R. (1), *Short History of Chinese Civilisation*, trans. J. Joshua, London, 1929.

Wilhelm, R. (2), *I Ching, or Book of Changes*, trans. C. F. Baynes, London, 1951 and 1968.

Wright, A. F. and Twitchett, D. (1) (eds), *Confucian Personalities*, Stanford, 1962.

Yang, C. K. (1), *Religion in Chinese Society*, Berkeley and Los Angeles, 1961.

Yoshikawa, K. (1), *An Introduction to Sung Poetry*, trans. B. Watson, Cambridge, Mass., 1967.

Yu Ying-Shih (1), *Trade and Expansion in Han China; a Study in the Structure of Sino-Barbarian Economic Relations*, Berkeley and Los Angeles, 1967.

Yule, Sir Henry (1), *Cathay and the Way Thither; being a Collection of Medieval Notices of China*, 4 vols, London, 1866, revised edition 1913–16. Includes Marco Polo, Odonic of Pordonone, John of Montecorvino, Ibn Buttutah and others.

Zimmer, H. (1), *Philosophies of India*, ed. J. Campbell, Princeton, 1951, Bollingen series.

Zimmer, H. (2), *Myths and Symbols in Indian Art and Civilization*, ed. J. Campbell, New York, 1946; New York, 1962; Bollingen series.

Zürcher, E. (1), *The Buddhist Conquest of China; the Spread and Adaptation of Buddhism in Early Medieval China*, 2 vols, Leiden, 1959; Sinica Leidensia, 11.

Index